CHILDREN CROSSING BORDERS

CHILDREN

CROSSING

BORDERS

Latin American Migrant Childhoods

EDITED BY

ALEJANDRA J. JOSIOWICZ AND IRASEMA CORONADO

THE UNIVERSITY OF
ARIZONA PRESS
TUCSON

The University of Arizona Press
www.uapress.arizona.edu

We respectfully acknowledge the University of Arizona is on the land and territories of Indigenous peoples. Today, Arizona is home to twenty-two federally recognized tribes, with Tucson being home to the O'odham and the Yaqui. Committed to diversity and inclusion, the University strives to build sustainable relationships with sovereign Native Nations and Indigenous communities through education offerings, partnerships, and community service.

ISBN-13: 978-0-8165-4620-6 (hardcover)
ISBN-13: 978-0-8165-4619-0 (paperback)
ISBN-13: 978-0-8165-4621-3 (ebook)

Cover design by Leigh McDonald
Interior designed and typeset by Sara Thaxton in 10/14 Warnock Pro with Brandon Grotesque

Publication of this book is made possible in part by the proceeds of a permanent endowment created with the assistance of a Challenge Grant from the National Endowment for the Humanities, a federal agency.

Library of Congress Cataloging-in-Publication Data
Names: Josiowicz, Alejandra J., 1981– editor. | Coronado, Irasema, editor.
Title: Children crossing borders : Latin American migrant childhoods / edited by Alejandra J. Josiowicz and Irasema Coronado.
Description: Tucson : University of Arizona Press, 2022. | Includes bibliographical references and index.
Identifiers: LCCN 2021061562 (print) | LCCN 2021061563 (ebook) | ISBN 9780816546206 (hardcover) | ISBN 9780816546190 (paperback) | ISBN 9780816546213 (ebook)
Subjects: LCSH: Immigrant children—United States—Social conditions—21st century. | Latin Americans—United States—Social conditions—21st century. | Immigrant families—United States—Social conditions—21st century.
Classification: LCC JV6600 .C55 2022 (print) | LCC JV6600 (ebook) | DDC 305.23086/9120973—dc23/eng/20220308
LC record available at https://lccn.loc.gov/2021061562
LC ebook record available at https://lccn.loc.gov/2021061563

Printed in the United States of America
♾ This paper meets the requirements of ANSI/NISO Z39.48-1992 (Permanence of Paper).

Alejandra's dedication:

To the memory of my grandfather Gunther Frey Engel.

To José Ceroli, for the bonds that we create, sometimes stronger than blood.

To my sons, Darío and Valentín, for their patience and love.

To all the children that have suffered losses and have been uprooted during the COVID-19 pandemic.

Irasema's dedication:

To migrant children all over the world and everyone who lives in a place other than where they were born.

To my mother, Lupita Coronado, and the memory of my father, Gonzalo Coronado.

CONTENTS

Part III. Best Interests of the Child Crossing Borders

ACKNOWLEDGMENTS

As we conclude this book in the fall of 2021, the COVID-19 pandemic is still raging, people are fleeing Afghanistan, a hurricane is looming near Louisiana, and the Supreme Court has ruled that the Biden administration cannot stop the "Remain in Mexico" policy and must return, for now, to the previous administration's policy of halting the arrival of asylum seekers and having them wait in Mexico. The Biden administration has kept Title 42 of the U.S. Code (a public health rule) in place, and over one million migrants at the border have been turned back. It is important to note that children arriving with one or two parents have also been sent back; however, unaccompanied minor children have been allowed to enter the United States. The effects of these public policy transformations on the lives of children have been enormous, pointing out the importance of disseminating knowledge and questioning still-prevalent prejudices and stereotypes surrounding migrant children.

We hope that this book draws attention to the plight of migrant children and their families and that it serves to help readers learn about the migratory challenges of our neighbors and friends in our communities and throughout the Americas. Contributors to this book shed light on the human and emotional toll that children experience as they crisscross the Americas. They look at the challenges these children face owing to border bureaucracies, educational establishments, and social institutions, as well as to the possibilities that they are capable of fulfilling in a more tolerant future world. Hopefully, this book will inspire policy makers to embrace humane immigration policies and avoid the unnecessary suffering of children in our world. It will also aid educators and communicators in problematizing their previous ideas on migrations and childhood and in viewing children's plights with respect and care.

We want to thank our multilingual colleagues and friends that contributed chapters to this book; all are scholars that enhance the academy theoretically and methodologically as well as have an impact on applied research and public policy. We enjoyed working with colleagues who are native Spanish, English, Portuguese, and French speakers, and yes, our book has a variety of accents. This is crucial to us as a diverse, transnational community of female intellectuals, a majority of whom are women of color, inspired by a social justice approach to different academic fields.

It is important to acknowledge our colleagues who reviewed drafts of chapters and provided feedback to us to strengthen our work: Kathy Staudt, Brendan O'Connor, Kamala Platt, Tony Payan, Hector Padilla, Mark Lusk, and Rosanna Kohl Bines. Nora Martinez and Carlos Hernandez deserve our utmost recognition for helping with research, citations, and editing. Special thanks to Professor Donna Guy for introducing us to each other and for helping conceive of this book and bring it to fruition and, of course, to the University of Arizona Press staff, especially Kristen Buckles for her support of this project.

CHILDREN CROSSING BORDERS

Introduction

This book on children on the borders in the Americas was planned and structured before the onset of the COVID-19 pandemic. However, it has been completed and will be published in a changed world, one in which considerations of the health and well-being of children in the Americas have become even more relevant and in which inequalities related to race, citizenship, ethnicity, social class, and gender have become even more intense and unavoidable. In 2020 millions of children in Latin America and the Caribbean suffered poverty, violence, and a lack of adequate health services. Over 154 million children in Latin America and the Caribbean were out of school during 2020. Serious consequences ensued for the most vulnerable, who depended on schools to access food and sanitary services as well as psychosocial support (UNICEF 2020a). Many have been denied their minimum needs and rights, such as food and adequate housing. According to the United Nations Children's Fund (UNICEF), owing to the impact of COVID-19, the number of children living in poor households will increase by 21.7 percent, from 71.6 million to 87.1 million children (UNICEF 2020b). At the same time, even those that enjoy relatively better economic positions suffer depression, isolation, and loneliness as rising unemployment, inflation, and the loss of millions of lives take a toll on all families across the Americas. Hate speech, racism, and intolerance have risen, too, amplifying the reverberation of racist and xenophobic discourses online as well as offline (UN 2019). As a result many children in the Americas have experienced the same physical and psychological instability that migrant children suffer.

Migrants and refugees across the region have been particularly exposed to the virus, as practicing social distancing is challenging for vulnerable communities. At the same time, border closures and increasing xenophobia have left many migrant families and children stranded when they are in need of protection and humanitarian assistance. Just like migrant families, children experiencing this pandemic have lost their sense of security, challenged by economic, political, spatial, or educational instabilities.

This book intends to reflect on children on the borders in the Americas through theoretical as well as empirical perspectives; it seeks to serve as a toolbox for those who work with children on the borders and to point out and challenge ways in which the media, literature, legislation, public policies, and everyday practices construct and deconstruct migrant childhoods. We seek to provide theoretical and practical tools for better understanding the way in which refugee and immigrant children are represented in different kinds of cultural and literary productions. One of our goals is to offer tools to help educators, social workers, policy makers, and advocates accompany immigrant children in their journeys of self-recognition, their searches for empowerment, and their struggles for rights and citizenship. We examine the way education, legislation, public policies, literature, and culture are potential tools for combating racism, nationalism, sexism, and xenophobia and for providing opportunities for children and their families to become aware of the experience of immigrants and refugees.

Intersectional Latin American and Latinx Childhood and Youth

Policy makers and academics only recently started to consider refugee and immigrant children in their singularities, as autonomous agents, given that many children and adolescents migrate by themselves, unaccompanied and independently, for a variety of reasons (Bhabha 2014; Chang et al. 2018). This relatively new way of considering immigrant and refugee children follows the paradigm shift in childhood studies that emphasizes children's agency as participants of society instead of seeing children as future adult citizens, with childhood as a preparatory stage (Qvortrup, Corsaro, and Honig 2009). This is the case of many "children on the move"—independent child migrants that cross borders in search of safety, educational opportunities, economic prospects, and family life (Bhabha 2014). It is also the case of historically marginalized boys, girls, and adolescents who work in the migrant-smuggling market, known as *niñez de circuito*, due to the lack of employment or occupational opportunities (DHIA 2019). Border studies that trace the limitations and complexities of nationalization—that is, of the political and social attempts to get people to identify with the nation-state—emphasize how the life experiences of children on the borders point to the flexibility and permanent contestation of identifications among borderland inhabitants (Venken 2017). According to these studies, borderland children, as historical actors whose practices often contest hegemonic meanings, offer creative alternatives that go beyond dichotomies (Venken 2017).

To avoid reductionisms and essentialisms, it is crucial to untangle how racism, heterosexism, imperialism, and xenophobia have all worked together throughout modern history in the Americas. The problems that affect Latin American refugee and immigrant children cannot be understood in isolation from national and international inequalities, in which geopolitical location is embedded in global power relations, which in turn entail economic, political, and ideological questions (Brah 1991). Childhood and youth cannot be thought of as unitary categories; rather, different social constructions of childhood and youth according to race, ethnicity, gender, citizenship status, and nationality should be considered, none of which is internally homogeneous (Bernstein 2011). Social class, racism, heterosexism, xenophobia, geopolitical location, and citizenship status determine different life opportunities for different children and young people (Brah 1991). Race, class, gender, and citizenship are interrelated with postcolonial and decolonial questions in the case of Latin American migrant children and youths, underscoring the role of imperialism and international power relations in the many layers of invisibility that affect these individuals. The many diasporas and diasporic experiences in Latin American history, related to human trafficking and slavery, colonialism, postcolonialism, and imperialism, are central to understanding how any theoretical consideration of immigrant children needs to simultaneously take into account race, ethnicity, class, gender, and global inequalities (Hollanda 2020).

Intersectionality and decolonial theory are crucial to these considerations. Instead of compartmentalizing different kinds of oppressions, these theories formulate strategies to face oppressions in articulated, interrelated ways (Brah 1991; Hill Collins and Andersen 2016; Lugones 2020). Intersectionality and decolonial theory show how race, class, gender, and geopolitics function as interconnected but distinctive structures of oppression expressed through relations of power that work in parallel, interrelated, simultaneous ways of subordination and domination, of inequality, power, exclusion, and privilege (Hill Collins and Andersen 2016; Lugones 2020). Their effects accumulate and overlap, while they configure social relations through multiple structurally interrelated levels of domination. The identities of immigrant and refugee children go beyond dichotomic, hierarchical conceptions; they juxtapose questions of race, gender, class, citizenship, and geopolitics.

In Latin America, Black and Indigenous women theorists and movements (Carneiro 2019; González 2020; Hollanda 2020) have denounced how racism, sexism, and colonialism together determine cultural representations. They also stress that Black and Indigenous peoples, particularly women in Latin America and the Caribbean and Latinxs in the United States, need to formulate their experiences through diasporic common histories. Global inequalities and hierarchies reinforce the centrality of Latin American and Caribbean Black and Indigenous women's struggles for reproductive freedom, political and civic rights, and cultural and economic participation (Carneiro 2019; Hollanda 2020). Black, Indigenous, postcolonial, and feminist movements in Latin American countries were pivotal in spreading awareness of the exclusion of nonwhite, non-middle-class children and youths from citizenship and rights (Lajolo and Zilberman 2017).

Childhood activists and scholars in the Americas point out that the historical experience of Black, Indigenous, and migrant children and youths does not fit within the parameters of childhood and youth modeled on white, westernized, middle-class boys and girls (Bernstein 2011; Higonnet 1998; Zapiola 2019). In the context of the multiracial, pluricultural, racist, and classist societies of Latin America, Black, Indigenous, and migrant children and youths are not considered pure, innocent, vulnerable creatures in need of protection. Instead they are frequently considered to be evacuated of innocence, stigmatized, and demeaned as nonchildren in need of punishment, discipline, and control (Guy 2002; Rizzini 2002).

This hegemonic model of childhood and youth was forged in the last decades of the nineteenth century in Latin America through laws; public policies; educational, health, and political institutions; and scientific discourses. According to this view, "normal" children were middle-class white children and young adults, who were both objects of family protection (as sons and daughters) and the objects of pedagogic care and control inside educational institutions (Carli 2002; Lionetti and Míguez 2010; Zapiola 2019). Governmental policies and scientific discourses during most of the twentieth century differentiated between children considered "normal" and others seen as "deviant" or "minors" (Zapiola 2019). Social and cultural representations implicitly or explicitly distinguished between those they saw as innocent, adaptable to social norms, and in need of family affection and those in institutional care and "minors," who were considered abnormal or sick, criminalized, and considered a potential threat to the social order and in need of correction, punishment, and control (Corrêa 1997; Rizzini 2002). Mothers, doctors, and educators were in charge of transmitting heteronormative, nationalist values to children and young people, and many authorities publicly encouraged the "right" kinds of births and discouraged others (Nari 2004).

After World War I and throughout the twentieth century, the juridical and penal category of the "minor" became the object of criticism and was questioned in favor of a more optimistic view of all children as educable (Carvalho 1997; Rizzini 2002). In connection with a worldwide movement for children's rights, international agreements on children were created. In 1924 the League of Nations adopted the Geneva Declaration of the Rights of the Child. A Pan American Children's Code was approved in 1948, and in 1989 the General Assembly adopted the United Nations Convention on the Rights of the Child (Qvortrup, Corsaro, and Honig 2009; Guy 2002). These conventions emphasized the specific needs of children—such as education, protection, and psychological and familiar care—irrespective of race; sex; language; national, ethnic, or social origin; or place of birth (Guy 2002; Rizzini and Kaufman 2009). Even though many countries signed treaties and conventions recognizing the rights of children and youths, as well as adopting progressive child-rights laws, the most basic rights of children continued to be violated on a daily basis throughout the Americas. Mass discrimination, hostility, and injustice endured (Rizzini and Kaufman 2009), especially for refugee and immigrant children, young girls, Black children, and Indigenous children, many of whom continue to lack access to basic services like health care, education, and nutrition.

Since World War II, and particularly in the last decades of the twentieth and the beginning of the twenty-first centuries, there was a process of incorporation and integration into the civil sphere of different communities of immigrants and refugees, as many voices emerged to defend their civil status, views, and rights as capable of participation in and needing protection from the state (Alexander 2013). Different conventions relative to the status of refugees were signed, granting equal treatment to refugees concerning employment, health, and education (Rocha Reis 2004). The Universal Declaration of Human Rights, signed by the United Nations in 1948, affirms the right to a nationality, to seek asylum, and to leave and return to the country of origin (Rocha Reis 2004). Additionally, in 1990 the United Nations approved the Convention on the Rights of Immigrants (Rocha Reis 2004). However, this process was not complete or without fissures. In recent decades these fissures have become apparent as backlash movements have emerged that reinforce stigmatizations and exclusions and distort and corrupt the images of poor, Black, Indigenous, refugee, and immigrant children and young people. These groups are seen as threats to the social order and to moral values, a view that conflates racism, sexism, xenophobia, and imperialism and reinforces hierarchies and rigid distinctions between races, ethnicities, gender roles, nationalities, and citizenship statuses (Alexander 2013). Many countries established additional barriers to the incorporation of immigrants and refugees, curbing their rights and their participation in democracies (Alexander 2013; Rocha Reis 2004). The narrative of a nonwhite immigrant invasion of the Western world is used to restrict immigrants' possibilities of integrating and becoming rightful members of the civic community. This narrative justifies the obstacles and barriers to naturalization and citizenship that generate exclusion, repression, and domination (Alexander 2018). These violent backlash movements and their policies, discourses, and laws, which so deeply affect Latin American refugee and immigrant children, cannot be understood without taking into account the historic legacy of colonialism. It is important to consider the way in which non-Western, nonwhite peoples have been submitted to systematic sexual and racial violence, perceived as passive, dependent, corrupted, irrational, nonhuman, hypersexual, savage, and incapable of self-rule (Hollanda 2020).

A Decolonial Perspective on Migrant Childhoods in the Americas

In this volume we approach migrant childhoods in the Americas through a decolonial perspective—that is, by considering the structure of social and economic inequalities that go back to the history of European imperialism and colonialism, which have shaped the circulation of children throughout the region at least since colonial times (Mignolo 2002; Rabello de Castro 2020). The main implication of this decolonial perspective is that we resist erasing differences between North and South or adhering to a notion of a prototypical (white, Anglo-Saxon, middle-class), definitive model of American or Latin American childhood against which other children would be compared. Our decolonial perspective on childhood migration in the Americas means that we seek to articulate North and South America through the unifying theme of migrant children, looking at children at the crossroads between colonialism and postcolonialism, diversity and oppression, invisibility and othering, and reappraising difference in migrant childhoods in the Americas in structural power relationships.

Our decolonial approach also has strong implications for our political economy of knowledge production: we incorporate theories and scholarship written in languages other than English and situated in North and South, as we reject essentializing difference and avoid reaffirming preferences, themes, and concepts that already circulate in international knowledge markets. We seek to create an egalitarian, collaborative space in which horizontal political and epistemic relations are possible regarding the international division of scientific labor. Our book strives to create bonds where long-standing structural and imperial divisions between North and South America exist, ones that have separated and interconnected these parts of the world. Thus, we assume the costs of dissenting and producing theory on children from within North and South.

Child Migration in the Americas Today

The Americas are witnessing an era of unprecedented human mobility. Between 2012 and 2015, 7.2 million people left their countries in the Americas, while 48 percent immigrated to the United States and Canada, 34 percent to Latin America, and 18 percent to Europe (SICREMI 2017).

In fiscal year 2020, the U.S. Border Patrol had encounters along the southwest border with approximately 52,000 families (children and adults, known as "family units") and 30,600 unaccompanied children. More than 328,000 people, including 13,000 unaccompanied children, were expelled to northern Central America and Mexico from the United States between March and November alone. This was an 85 percent decrease from fiscal year 2019, when 474,000 family units and 76,000 unaccompanied minors were apprehended (Batalova, Hanna, and Levesque 2021).

Gangs' threats of sexual violence toward young women and their exploitation of young men for criminal purposes are significant factors which led, by the end of 2019, to over eight hundred thousand people from El Salvador, Guatemala, and Honduras seeking to escape their home countries. COVID-19 restrictions on international travel only exacerbated the situation by limiting opportunities for fleeing danger and increasing incidence of persecution in this same region (UNHCR 2020).

The Trump administration inflicted inordinate human suffering and pain on families seeking asylum in the United States. Over 2,500 migrant children were separated from their families in 2017 and 2018. Children were kept in cages and in inhumane conditions, with reports of limited food and exposure to cold and hot temperatures in detention facilities. Jack Shonkoff, director of the Harvard University Center on the Developing Child, reports that separation from a parent removes the connection children need with a primary caregiver and subjects them to an onslaught of elevated stress. This stress can cause short-term physical health problems, like high blood pressure, headaches, and stomachaches, as well as mental health problems, like anxiety and depression. The trauma of separation, especially for children under five, can cause long-term impacts on health and well-being, including posttraumatic stress disorder, heart disease, and diabetes (Bassett and Yoshikawa 2020).

In Latin America the Venezuelan political crisis has sent millions of Venezuelans fleeing to neighboring states to escape violence and hardship. However, instead of a humane and effective approach to immigration, systematic violations of the human rights of migrants, refugees, and other vulnerable and displaced populations abounded. In 2018 Brazil reached the mark of 11,231 refugees recognized by the Brazilian state. The migration of Venezuelans has risen exponentially, with more than sixty thousand requests in 2019 (ACNUR, n.d.). This has impacted children, particularly young girls, in especially serious ways: they face death, extortion, xenophobia, trafficking, separation of families, and forced return to their country of origin.

The COVID-19 pandemic aggravated racism and xenophobic violence, leading to stigmatization and border closures, as many states associated the coming of migrants with health risks (Rodrigues, Cavalcante, and Faerstein 2020). This has been the case not only in Brazil but also across the Americas.

During the past decades, many countries have established additional barriers to the incorporation of immigrant and refugee children, curbing their rights and participation in democracies (Alexander 2013; Rocha Reis 2004). Furthermore, the detention of children and their separation from families has been used as a way to deter illegal crossings, punishing and controlling immigrants and asylum seekers. These practices have led to heartache and trauma, which can have lifelong negative consequences for children and their families.

Border Children in the Americas: An Interdisciplinary, Intersectional, Transnational Approach

This book approaches the border as a dynamic concept, a central site of power struggles, as well as a flexible theoretical tool with which to conceptualize diverse representations of childhood. It also traces the perspectives, legislations, and policies toward migrant and refugee children on the move for social, ethnic, political, or economic reasons and links these meanings to the representation of marginalized children in Latin America. Long before the policies controlling the international migration of children became global news, poor, abandoned, vulnerable, and illegitimate children had historically been regarded as "minors": outsiders of the civic community who were abnormal, problematic, potentially dangerous to the social order, and in need of discipline, punishment, and control (Guy 2002; Rizzini 2002; Zapiola 2019). These discriminatory and punitive views of marginalized children—those who fall outside the determinations of normality made by state institutions such as the school—still predominate in some media outlets. The results are police violence and the pervasive incarceration of young people.

This book explores the different meanings of the lives of borderland children in the Americas, paying special attention to their nonhegemonic practices and exploring how they present alternatives to identification with the nation-state insofar as they inhabit borders that are not only geographic but also civic, racial, ethnic, and sexual. The edited volume showcases scholars from Latin America, the United States, and Canada and their thoughts about child migration in the Americas. The authors utilize an intersectional approach that regards migrant and refugee children in terms of gender, race and ethnicity, nationality, and citizenship. With this approach they consider the lives of child migrants and children of deportees to understand their family and school lives, their experiences as wage laborers, and the legislation and policies that affect them. Additionally, the authors explore cultural and literary works that have migration and other related topics as a central theme. They employ a variety of approaches, including historical, anthropological, sociological, political, and cultural studies perspectives.

Seldom does a unique social phenomenon invite research and inquiry from an interdisciplinary approach to such a degree as does the current migration crisis, which challenges and interrogates legislation, public policies, and representations regarding the rights of children. The book invites reflections from a transnational perspective that also considers the unique ways in which the question of child migration impacts each location at different times and in distinct sociopolitical contexts. Exploring the connections between educational history, policy making, cultural studies, and anthropology, the essays in this volume navigate a space of transnational children's rights critical to life in the Americas in the twentieth and twenty-first centuries.

The migration of children is fueled by conflict, poverty, family reunification efforts, and a plethora of other reasons. We argue that child migration should take place following the Best Interests of the Child protocols and that all nations should come together to facilitate the movement of children and quickly settle them in their new home countries, wherever those may be. We also would like to disentangle previous ideas about what migrant children are and need, disseminated in communication media, which see them either as potential threats to the social order or as helpless victims, and to underline the importance of listening to their voices and taking their perspectives into account.

Contributors to this book come from various linguistic backgrounds. They are native Spanish, Portuguese, French, and English speakers. **If our book could speak, it would have a variety of accents**. We all come from diverse academic disciplines and share a common interest in the well-being of children; most of us have interacted directly with children in the course of our data gathering. Contributors employ a variety of methodologies in order to understand the migratory experience from the point of view of children. Ethnography, participant observation, formal and semistructured interviews, longitudinal studies, cultural studies, and case studies all inform the research process. It is important to highlight the fact that these scholars have expended an inordinate amount of emotional labor as they conducted their research. Many children shared with them their hardships and the pain that they endured as they crossed borders as migrants, while children of deportees shared that their new home is not as welcoming as it could and should be. Lessons learned from these chapters can be applied to children in a variety of international settings: refugee children arriving in European countries; Syrians fleeing their war-torn country; Central Americans traveling through Mexico on their way to the United States, where many of them decide to stay rather than risk family separation.

The chapters in this book are arranged in three parts. The first part focuses on the educational experiences of migrant children—many of them U.S. citizens who are now living in Mexico—and children from Latin America attending schools in the United States. Kathleen Tacelosky discusses how Spanish, the home language used by many migrants in the United States, is reserved for intimate and familial encounters and emphasizes the difficulty in adapting Spanish into a new academic context in Mexico. Taking a social constructivist approach and recognizing that language is central to individual identity construction, she examines "return" migration as experienced by schoolchildren, especially as it pertains to language. How do schoolchildren manage the social and linguistic border crossing from U.S. schools to Mexican institutions? Marissa Bejarano-Fernbaugh provides insights into the experiences of Central American migrants in the United States. She presents the challenges of educating children that have never attended schools in their home country and the trauma of migration and detention in U.S. government-funded facilities. She also offers successful strategies for schools and teachers. Marta Rodríguez-Cruz demonstrates the challenges that children whose educational experiences unfolded in the United States face and highlights the processes of construction of borders and cultural racialization in the schools of the state of Oaxaca, Mexico—one of the states that receives the most return migration today.

In the second part of the book, we include chapters that focus on literature, art, and culture and the depiction of migration in the Americas across several media. Alejandra Josiowicz reviews U.S. Latinx and Latin American children's and young adult literature on migration, examining how these texts underline the struggles and challenges of migrant children, the search for belonging, and denunciation of xenophobia and racial oppression. The chapter offers tools and practices for teachers working on migration by exploring the concept of resilience. Élisabeth Vallet and Nancie Bouchard highlight a border art project that took place in Montreal, Quebec, Canada, with school-age children in order to bring awareness to migration and border issues. Valentina Glockner shares an art project that took place in Nogales, Sonora, Mexico, in a shelter that houses migrant children, some of whom have been deported several times by U.S. authorities. The artwork depicts how children understand the migration process, the border wall, and migration policies in the United States. Glockner discusses the internal and international (im)migration dynamics and public policies of Mexico and its borderlands, as well as the lived experiences of children affected by them.

The principle of the best interests of the child is the unifying theme of the third part of the book. Patrícia Nabuco Martuscelli examines Brazil's policy vis-à-vis refugee children. With the lenses of child rights and the best interests of the child, this chapter analyzes whether the family reunification procedure for refugees is child-friendly. She complements the documental analysis of Brazilian laws on family reunification with semistructured in-depth interviews with Brazilian authorities, experts, and staff working in international organizations. Lina M. Caswell and Emily Ruehs-Navarro volunteered to serve as child advocates in the United States. They met children in detention facilities or at their homes after they had been released from federal custody. In their chapter, their advocacy work with children within the confines of U.S. government policies demonstrates the importance of the support that migrant children need in order to have positive outcomes. Through their work they gathered the story of the migration process, accompanied migrant children to court, clarified their case concerns, communicated the needs of the children to officials, and provided best-interests recommendations to interested parties. Irasema Coronado portrays the plight of U.S.-citizen children of deportees that reside in northern Mexico. She argues that both the United States and Mexico have implemented policies and practices that are not in the best interests of the child, concluding with public policy recommendations for both parties. María Inés Pacecca focuses on Bolivian teenagers' independent international work-driven migrations. Child protection agencies were alerted to these Bolivian teenagers working in Argentine sweatshops, vegetable farms, retail stores, and homes, and as a consequence, they intervened. The negative and positive consequences of these teenagers' migratory plight demonstrate the challenges of all economic migrants.

This book is dedicated to the migrant child that was Alejandra Josiowicz's grandfather Gunther Frey Engel. He was deported from Germany with his family after his father, Karl, was taken to a concentration camp, and all of them were stripped of their citizenships. Gunther was nine years old when a ship took him from the port of Marseille to Bolivia, where he arrived without any means or personal connections. In Bolivia Gunther started working right away, first as a waiter, afterward as an assistant tailor. He also sold paper bags that his family assembled while he studied at night. Although he studied and went on to become the first Jewish lawyer in Cochabamba, Gunther never felt a sense of belonging to any nation in the world. He belonged neither to Bolivia nor to Argentina, where he lived all his adult life, nor to Germany. Instead he was a man from the diaspora, a cosmopolitan, who knew about many nations, cultures, and languages while belonging to none. He was a model of resilience in the face of adversity. This is why, through him, this book is dedicated to migrant children's struggle to build a sense of belonging while confronting racism and estrangement every day of their lives.

References

ACNUR (Agência da ONU para Refugiados). n.d. "Dados sobre refúgio no Brasil." Accessed June 20, 2021. https://www.acnur.org/portugues/dados-sobre-refugio /dados-sobre-refugio-no-brasil/.

Alexander, Jeffrey. 2013. "Struggling over the Mode of Incorporation: Backlash Against Multiculturalism in Europe." *Ethnic and Racial Studies* 36 (4): 531–56.

Alexander, Jeffrey. 2018. "Frontlash/Backlash: The Crisis of Solidarity and the Threat to Civil Institutions." *Contemporary Sociology* 48 (1): 5–11.

Bassett, Lucy, and Hirokazu Yoshikawa. 2020. "Our Immigration Policy Has Done Terrible Damage to Kids." *Scientific American,* December 1, 2020. https://www.scientific american.com/article/our-immigration-policy-has-done-terrible-damage-to-kids/.

Batalova, Jeanne, Mary Hanna, and Christopher Levesque. 2021. "Frequently Requested Statistics on Immigrants and Immigration in the United States." Migration Policy Institute. Migration Information Source, February 11, 2021. https:// www.migrationpolicy.org/article/frequently-requested-statistics-immigrants -and-immigration-united-states-2020#children-immigrants.

Bernstein, Robin. 2011. *Racial Innocence: Performing American Childhood from Slavery to Civil Rights.* New York: New York University Press.

Bhabha, Jacqueline. 2014. *Child Migration and Human Rights in a Global Age.* Princeton, N.J.: Princeton University Press.

Brah, Avtar. 1991. "Difference, Diversity, Differentiation." *International Review of Sociology* 2 (2): 53–71.

Carli, Sandra. 2002. *Niñez, pedagogía y política: Transformaciones de los discursos acerca de la infancia en la historia de la educación argentina entre 1880 y 1955.* Buenos Aires: Miño y Dávila.

Carneiro, Sueli. 2019. "Enegrecer o feminismo: A situação da mulher negra na América Latina a partir da perspectiva de gênero." In *Pensamento feminista: Conceitos fundamentais*, edited by Heloisa Buarque de Hollanda, 313–21. Rio de Janeiro: Bazar dos Tempos.

Carvalho, Marta Maria Chagas de. 1997. "Quando a história da educação é a história da disciplina e da higienização das pessoas." In *História social da infância no Brasil*, edited by Marcos Cezar de Freitas, 269–87. São Paulo: Cortez.

Chang, Stewart, Amy Woo Lee, Cynthia Holton, and Craig Arthur. 2018. "Families Across Borders: When Immigration Law and Family Law Collide—Minors Crossing Borders." *Whittier Journal of Child and Family Advocacy* 17, no. 1 (Spring): 138–62.

Corrêa, Mariza. 1997. "A cidade de menores: Uma utopia dos anos 30." In *História social da infância no Brasil*, edited by Marcos Cezar de Freitas. São Paulo: Cortez Editora.

DHIA (Derechos Humanos Integrales en Acción). 2019. "Boys, Girls and Adolescents in the U.S.-Mexico Border Migrant Smuggling Market." In *Critical Insights on Irregular Migration Facilitation*, edited by Gabriella Sanchez and Luigi Achilli, 37–40. Florence: European University Institute.

González, Lélia. 2020. "Por um feminismo afro-latinoamericano." In *Pensamento feminista hoje: Perspectivas decoloniais*, edited by Heloisa Buarque de Hollanda, 38–51. Rio de Janeiro: Bazar dos Tempos.

Guy, Donna. 2002. "The State, the Family, and Marginal Children in Latin America." In *Minor Omissions: Children in Latin American History and Society*, edited by Tobias Hecht, 139–64. Madison: University of Wisconsin Press.

Higonnet, Anne. 1998. *Pictures of Innocence: The History and Crisis of Ideal Childhood*. London: Thames and Hudson.

Hill Collins, Patricia, and Margaret L. Andersen. 2016. *Race, Class, and Gender: An Anthology*. 9th ed. Boston: Cengage Learning.

Hollanda, Heloisa Buarque de, ed. 2020. *Pensamento feminista hoje: Perspectivas decoloniais*. Rio de Janeiro: Bazar dos Tempos.

Lajolo, Marisa, and Regina Zilberman. 2017. *Literatura infantil brasileira: Uma nova outra história*. Curitiba, Brazil: Editoria Universitária Champagnat.

Lionetti, Lucía, and Daniel Míguez, eds. 2010. *Las infancias en la historia argentina: Intersecciones entre prácticas, discursos e instituciones (1890–1960)*. Rosario, Argentina: Prohistoria.

Lugones, María. 2020. "Colonialidade e gênero." In *Pensamento feminista hoje: Perspectivas decoloniais*, edited by Heloisa Buarque de Hollanda, 52–83. Rio de Janeiro: Bazar dos Tempos.

Mignolo, Walter. 2002. "Geopolitics of Knowledge and the Colonial Difference." *South Atlantic Quarterly* 100 (1): 1–40.

Nari, Marcela. 2004. *Políticas de maternidad y maternalismo político: Buenos Aires, 1890–1940*. Buenos Aires: Biblos.

Qvortrup, Jens, William A. Corsaro, and Michael-Sebastian Honig. 2009. "Why Social Studies of Childhood? An Introduction to the Handbook." In *The Palgrave*

Handbook of Childhood Studies, edited by Jens Qvortrup, William A. Corsaro, and Michael-Sebastian Honig, 1–18. New York: Palgrave Macmillan.

Rabello de Castro, Lucia. 2020. "Why Global? Children and Childhood from a Decolonial Perspective." *Childhood* 27 (1): 48–62.

Rizzini, Irene. 2002. "The Child-Saving Movement in Brazil: Ideology in the Late Nineteenth and Early Twentieth Centuries." In *Minor Omissions: Children in Latin American History and Society*, edited by Tobias Hecht, 165–80. Madison: University of Wisconsin Press.

Rizzini, Irene, and Natalie Kaufman. 2009. "Closing the Gap Between Rights and the Realities of Children's Lives." In *The Palgrave Handbook of Childhood Studies*, edited by Jens Qvortrup, William A. Corsaro, and Michael-Sebastian Honig, 422–34. New York: Palgrave Macmillan.

Rocha Reis, Rosanna. 2004. "Soberania, direitos humanos e migrações internacionais." *Revista brasileira de ciências sociais* 19 (55): 149–64.

Rodrigues, Igor de Assis, João Roberto Cavalcante, and Eduardo Faerstein. 2020. "Pandemia de Covid-19 e a saúde dos refugiados no Brasil." *Physis: Revista de saúde coletiva* 30, no. 3. https://doi.org/10.1590/S0103-73312020300306.

SICREMI (Continuous Reporting System on International Migration in the Americas). 2017. *International Migration in the Americas: Fourth Report of the Continuous Reporting System on International Migration in the Americas (SICREMI)*. Washington, D.C.: OAS. http://www.oas.org/documents/eng/press/SICREMI-2017-english-web-FINAL.pdf.

UN (United Nations). 2019. *United Nations Strategy and Plan of Action on Hate Speech*. May 2019. https://www.un.org/en/genocideprevention/documents/advising-and-mobilizing/Action_plan_on_hate_speech_EN.pdf.

UNHCR (United Nations High Commissioner for Refugees). 2020. "Death Threats and Gang Violence Forcing More Families to Flee Northern Central America— UNHCR and UNICEF Survey." Press release, December 17, 2020. https://www.unhcr.org/en-us/news/press/2020/12/5fdb14ff4/death-threats-gang-violence-forcing-families-flee-northern-central-america.html.

UNICEF (United Nations Children's Fund). 2020a. "COVID-19: Más del 95 por ciento de niños, niñas y adolescentes está fuera de las escuelas en América Latina y el Caribe." Press release, March 23, 2020. https://www.unicef.org/chile/comunicados-prensa/covid-19-m%C3%A1s-del-95-por-ciento-de-ni%C3%B1os-ni%C3%B1as-y-adolescentes-est%C3%A1-fuera-de-las.

UNICEF (United Nations Children's Fund). 2020b. "COVID-19: Number of Children Living in Household Poverty to Soar by up to 86 Million by End of Year." Press release, May 27, 2020. https://www.unicef.org/press-releases/covid-19-number-children-living-household-poverty-soar-86-million-end-year.

Venken, Machteld, ed. 2017. *Borderland Studies Meets Child Studies: A European Encounter*. Frankfurt am Main: Peter Lang, 2017.

Zapiola, María Carolina. 2019. *Excluidos de la niñez: Menores, tutela estatal e instituciones de reforma; Buenos Aires, 1890–1930*. Buenos Aires: Ediciones UNGS.

PART I

Educational Experiences on the Borders

The three chapters in this first section focus on the educational challenges that migrant children face as they and their families are uprooted, deported, or repatriated. Based on different ethnographic approaches, the three point to difficulties and possibilities for working with migrant children in the educational environment. Kathleen Tacelosky explores the school experiences of children who inhabit transnational borders, emphasizing the linguistic and social issues child migrants face in Mexican schools. Tacelosky discusses borders as historical and cultural constructions and adds specific depth to understanding the process of "crossing back," that is, return migration, as one that creates linguistic and cultural disruption. She stresses the adaptability and resilience of children confronted with competing national and cultural loyalties as they construct and reconstruct their identities.

Marissa Bejarano-Fernbaugh presents the challenges English language educators encounter when working with Central American children as they arrive in the United States and face traumatic situations. She stresses the need to avoid labeling children as migrant "others" and offers successful strategies for encouraging children and young people to build the futures they envision.

Marta Rodríguez-Cruz looks at children that were born in the United States and had to return to Mexico due to immigration enforcement, pointing to the cultural racism and exclusion they face at school in Mexico. Rodríguez-Cruz zooms in on the linguistic and cultural challenges these children encounter, separated by language, food, sports, and other cultural markers, as they struggle to assimilate and internalize Mexican identity.

These three chapters underline the pain and stress children face as they grow up along racial, linguistic, cultural, and social borders and as educational authorities, parents, and even their peers try to label and classify them in an attempt to define them in fixed terms. However, they also offer strategies of resilience and adaptability through which teachers and students can work together to build and rebuild new meanings, ways of communicating and experiencing that can encourage children and young people to pursue their dreams.

CHAPTER 1

Children of Return Migrants Crossing the Linguistic and Cultural Border in the Mexico – United States Context

KATHLEEN TACELOSKY

Introduction

Borders define, distinguish, delineate, partition, divide, separate, contain, restrict, and even unify. Whether conceived from war-ending treaties, tyrannical will, or cartographic estimates, these "imagined projections" (Baud and Van Schendel 1997, 211) are a way of life for people who dwell in the real or symbolic world of transnational spaces, where political, psychological, social, and emotional ties are interconnected in spite of geopolitical, international boundary lines. The experiences represented in this chapter, mostly in the voices of children and adolescents who inhabit borders broadly defined, are those of transnational students and their school experiences. However, each and every one has crossed a political land border, specifically the Mexico-U.S. border, at least once and often various times.

Return migrants are, strictly speaking, people who return to their country of origin after having emigrated to and lived in another. Their children may or may not have lived in or ever even visited the parental homeland. The literature of second-generation return migration tends to focus on adults who go to the ancestral or parental home country, usually by choice (King and Christou 2010; Takamori 2010). Thus, I refer to the youngsters as "children of return migrants." The field of transnational education is where most of the research regarding children who return or go to the parental homeland is housed. Thus, following common practice in this field, I use the term *transnational students* because these children have been schooled in both the United States and Mexico.

As any student who has ever looked at a map understands, nation-states are delimited by some sort of boundary—perhaps a natural body, such as a river or mountain range, but more often a wall, a fence, or guard stations. At times the boundary is imperceptible. When families cross borders to immigrate to a new place and way of life, their children might journey with them. Likewise, children are born in the new place. The identities of these children are at once linked to their immediate surroundings and influences as well as informed by the stories, artifacts, celebrations, customs, relatives, and values of the parental homeland. When their parents return to their homeland, the children and adolescents often accompany them, often, but not always, without being given a choice. For these children this means being uprooted from home, community, and school. Children spend the better part of their waking lives in school and school-related activities, and changing schools can have an enormous impact and be very difficult. To relocate / be relocated to a new school in another country and another language is a particular challenge.

This chapter highlights the linguistic and social issues facing the children of Mexican migrants in the Mexican educational context. Return migration from the United States to Mexico affects millions of people of all ages (Gonzalez-Barrera 2015). The focus here is school-age children. Employing the befitting figurative language of borders and border crossing, I explore the question of how schoolchildren negotiate the social and linguistic border crossing from U.S. educational institutions to Mexican ones. In other words, how do they navigate crossing the border from one school system to another?

Organization of the Chapter

The chapter begins with an explanation of the fieldwork and theoretical lens that undergirds the research. Next, I undertake an exploration of the United States–Mexico border because, though physically distant from where they reside, the border is a real force in the lives of transnational students. After contextualizing the existence and importance of the border, I briefly trace the history of migration and return migration across it. I explore theories of return migration and recognize children in the process, examining the various linguistic trajectories of transnational students. The linguistic and cultural implications of school transition are then considered. The chapter concludes by positioning school entry as a type of border crossing; it takes the civic event of *honores a la bandera* (honoring of the flag) as a type of induction ceremony for newly arrived transnationals and considers how transnational students negotiate participation in the ceremony. Throughout the chapter I incorporate examples from the lives of transnational students, from both the literature and my own interviews with them, because first and foremost, this is their story.

Fieldwork and Theoretical Lens

This chapter is informed by ethnographic fieldwork I carried out in Mexico from 2010 to 2020 that includes extended interaction with over fifty transnational students in the form of interviews (some on more than one occasion and over the course of several years), school observations, home visits, and workshop offerings. I also interviewed teachers and school administrators. In late 2019 and early 2020, my colleague Joel del Villar and I administered a survey that yielded results from 592 transnational students in the state of Zacatecas. Some pertinent preliminary results are shared here, though analysis is ongoing.

Initial interviews took place in the state of Puebla during the academic year of 2010–11 and then during annual summer visits through 2017 and in the state of Zacatecas during the first six months of each year from 2018 to 2020. (The work in 2020 was interrupted in mid-March due to the pandemic.) In Puebla sampling was done by reference (school principals introduced me to transnational families) and snowball sampling (families introduced me to other families) (Johnson 2014). In Zacatecas, at the invitation of the Secretaría de Educación Pública, I visited schools in which officials supported me with the task of finding transnational students in municipalities with high return migration. This "purposeful sampling" is appropriate when seeking a very specific population (Palinkas et al. 2015), in this case students who have studied in the United States. The language of the interview depended on the preference of each participant; many chose a combination of English and Spanish in the same interview, or English in the early years and then Spanish as their own linguistic repertoire shifted to predominantly Spanish.

The average age of participants at the time of the first interview was twelve years and nine months. On average, participants had lived in the

United States for just under five years (4.93), with a range of one to eleven years. They had been (back) in Mexico from two months to six years. Participants' names have been changed to protect their anonymity. In some instances the students chose their own pseudonyms.

Approximately 3 percent of students in Mexican schools have school experience in the United States (Jensen, Mejía Arauz, and Aguilar Zepeda 2017). Some states, like Zacatecas, have high concentrations of return migration, but this does not necessarily translate into high numbers of students in any given school. In other words, many transnational students did not know other students with life experiences similar to their own, apart from a few exceptions.

A sociocultural lens is used to focus on the examination of schools and schooling as experienced by transnational students. Distilled to its simplest terms, socioculturalism recognizes that humans develop and learn when positioned within a social context and that meaning-making/learning happens through interaction with others (Vygotsky 1978). This "mediation," as Vygotsky (1978) called it, is "the process through which the social and the individual mutually shape each other" (Daniels 2015, 34). Thus, transnational children shape and are shaped by their movement (migration) and their binational educational experiences and interactions.

Transnationalism and Second-Generation Returnee Children

Persons born in the "host" country of immigrant parents who go to live in the homeland of their parents are considered second-generation return migrants, although the use of the term *return* is contested, since some are going for the first time. Second-generation return migration has been little studied and theorized as part of the return migration literature. When second- and third-generation individuals and populations, the "counter-diaspora" (King and Christou 2010), do appear in the literature, the studies tend to be about adults who go to the ancestral homeland (King and Christou 2010; Takamori 2010). However, there is a rich and growing body of empirical, school-based research regarding second-generation students in Mexican schools that began with the groundbreaking work of a binational team of scholars in the first decade of the twenty-first century (Hamann, Zúñiga, and Sánchez García 2006, 2008; Zúñiga and Hamann 2006; Zúñiga, Hamann, and

Sánchez García 2008) and continues with contributions from academicians, sociologists, linguists, anthropologists, policy makers, activists, and educators, many of whom work with the express purpose of effecting systematic change to help improve the lives of transnational students.

The people and processes presented in this chapter are seen through a transnational lens. The proximity of Mexico and the United States, historically, physically, and emotionally in the collective imagination of both countries, lends itself uniquely to a transnational vision. The overlapping histories, shared geography—most notably 1,950 miles of common border spanning four U.S. states and six Mexican states—interdependent economies, and intertwined policies correspond to migratory experiences that include feelings of connection with both places, or what Hamann and Zúñiga (2021) call a "durable attachment on both sides of the border."

The prefix *trans-* implies movement and/or change, as in across, beyond, or through. The adjective *transnational* intentionally minimizes the focus on nation-states and nationalism (Glick Schiller, Basch, and Blanc-Szanton 1995) while recognizing the world's growing interconnection in "politics, economy, and family" (Anghel, Fauser, and Boccagni 2019, 7). I use the word *transnational* as an adjective to describe students who have had certain life experiences, specifically those who have had some or all of their schooling in the United States and who are currently enrolled in school in Mexico (or were at the time I first interviewed them).

The United States–Mexico Border: Real and Imagined Space

To describe the Mexico–United States border is to describe not only a physical place but also a relationship, one so interwoven that for many years, and even now in some places, the line is unidentifiable (St. John 2011). What is commonly accepted as the current, official border began first with the U.S. annexation of Texas in 1845 and then the land acquisition of the Treaty of Guadalupe, the pact that ended the Mexican-American War in 1848. Thus, Mexican citizens who were living in Mexican territory abruptly found themselves inhabitants of the United States without having crossed the border; the border had crossed them (Chanbonpin 2005). To remain in the homeland, Mexico, they had to move. A small number, about three thousand, or 3 percent, chose to do so (Rosales 2007, 400).

The connection of the two countries in the collective and individual imaginations of persons of both countries is one where experiences and sentiments include at once both places and neither, or rather a new, hybrid sphere (Bhabha 2012). Transnationals may find themselves most at home in "third intercultural spaces . . . where identities are no longer fixed" (Despagne and Jacobo-Suárez 2016, 10).

Although many transnational students in Mexico inhabit the border regions in states close to the dividing line, the students in my research do not reside or attend school in the physical borderlands. However, they understand the power of the border as representative of the regulations regarding its crossing. *Al otro lado* is an expression, common in all parts of Mexico, that refers to life "on the other side." In this way the border, like *papeles* (papers), is symbolic in that it represents the restriction of movement and the documentation associated with immigration, residency, or citizenship status.

On the other hand, minimizing the power of the border and its restrictions could be an attempt to grapple with an identity that is not so easily defined. "To me the border . . . is just a piece of land. That's all it is. A piece of land where I can cross. No one can tell me, 'Why are you here? You're not supposed to be here'" (Melchor, a transnational high school student in the documentary *Una vida, dos países*, Kleyn 2016).

Kasun and Mora Pablo (2020) share an example from a university student illustrating the struggle to identify: "*Soy indecisa de quién soy*" (I'm indecisive about who I am). Using similar language, Wendy, a transnational young adult that I interviewed, spoke at length about her identity in relation to place: "*No tengo una identidad muy definida en cuanto a de dónde soy*" (I don't have a well-defined identity regarding where I'm from). She explained that "*la migración afecta las amistades*" (migration affects friendships). Her friends whose life experiences do not include moving and migration press her for specifics regarding a locale, a bounded space. She recounted in Spanish a conversation with friends, which I approximate here in English:

"You were born in [city in Zacatecas]. So you are from there?"

"I was born there, but I never lived there."

"OK, so you are from here in this place?"

"Yes, I have lived here, but that's not the whole story. I also lived in the United States for many years."

"Surely you are not from the United States, are you?"

At this point in the interview, she pondered a moment, stretched her hands above her head, and looked up: "*Se me hace un mapa así y ¿cómo les explico tanto?*" (It seems to me a map, like this, and how do I explain so much to them?). She paused and then said, "*No soy ni de aquí ni de allá. Es raro. Pero es bonito. Me gusta la multiculturalidad*" (I am from neither here nor there. It's odd. But it is beautiful. I like multiculturality).

The "neither here nor there" identities found in Wendy's sentiment are echoed in the research of other authors who investigate transnationalism and migration. Gema, the participant in Kasun and Mora Pablo's study, felt her identity shift in the movement toward or away from the border: "*De aquí a la frontera soy mexicana. Y de la frontera para allá, soy americana*" (From here to the border, I'm Mexican. And from the border onward, I'm American).

Offering an alternative to the "neither here nor there" narrative, some researchers and activists propose a both/and statement to describe those who live transnational lives: "*Soy de aquí y de allá*" (I'm from here **and** there) (Kasun and Mora Pablo 2020). Otros Dreams en Acción, a political action group by and for young people who grew up in the United States and are now in Mexico, uses the hashtag *#DeAquíyDeAllá*. Kiara, a participant in my study, appears to have found herself and a sense of belonging with a dual approach to identity. When I asked her whether she considers herself to be from any one place, she replied:

> Not really, because since I was little, even though I was born in the United States, I used to say, "I'm from Mexico." And people were like, "Really?" And I was like, yeah, I was born there.... I felt proud of myself for being Mexican or part Mexican. No, I feel like half and half. I don't usually say it, but I'm really proud because I have ... two kinds of cultures. So I'm really proud of both sides, the Mexican side and the U.S. side. (Kiara, age fourteen)

While it may be that "national borders are political constructs, imagined projections of territorial power" (Baud and Van Schendel 1997, 211), the long reach of the power of the border and the controls implemented by those in authority are very real to transnational children and their family members. Aricel, age thirteen and a U.S. citizen, told me that she had to go back to the United States to "change [her] papers." When I asked her to explain, she said, "I only have five years to stay here [Mexico]. If I don't go back, I'm not from the USA. I'm from here. Or I get los[t]." If that happened, she said, she would have to *"pedir permiso."* I asked her from whom she would need to get permission, and she replied, "The president of the United States." She believed that if she did not take appropriate action in the time allotted, "they" would come looking for her. I asked her how that made her feel. Her reply: "Like I'm in a cage." Although her understanding of the laws governing immigration appear to be somewhat hazy, her feelings are valid, and common.

Melchor, the high school student from the documentary *Una vida, dos países*, also shared feelings of confinement regarding his status, this time in the United States: "I realized that we were different. It felt like there was an invisible wall around us, and we could not do the same things as other people" (Kleyn 2015). Transnational families regularly share with me their fears and worries regarding their lack of freedom of movement. Even policy analysts use the term "caging effect" to explain why immigrants residing in the United States without legal documentation stay longer rather than return when border policies and practices tighten (Rosenblum 2012). They are afraid to move.

In November of 2019, my colleague and I conducted a survey in the north-central Mexican state of Zacatecas to which 592 transnational students enrolled in that state's elementary and middle schools (first through ninth grade) responded. We asked them in an open-ended question why they had to go/return to Mexico. Of the 371 answers that were readily categorizable, almost one-fifth (about 18 percent) pertained to legal matters. Even very young children, ages six and seven, responded with answers such as *"porque a mis papás se les acabó un permiso"* (because my parents' authorization ran out) and *"para arreglar papeles"* (to take care of paperwork) and *"se vensio [venció] mi pasaporte"* (my passport expired). One eight-year-old wrote, *"porque mi mamá era illegal"* (because my mom was illegal).

Takamori (2010, 232), who studies language and identity of Japanese American adults living in Japan, claims that "it is precisely in their in-between-ness and with unclear boundaries of identity that they also find creative ways to navigate, subvert." Students in my work told me that they sometimes pretend they do not understand English, especially in English classes, so other students will not pester them for help and answers. Ana, who lived in New Jersey for ten years and had been in Mexico for two months when I met her, told me that during Simon Says games in English class, she makes mistakes on purpose. When I asked her why, she said it was so the other students could learn, and that they should pay attention to the game and not just copy her. Unlike the Japanese American adults of Takamori's study, the children who practice these subversive tactics do not always end up feeling triumphant or agentive. When I asked her how that makes her feel, Ana said, "Bad! Bad! . . . Because I really like to participate in everything, but not with everyone copying me. I don't feel good."

Migration: Crossing the Border

In the late nineteenth and early twentieth centuries, push factors in Mexico—such as a revolutionary war that left many dispossessed of their land—and pull factors in the United States—such as the need for labor for railroads and agriculture—resulted in increased immigration (Rodríguez, Sáenz, and Menjívar 2007). Temporary labor attracted mostly single young men, for many of whom return to Mexico always was part of the migration project. Thus, the first 130 years of Mexico–United States immigration was marked by this circular migration of coming and going, sometimes formally sanctioned, as with the guest worker Bracero Program implemented during World War II (Calavita 2010).

However, in the late 1980s, with the passage of the Immigration Reform and Control Act, the practice of repeated return and reentry waned considerably. The act not only required employers to demonstrate legal status of employees but also tightened border control, making passage difficult and dangerous (Gutiérrez 2019). Return migration decreased, and what had been a back-and-forth migration of single men drawn to certain regions of the United States became an establishment of family units all over the country (Massey 2015).

In the first decade of the twenty-first century, the period when most of the students in my research were born, new laws increased the punishment and criminality extended beyond immigrants themselves when the Border Protection, Antiterrorism, and Illegal Immigration Control Act of 2005 was established. This law introduced ten-year prison sentences for those who enter the United States with false documentation (Gutiérrez 2019).

Due to a 2012 policy established by then President Obama known as Deferred Action for Childhood Arrivals (DACA), children taken to the United States when they were under the age of sixteen and who meet certain requirements are permitted to apply for the right to remain in the country, be exempt from deportation, and apply for a work permit. During his time in office, President Trump attempted to reverse DACA waivers through executive order, but the order was struck down by the Supreme Court (O'Toole 2020). President Biden has promised to protect DACA and provide a path to citizenship for DACA recipients (Biden 2021).

In recent years an unstable economy in the United States and a president unfriendly to immigrants, coupled with enduring factors such as familial illness and death, are influences that contribute to Mexican immigrants' going back to their homeland in greater numbers than ever. This phenomenon—return migration—is explored and theorized in the next section.

Return Migration: Crossing Back

For as long as there has been immigration from Mexico to the United States, there has been return. Due to the proximity and relative ease of movement across the border, Mexican citizens have immigrated and repatriated for more than a century and a half.

In its broadest sense, return migration is defined simply as the return to the country of origin of people who had previously left it. Distinctions are made between forced and voluntary return. Deportation, or repatriation, is perhaps the most obvious type of forced or involuntary return, but there are other ways that individuals and families feel compelled to remigrate to their homelands. People who leave to be with a spouse who has been deported might not believe that they have much choice in the matter. Likewise, children are often not directly consulted when parents contemplate remigration, or the choices they are given are exceedingly difficult ones. Some researchers suggest that "children influence return plans" of their parents (Dustmann 2003, 817). Andrés, a participant in my research, was seven years old and had lived in the United States for two years when his mom asked him whether he wanted to stay in North Carolina with his grandparents or go back to Mexico with her. One might argue that asking a seven-year-old whether he wants to be with his mother or not does not constitute much of a choice. He went with his mother and brother.

Lina, a mother I interviewed in Zacatecas, told me that while living in Oklahoma, her husband left home one morning to drive to work. He failed to turn on his signal when he made a turn and was stopped by police. The next time she heard from him, he was in a detention center. He was held for several months. Without his income and participation in family life, she could not stay in the United States. So she took a second job for a few months, saved enough money to pack up her two school-age children and some of their possessions, and moved back to her home state in Mexico. Her children, and many like them, had never been to Mexico, and they did not leave voluntarily. "This forced/voluntary dichotomy inadequately captures the many complexities of transnational movement" (Boehm 2016, 7).

Theories of Return Migration

One-quarter of all immigrants in the United States, or 11.2 million people, are from Mexico (Budiman 2020). However, this number reflects a reduction by two million in unauthorized immigrants from Mexico compared with a decade prior (Budiman 2020). This decrease is mainly due to Mexican immigrants' return to their homeland. In the five-year period from 2005 to 2010, the number of Mexicans and their children who moved from the United States to Mexico was, at 1.4 million, about twice that of a decade prior (Passel, Cohn, and Gonzalez-Barrera 2012). For much of the twenty-first century, migration of Mexicans north to south—from the United States to Mexico—has been greater than that of south to north—from Mexico to the United States (Gonzalez-Barrera 2015). In other words, more Mexicans have been leaving the United States than arriving. Very recently, Pew Research Center released the latest data on return migration, suggesting that from 2013 to 2018, there was a slight reversal of the trend, meaning that more Mexicans came to the United States than returned home (Gonzalez-Barrera 2021). The effects of the COVID-19 pandemic on migration patterns are not yet fully known, but at least one survey that included Mexicans suggested that "the pandemic affected the migration plans of 57% of people with the intention of migrating" (International Organization for Migration 2020, 15).

Theories attempt to make sense of the complex issues by distilling them down to comprehensible essentials. Early ideas of return migration, specifically neoclassical theory, focused on labor economics: following a cost-benefit analysis, individuals decide that to reach certain economic goals, they should migrate. If they return, it is because they failed to achieve their financial goals (Cassarino 2004). Scholars who ascribe to structuralist perspectives consider how structures or systems like economics and politics affect return migration. For example, limited job opportunities or changing immigration laws might precipitate a return to new opportunities at home or to a life safe from fears of being detained or deported.

In the early 1990s, transnational perspectives began to draw attention to the way migrants interact with both countries by maintaining strong ties to both places (Glick Schiller, Basch, and Blanc-Szanton 1992). Sometimes travel back and forth is permitted, especially for the second generation, whose immigration status allows for ease of entry and reentry. As such, return is theorized as an expected feature of the back-and-forth journey rather than a detour or dead end (Cassarino 2004). Transnational spaces are those, real or imagined, that are stable and enduring and include "dense sets of ties reaching beyond and across borders of sovereign states" (Faist 2010, 13). In more recent decades, research on the "Digital Diaspora" (Moreno-Esparza 2019, 415) has demonstrated how families not only maintain transnational ties but create new "transnational social spaces" (Christiansen 2017) through social media–based communication. From a transnational perspective, migrants are at the center, viewed as agents with decision-making power (Glick Schiller, Basch, and Blanc-Szanton 1992; Smith and Guarnizo 1998) that includes both the going and the coming back.

Implications of Return Migration for the Mexican Education System

As mentioned, when "established" migrant families began to leave the United States in large numbers, often, but not always, their children accompanied them, and this continues to hold true. Data from 2015 indicate that 550,000 U.S.-born children younger than age eighteen were living in Mexico (Masferrer, Hamilton, and Denier 2019). The exact number of students in the public school system in Mexico who have received some or all of their education in the United States is unknown. This lack of information suggests that the arrival of these students in Mexican classrooms has not been properly considered or documented because the administrative instrument to include relevant questions in the census or school enrollment forms is lacking. However, extrapolations from census data indicate that hundreds of thousands (Alba 2013), perhaps up to six hundred thousand (Jensen and Jacobo-Suárez 2019), students with educational experience in the United States currently attend Mexican schools. The school experiences and language trajectories of transnational students, which differ considerably from those of their mononational schoolmates, are the focus of the remainder of this chapter.

School as Border Crossing

School-age children who transition between two countries with different languages experience multiple disruptions, linguistic and otherwise (Hamann and Zúñiga 2011). Unlike learners in bilingual programs, whose curriculum is designed for the purposeful use of both languages, these transnational students find themselves handling one monolingual academic environment at a time—English in U.S. schools and Spanish in Mexican schools. These disruptions can interrupt linguistic development (Montrul 2008; Potowski, Jegerski, and Morgan-Short 2009) as well as academic achievement. Starting out in any new situation can be challenging. First days, weeks, and even months in a new school, especially when a child is among a handful of new students and the language is not the one they are accustomed to using, can be scary and nerve-racking. As such, transnational children must develop strategies for social and school success.

Though transnational students reside throughout Mexico, I met all the participants in one of two Mexican states—Puebla or Zacatecas. Before delving into the educational and linguistic trajectories of the participants, a word about home language. The transnational students in my study learned to speak Spanish at home because at least one and usually both of their parents are Spanish-speaking Mexicans. However, the acquisition and use of Spanish may vary among transnational students / children of return migrants. The proficiency and comfort level with Spanish of transnational students when they migrate to Mexico is a product of many variables, including how much exposure they have to written Spanish, whether they have siblings in the household with whom they speak English, and the variety of Spanish they learned (discussed in detail later in the section called "Language: The Spanish of Transnational Students"). Further, I have found that sometimes teachers claim that transnational students do not know any Spanish at all, which, while possible, is more likely an interpretation on their part that students do not know enough (quantity) academic (register) Spanish to be successful in school. This point, likewise, is addressed in the language section later.

Trajectory One: Second Generation: Born United States, First Schooling United States, Second Schooling Mexico

The majority of both the students that I interviewed (75 percent) and those that completed the written survey (87 percent) were born in the United States into a Spanish-speaking home. Kiara is an example of such a student. She was born in Pasadena, California, spoke only Spanish until age five, and then learned English at school. Generally speaking, the longer a student stays in school in the United States, the more their English language skills and identity as English speakers develop. Such is the case for Kiara. When she was eleven, her parents decided to return to Mexico for a variety of reasons, the main one being that Kiara's maternal grandmother had cancer and was dying. Kiara's father stayed behind so he could send them money to continue construction on their home in Mexico. Kiara and her mother went to say goodbye to her grandmother. For Kiara's mom this was a one-way trip back to Mexico after twenty-five years in the United States because she did not have any legal way to reenter. For Kiara the move meant leaving behind the only home she had ever known and crossing a cultural and linguistic border into an educational system that had not been designed with her in mind (see table 1.1, Trajectory 1). Specifically, she was expected to behave, linguistically and socially, like her mononational counterparts without any kind of orientation or assistance.

Trajectory Two: Immigrants to the United States: Born Mexico, First Schooling Mexico, Second Schooling United States, Third Schooling Mexico

For transnational students born in Mexico, both home language and first school language are Spanish. This is the case for Julieta: she started school in Mexico and attended through second grade. When she and her family immigrated to California, she started third grade. By the time her family returned to Mexico, she had attended third, fourth, fifth, sixth, and half of seventh grade in the United States, in English. Upon return, she entered middle school at midyear and had to manage Spanish as the school language. (See table 1.1, Trajectory Two.)

Trajectory Three: 1.5 Generation: Born Mexico, Taken to the United States at a Young Age, First Schooling United States, Second Schooling Mexico

Children taken to the United States at a young age are sometimes referred to as the 1.5 generation, born in Mexico but taken to the United States at such a young age that most life experience and memory is in the United States. Andrés was born in Mexico, where he attended preschool (in Mexico preschool starts at age two or three) but left before he was old enough to learn to read. He immigrated with his mother and brother to North Carolina when he was quite young, at age five, so his earliest recollection of school is in English. Regarding his first days in U.S. school, he said, "It was very hard to me to communicate because it was like I [didn't] have a voice" (Andrés, age fourteen). Eventually, he did learn English. In North Carolina he continued to speak Spanish at home with his mother, but as their English improved due to school and community exposure, he and his older brother began to speak English to each other, even at home. When the three of them returned to Mexico, the boys were required to use Spanish for schooling. (See table 1.1, Trajectory Three.) They continued speaking both languages at home: English with each other and Spanish with their mother.

TABLE 1.1 The linguistic journey of children of Mexican immigrants: Possible trajectories

	Trajectory 1: Kiara	Trajectory 2: Julieta	Trajectory 3: Andrés	Trajectory 4: Nicole
Born	United States	Mexico	Mexico	United States
Home language	Spanish	Spanish	Spanish	Spanish
First school language	English (United States)	Spanish (Mexico)	English (United States)	English (United States)
Second school language	Spanish (Mexico)	English (United States)	Spanish (Mexico)	Spanish (Mexico)
Third school language	—	Spanish (Mexico)	—	English (United States)

Trajectory Four: Full Circle: Born United States, First Schooling United States, Second Schooling Mexico, Third Schooling United States

A few students in my longitudinal study have returned to the United States, their country of birth and first schooling. (See table 1.1, Trajectory Four.) I met Nicole at her elementary school in Zacatecas in 2018, when she was in fourth grade. She had been living in Mexico for just a few months, having been born and raised by her Mexican mother in the United States. She attended a writing workshop I was teaching and wrote about leaving the United States, the journey across the border, and her initial reactions to Mexico:

> I remember one day after school I was doing my homework. . . . My mom said she wanted to move to Mexico. I never thought she was serious. . . . We were crossing the border and we took a bus right outside of El Paso [Texas]. I think it was already Mexico. It took like three days. It felt like ten thousand years. I was so bored. . . . When I got out, we got to Zacatecas. I got very excited. My uncle was waiting for us at the bus station. I ran to him and gave him a big hug. We went straight to my great grandmother's house, and . . . she was trying to talk to me, but I felt weird, and it was strange because she was making weird expressions that made me not understand. (Nicole, age ten)

Nicole's words demonstrate the impact that the linguistic repertoires transported across borders may engender when children of return migrants attempt to communicate with family members and others. Nicole entered fourth grade in Mexico and had a mixed experience, struggling with adjustment to the new school and the language of school. Fifth grade proved increasingly difficult academically, though she had been an excellent student in the United States. Finally, her mother decided to send her and her sister to live with family back in New Mexico. Nicole's mother cannot leave Mexico while she waits for her visa to be processed. Thus, they are another family "divided by borders" (Dreby 2010).

There are, of course, many other possible scenarios. For example, I met students in school in Mexico who had been born in the United States and lived there for a very short period of time (months or a few years) before being taken to Mexico, starting school and living only there. I did not interview children who had had no U.S. schooling, since my focus is on the linguistics of school. There are also students who return and either do not enter school or drop out before completion.

Transition: New School

After crossing into Mexico, transnational families have to traverse the border of school admission. Not unlike officials at political borders who demand entry permits, school administrators require appropriate documentation for entrance. Until 2015 the obstacles for school acceptance were onerous—birth certificates, report cards, and Mexican and U.S. identification. In the past some of these documents had to be stamped with a raised seal of authenticity, an apostille. Nicole's mother told me that when they arrived in 2017, her daughters were denied access at two different schools because their report cards from New Mexico did not have the required seal. She was told she would have to get this seal from the capital of the state where she and the girls had lived. No kind of administrative procedure exists to get children's report cards validated in such a way, to say nothing of the impossibility of returning to the United States for such a procedure. Although laws had been changed two years prior to provide more ready access and state-level departments of education have made efforts to educate school administrators, practices on the ground lag behind, and in some places returning families continue to encounter obstacles.

Once enrolled, transnational students have other social, cultural, and linguistic challenges:

> Thinking about being in school here in Mexico made me sick, nervous. I was scared of being alone. I was scared of everyone. The first day I saw some girls from third grade, and they asked me if I was new. I stayed quiet. They grabbed me by the hand and showed me the classrooms and the bathrooms. I wish I spoke Spanish. It would have been a lot easier to make a friend. When I went inside the classroom everybody was staring at me, and my head was hot, my hands were shaking, my mouth was dry, and I was thinking so many things that I got dizzy. The teacher asked me some questions, but all I wanted to do was go home. (Nicole, age ten)

As newcomers, transnational students might be positioned as neophytes—ignorant and inexperienced—by teachers and classmates. However, they bring prior knowledge and experience. The linguistic and cultural knowledge they carry with them is sometimes not recognized as valid or valuable by classmates and teachers. Nicole's sister, Jade, found school in Mexico difficult at first too:

> My first day of school was sad because . . . I thought my teacher was mean and all the kids were making fun of me every day, and I felt sad, and I go to the bathroom, and I cry and cry. . . . It took me a long time to make friends and the teacher started to like me too. By the time I started to get along and get comfortable at school, it was time for summer vacation. (Jade, age eight)

Furthermore, their language, having been acquired in their U.S. homes and Spanish-speaking communities, is a contact variety, formed as groups with more than one linguistic repertoire (language or variety) interact with one another (Weinreich 1953; Winford 2003). This Spanish, then, is distinct from that of their mononational classmates in Mexico. It is influenced by English and, in some communities, by multiple Spanish varieties and other foreign languages (Lipski 2008; Otheguy and Zentella 2012). As such, individual speakers have a range of experiences in terms of contact with variations inside and outside their homes.

Language: The Spanish of Transnational Students

In addition to learning Spanish at home from their Mexican parents in the United States, transnational students learn from encounters in the community. The richness of a bilingual library, bilingual support staff at school, and church services in Spanish potentially support the development of Spanish. However, transnational students do not necessarily have access to these linguistic resources. Many do not live in an environment where Spanish is part of their daily sphere outside of the home. Furthermore, as a contact variety, the Spanish that they encounter in the United States is marked by lexical, semantic, syntactic, and prosodic features influenced by its creation in a community where other languages and varieties, in this case mostly English, are spoken (Otheguy and Zentella 2012).

In sum, the Spanish that transnational students take (back) with them to Mexico is not the same Spanish they encounter in social/familial situations in Mexico or in Mexican academic settings. Nicole, the fourth grader from

Zacatecas, could not understand her great-grandmother or her classmates at recess. The language of playground and social events—jokes, plays on words, and double meanings—are lost on children who use mostly English in those domains. Transnational students are accustomed to English at school and Spanish at home.

The Spanish required for school success, especially in later school years, has to be learned. Home language may be marked by informality and lexical variation limited to the quotidian sphere. For example, discussions about daily life and familial decisions require a kind of vocabulary and grammar different from school language. Academic language is not simply a more complicated and more specialized lexicon. Academic language includes complex clauses held together by subordinating and coordinating conjunctions; discourse markers for paragraph and essay comprehension; figurative language, like metaphors and similes; and writing in a sophisticated style to compare and contrast, analyze, persuade, and so on. Simply put, the Spanish learned at home is not readily transferable to a school context, and the English learned in school is not simply translatable to Spanish. As a result a student with years of schooling in the United States likely will encounter significant challenges in Mexican schools. Although the Mexican education system has begun to pay attention to the changing needs of this international population, much needs to be done to assist newcomers and returnees from the United States in their transition to Mexican academic life and language. Mexican teachers of all grades must be trained to teach reading in Spanish. Instructional support is needed to fill gaps in learning, such as Mexican history and geography. However, what students tell me they want most is for teachers to be patient and respectful with them and to be kind to them.

Honores a la Bandera: A School-Based Citizenship Test

Although Mexican schools may be seeing a shift away from assimilationist policies, if not practices, toward more inclusive ones (Levinson, Luna Elizarrarás, and Hamann 2020), schools continue to be sites where national loyalty is expected and tested. Perhaps this is never more palpable than during the *honores a la bandera*, the flag ceremony.

No one emblem represents a nation quite like its flag. Flags are imbued with symbolism and history and are accompanied by a narrative that interweaves its colors and images. When, where, and how the flag is to be displayed and handled are matters of serious consideration. In Mexico guidelines and specifics of how to honor the flag were written into law in 1984 (Hurtado 1984), though school ceremonies honoring the flag predate the law by several decades. The law requires the ceremony be held every Monday morning and on thirty-one other dates during the academic year in all schools.

Dana, a middle schooler in Zacatecas, knew nothing about the law or the practice when she arrived at a Mexican school at age twelve after having been born and raised in the United States. All she knew was that on the first day of the school year in her first year of middle school, about a year and a half before I met her, she found herself standing in the school courtyard at a ceremony that she did not understand. She brought it up when I asked her about her first day of school in Mexico:

> They have a thing called "honors," like when they go out, where they do soccer and PE, it's kind of like the field, but it's not grass. It's concrete, and there is this thing where they honor the flag. I wasn't used to that because we wouldn't do that, we wouldn't honor the flag the way they do, and they would just do stuff like sing a song, and I didn't know what to do. I was just confused and trying to follow the others. (Dana, age thirteen)

Dana endeavored to situate this highly symbolic ceremony in which schoolchildren place their hands over their hearts and solemnly swear to honor and defend the flag with loyalty and perseverance (Hurtado 1984, 13). She tried to make sense of it by comparing it to her prior experiences. Her use of "they" to describe students in Mexican schools and "we" to talk about her life in the United States suggests that she continues to identify with U.S. practices, the ones she understands. It is also possible that she is seeking or expressing solidarity with me, a native English-speaking researcher from the United States.

Dana went on to explain that the concrete area where the event takes place is "like the field." Fields are places with grass, in her experience, and here there is only concrete. In most Mexican schools, a concrete patio in the middle of a rectangle of buildings that house the classrooms serves as a recess yard, sports field, eating area, dance floor, stage, and, on Monday mornings, flag-ceremony site.

When she did not know what behavior was expected, Dana attempted to "follow the others." Conforming to the practices at a new school is an important part of fitting in, as Dana tried to do. In an interview with a different student, the issue of the flag ceremony likewise came up. When the student told me that he did not know the words to the national anthem, I asked whether he would like to learn them. He said that during the ceremony he prefers to "watch other people sing; but also no one like looks at me or tells me to sing, so it's still not on my top list [of things I need to learn] even though I don't know it" (Benito, age fourteen). He went on to express that he had more pressing needs, like improving his reading comprehension in Spanish.

Dana continued her comparison when I asked her to talk about activities associated with the flag in school in the United States: "We would say the Pledge of Allegiance, but it's pretty different here because here some girls . . . walk around with the flag." Dana likely will discover that what she interpreted as girls walking around with the flag is called the *escolta* (color guard) and involves many hours of training and practice. A forty-page manual from another state prescribing flag protocol contains 153 mentions of the *escolta* (Gómez Tejeda 2017).

I asked her whether anyone helped her during the ceremony. She said yes, that a girl who had spoken to her earlier gave her some guidance on what to do, and she said, "I felt pretty glad because I didn't really have to struggle to find a friend."

Dana's response to the assistance was a positive one, not expressly because it helped her be able to participate in the event but rather because she made a friend. A ceremony whose main purpose is to "educate . . . children and youth in the practice of civic values and to promote love of Country among all Mexicans"[1] (Gómez Tejeda 2017, 3) likely does not carry the same meaning for transnational students that it does for their mononational counterparts. Both Dana and Benito were born in the United States and lived there for twelve years. Each of them had been in Mexico for about one and a half years when we spoke, Dana in 2020 and Benito in 2018. It is possible that their identification with the United States after six to seven years of public education there, saluting the U.S. flag and singing the U.S. national anthem, meant that they did not want to engage too deeply or claim an allegiance that might make them feel uncomfortable or disloyal.

The emotion that is supposed to swell in the hearts of children and adolescents across Mexico during the *honores* is lost on those with a different history and context. However, that does not mean that the exercise is devoid of significance for them. Transnational students situate themselves to the best of their ability and according to their own desire to integrate. It is easy to imagine why a new student would view making a friend on the first day of school as more pressing than learning the words and gestures of the flag salute.

In this brief examination, we observe how on one level transnationals and other newcomers are integrated into the community. On another level they demonstrate autonomy by prioritizing what is important. In this way transnational students correspond to Vygotsky's (1978) description of independent and interdependent social agents who act and interact to negotiate their identities, create meaning, and respond to their new situation.

Transnational students who have adapted to the Mexican school system after a time might be excellent sources of expertise, given their previous experiences as scholars of culture. During our conversation Dana revealed that the girl who helped her was another transnational student who herself had lived in the United States. Thus, at one point she also had been the new girl and likely had had to figure out the flag ceremony on her first day.

Conclusion

In addition to being delimiters of geopolitical boundaries, borders have a sociocultural function, marking belonging and exclusion. Borders are "ambiguous human constructions, produced, reproduced, and justified through social practices and discourses" (Haselberger 2014, 518). They represent transnational spaces as migrants symbolically cross and recross through interconnected political, social, cultural, and linguistic transfer.

From day one, transnational students are faced with the reality that "transnational migration entails crossing national borders as well as the boundaries of 'us' versus 'them'" (Chee and Jakubiak 2020, 119). The example of the flag ceremony, beyond being an unfamiliar cultural practice, is a de facto citizenship test, a site where demonstration of loyalty is exacted through what is arguably the "most potent moment of civic education" in the life of a student (Bybee et al. 2020, 137). Transnational students exercise agency as they choose how and whether to participate.

Every day in Mexico and the United States, hundreds of thousands of children wake up and go to school in a country where they were not born and raised. These international "sojourners" (Hamann 2001) find themselves in classrooms with mononational classmates and teachers whose values and life experiences vary widely from their own. As such, every day at school is a type of cultural and linguistic border crossing.

Note

1.   Translation mine.

References

Alba, Francisco. 2013. "Mexico: The New Migration Narrative." Migration Policy Institute. Migration Information Source, April 24, 2013. https://www.migration policy.org/article/mexico-new-migration-narrative.

Anghel, Remus G., Margit Fauser, and Paolo Boccagni, eds. 2019. *Transnational Return and Social Change: Hierarchies, Identities, and Ideas.* New York, N.Y.: Anthem Press.

Baud, Michiel, and Willem Van Schendel. 1997. "Toward a Comparative History of Borderlands." *Journal of World History* 8 (42): 211–42.

Bhabha, Homi K. 2012. *The Location of Culture.* New York, N.Y.: Routledge.

Biden, Joe R. 2021. "Preserving and Fortifying Deferred Action for Childhood Arrivals." Memorandum, January 20, 2021. Federal Register. https://www.federalregister .gov/documents/2021/01/25/2021-01769/preserving-and-fortifying-deferred -action-for-childhood-arrivals-daca.

Boehm, Deborah A. 2016. *Returned: Going and Coming in an Age of Deportation.* Oakland: University of California Press.

Budiman, Abby. 2020. "Key Findings About U.S. Immigrants." Pew Research Center, August 20, 2020. https://www.pewresearch.org/fact-tank/2020/08/20/key -findings-about-u-s-immigrants/.

Bybee, Eric Ruiz, Erin F. Whiting, Bryant Jensen, Victoria Savage, Alisa Baker, and Emma Holdaway. 2020. "'Estamos aquí pero no soy de aquí': American Mexican Youth, Belonging and Schooling in Rural, Central Mexico." *Anthropology and Education Quarterly* 51 (2): 123–45.

Calavita, Kitty. 2010. *Inside the State: The Bracero Program, Immigration, and the INS.* New Orleans, La.: Quid Pro.

Cassarino, Jean-Pierre. 2004. "Theorising Return Migration: The Conceptual Approach to Return Migrants Revisited." *International Journal on Multicultural Studies* 6 (2): 253–79.

Chanbonpin, Kim D. 2005. "How the Border Crossed Us: Filling the Gap Between Plume v. Seward and the Dispossession of Mexican Landowners in California after 1848." *Cleveland State Law Review* 52 (2): 297–320.

Chee, Wai-Chi, and Cori Jakubiak. 2020. "The National as Global, the Global as National: Citizenship Education in the Context of Migration and Globalization." *Anthropology and Education Quarterly* 51 (2): 119–22.

Christiansen, Martha S. 2017. "Creating a Unique Transnational Place: Deterritorialized Discourse and the Blending of Time and Space in Online Social Media." *Written Communication* 34 (2): 135–64.

Daniels, Harry. 2015. "Mediation: An Expansion of the Socio-Cultural Gaze." *History of the Human Sciences* 28 (2): 34–50.

Despagne, Colette, and Monica Jacobo-Suárez. 2016. "Desafíos actuales de la escuela monolítica mexicana: El caso de los alumnos migrantes transnacionales." *Sinéctica* 47. https://sinectica.iteso.mx/index.php/SINECTICA/article/view/645.

Dreby, Joanna. 2010. *Divided by Borders: Mexican Migrants and Their Children*. Los Angeles: University of California Press.

Dustmann, Christian. 2003. "Children and Return Migration." *Journal of Population Economics* 16 (4): 815–30.

Faist, Thomas. 2010. "Diaspora and Transnationalism: What Kind of Dance Partners?" In *Diaspora and Transnationalism: Concepts, Theories, and Methods*, edited by Rainer Bauböck and Thomas Faist, 9–34. Amsterdam: Amsterdam University Press.

Glick Schiller, Nina, Linda Basch, and Cristina Blanc-Szanton. 1992. "Transnationalism: A New Analytic Framework for Understanding Migration." *Annals of the New York Academy of Sciences* 645 (1): 1–24.

Glick Schiller, Nina, Linda Basch, and Cristina Blanc-Szanton. 1995. "From Immigrant to Transmigrant: Theorizing Transnational Migration." *Anthropological Quarterly* 68 (1): 48–63.

Gómez Tejeda, David. 2017. "Protocolo para ceremonias con presencia de la bandera nacional." Pachuca de Soto, Mexico: Secretaría de educación pública del estado de Hidalgo.

Gonzalez-Barrera, Ana. 2015. "More Mexicans Leaving than Coming to the U.S." Pew Research Center. Research report, November 19, 2015. https://www.pewresearch .org/hispanic/2015/11/19/more-mexicans-leaving-than-coming-to-the-u-s/.

Gonzalez-Barrera, Ana. 2021. "Before COVID-19, More Mexicans Came to the U.S. Than Left for Mexico for the First Time in Years." Pew Research Center, July 9, 2021. https://www.pewresearch.org/fact-tank/2021/07/09/before-covid-19-more -mexicans-came-to-the-u-s-than-left-for-mexico-for-the-first-time-in-years/.

Gutiérrez, Ramón A. 2019. "Mexican Immigration to the United States." In *Oxford Research Encyclopedia of American History*. Article published online July 29, 2019. Oxford: Oxford University Press. https://doi.org/10.1093/acrefore/9780199329 175.013.146.

Hamann, Edmund T. 2001. "Theorizing the Sojourner Student (with a Sketch of Appropriate School Responsiveness)." In *Negotiating Transnationalism: Selected Papers on Refugees and Immigrants*, edited by MaryCarol Hopkins and Nancy Wellmeier, 32–71. Arlington, Va.: American Anthropological Association.

Hamann, Edmund T., and Víctor Zúñiga. 2011. "Schooling and the Everyday Ruptures Transnational Children Encounter in the United States and Mexico." In *Everyday Ruptures: Children, Youth, and Migration in Global Perspective*, edited by

Cati Cole, Rachel R. Reynold, Debora A. Boehm, Julia Meredith Hess, and Heather Ray Espinoza, 141–60. Nashville, Tenn.: Vanderbilt University Press.

Hamann, Edmund T., and Víctor Zúñiga. 2021. "What Educators in Mexico and in the United States Need to Know and Acknowledge to Attend to the Educational Needs of Transnational Students." In *The Students We Share: Preparing U.S. and Mexican Educators for Our Transnational Future*, edited by Patricia Gándara and Bryant Jensen, 99–117. Albany, N.Y.: SUNY Press.

Hamann, Edmund T., Víctor Zúñiga, and Juan Sánchez García. 2006. "*Pensando en Cynthia y su hermana*: Educational Implications of United States–Mexico Transnationalism for Children." *Journal of Latinos and Education* 5 (4): 253–74.

Hamann, Edmund T., Víctor Zúñiga, and Juan Sánchez García. 2008. "From Nuevo León to the U.S.A. and Back Again: Transnational Students in Mexico." *Journal of Immigrant and Refugee Studies* 6 (1): 60–84.

Haselberger, Beatrix. 2014. "Decoding Borders: Appreciating Border Impacts on Space and People." *Planning Theory and Practice* 15 (4): 505–26.

Hurtado, Miguel. 1984. "Ley sobre el escudo, la bandera y el himno nacionales." Decree, Congreso General.

International Organization for Migration. 2020. *Effects of COVID-19 on Migrants: Survey in Central America and Mexico*. San José, Costa Rica: International Organization for Migration.

Jensen, Bryant, and Mónica Jacobo-Suárez. 2019. "Integrating American–Mexican Students in Mexican Classrooms." *Kappa Delta Pi Record* 55 (1): 36–41.

Jensen, Bryant, Rebeca Mejía Arauz, and Rodrigo Aguilar Zepeda. 2017. "Equitable Teaching for Returnee Children in Mexico." *Sinéctica* 48. https://sinectica.iteso.mx/index.php/SINECTICA/article/view/757.

Johnson, Timothy P. 2014. "Snowball Sampling: Introduction." *Wiley StatsRef: Statistics Reference Online*, first published September 29, 2014. https://doi.org/10.1002/9781118445112.stat05720.

Kasun, G. Sue, and Irasema Mora Pablo. 2020. "El anti-malinchismo en contra del ser mexicano-transnacional: Cómo transformar esa frontera limitante." Zoom conference presentation at Instituto Investigativo de Antropología, UNAM, May 13, 2020.

King, Russell, and Anastasia Christou. 2010. "Cultural Geographies of Counter-Diasporic Migration: Perspectives from the Study of Second-Generation 'Returnees' to Greece." *Population, Space, and Place* 16 (2): 103–19.

Kleyn, Tatyana, ed. 2015. "Guía de apoyo a docentes con estudiantes transfronterizos: Alumnos de educación básica y media" [Guide to Support Teachers of Transborder Students: Primary and Secondary Students]. http://www.unavidathefilm.com/s/Guia-Final-3-18-16_Small.pdf.

Kleyn, Tatyana, dir. 2016. *Una vida, dos países: Children and Youth (Back) in Mexico*. Filmed in Oaxaca, Mexico. 30 min. http://www.unavidathefilm.com/#watch-the-film.

Levinson, Bradley A., María E. Luna Elizarrarás, and Edmund T. Hamann. 2020. "Transnational Migration and Civic Education in Mexico: An Evolving Story." *Intercultural Education* 31 (5): 533–47.

Lipski, John M. 2008. *Varieties of Spanish in the United States*. Washington, D.C.: Georgetown University Press.

Masferrer, Claudia, Erin R. Hamilton, and Nicole Denier. 2019. "Immigrants in their Parental Homeland: Half a Million U.S.-Born Minors Settle Throughout Mexico." *Demography* 56 (4): 1453–61.

Massey, Douglas S. 2015. "A Missing Element in Migration Theories." *Migration Letters* 12 (3): 279–99.

Montrul, Silvina A. 2008. *Incomplete Acquisition in Bilingualism: Re-Examining the Age Factor*. Philadelphia: John Benjamins.

Moreno-Esparza, Gabriel. 2019. "Digital Diasporas: Accounting for the Role of Family Talk in Transnational Social Spaces." In *The Handbook of Diasporas, Media, and Culture*, edited by Jessica Retis and Roza Tsagarousianou, 415–28. Hoboken, N.J.: John Wiley and Sons.

Otheguy, Ricardo, and Ana C. Zentella. 2012. *Spanish in New York: Language Contact, Dialectical Leveling, and Structural Continuity*. New York: Oxford University Press.

O'Toole, Molly. 2020. "The Supreme Court Rejected Trump's Attempt to End DACA. Now What?" *Los Angeles Times*, June 18, 2020. https://www.latimes.com/politics/story/2020-06-18/the-supreme-court-rejected-trumps-attempt-to-end-daca-now-what.

Palinkas, Lawrence A., Sarah M. Horwitz, Carla A. Green, Jennifer P. Wisdom, Naihua Duan, and Kimberly Hoagwood. 2015. "Purposeful Sampling for Qualitative Data Collection and Analysis in Mixed Method Implementation Research." *Administration and Policy in Mental Health and Mental Health Services Research* 42 (5): 533–44.

Passel, Jeffrey S., D'Vera Cohn, and Ana Gonzalez-Barrera. 2012. "Net Migration from Mexico Falls to Zero—and Perhaps Less." Pew Research Center. Research report, April 23, 2012. https://www.pewresearch.org/hispanic/2012/04/23/net-migration-from-mexico-falls-to-zero-and-perhaps-less/.

Potowski, Kim, Jill Jegerski, and Kara Morgan-Short. 2009. "The Effects of Instruction on Linguistic Development in Spanish Heritage Language Speakers." *Language Learning* 59 (3): 537–79.

Rodríguez, Havidán, Rogelio Sáenz, and Cecilia Menjívar, eds. 2007. *Latinas/os in the United States: Changing the Face of America*. New York, NY: Springer.

Rosales, F. Arturo. 2007. "Repatriation of Mexicans from the U.S." In *The Praeger Handbook of Latino Education in the U.S.*, edited by Lourdes Diaz Soto, 400–403. Westport, Conn.: Greenwood.

Rosenblum, Mark R. 2012. "Border Security: Immigration Enforcement Between Ports of Entry." Washington, D.C.: Congressional Research Service.

Smith, Michael P., and Luis E. Guarnizo, eds. 1998. *Transnationalism from Below*. New York: Routledge.

St. John, Rachel. 2011. *Line in the Sand: A History of the Western U.S.-Mexico Border*. Princeton, N.J.: Princeton University Press.

Takamori, Ayako. 2010. "Rethinking Japanese American 'Heritage' in the Homeland." *Critical Asian Studies* 42 (2): 217–38.

Tsuda, Takeyuki. 2003. *Strangers in the Ethnic Homeland: Japanese Brazilian Return Migration in Transnational Perspective.* New York: Columbia University Press.

Vygotsky, Lev S. 1978. *Mind in Society: The Development of Higher Psychological Processes.* Edited by Michael Cole, Vera John-Steiner, Sylvia Scribner, and Ellen Souberman. Cambridge, Mass.: Harvard University Press.

Weinreich, Uriel. 1953. *Languages in Contact.* The Hague: Mouton.

Winford, Donald. 2003. *An Introduction to Contact Linguistics.* Malden, Mass.: Blackwell.

Zúñiga, Víctor, and Edmund T. Hamann. 2006. "Going Home? Schooling in Mexico of Transnational Children." *CONfines de relaciones internacionales y ciencia política* 2 (4): 41–57.

Zúñiga, Víctor, Edmund T. Hamann, and Juan Sánchez García. 2008. *Alumnos transnacionales: Las escuelas mexicanas frente a la globalización.* Mexico City: Secretaría de Educación Pública.

CHAPTER 2

Be the Buffalo

Working for EL Success in the South

MARISSA BEJARANO-FERNBAUGH

As an educator who lived on the United States–Mexico border, I became familiar with the plight of English learners (ELs). As a middle and high school student in the border town of Nogales, Arizona, I learned of the challenges that my peers faced because they did not speak English. In middle school the ELs were segregated and had their own building and even their own student government. In high school our bilingual principal refused to speak Spanish to students and would ignore requests to translate for our peers. Being raised in a border town, everyone was related to or knew someone who did not speak English. So as a high school community, we took it upon ourselves to help our classmates. At that time I also volunteered during community-based naturalization/U.S.-citizenship workshops and helped future citizens complete forms that were available only in English. Hence, I am familiar with the barriers that ELs face when trying to learn English and navigate a new society, country, and culture.

My reintroduction to the challenges and barriers faced by ELs fully crystallized when I became a teacher in Louisiana. In 2005, amid the devastation of Hurricane Katrina, the rebuilding of neighborhoods and communities led to the recruitment of immigrant workers from Mexico and Central America. Louisianans embraced the arrival of workers who helped with the cleanup efforts. Subsequently, these immigrants changed the demographics of Louisiana since many of their families joined them once they were settled (Grimm 2019).

This demographic change became evident in classrooms, and lamentably, teachers and administrators were not prepared to integrate and adjust to this new student population. In 2012 the Southern Poverty Law Center filed two complaints alleging that Jefferson Parish School System in Louisiana failed to provide adequate translation and interpretation services for EL students and their families. The complaint noted that staff interrogated students about their citizenship status as a condition of enrollment and graduation. School officials failed to take any action against a teacher who called a student a "w**back" during class and refused to place the student in another classroom. The complaint also noted that the school district staff created a hostile learning environment for Hispanic students, citing a high rate of long-term suspensions as one example, and indicated that special education materials were provided only in English to Spanish-speaking parents (SPLC 2012).

The Department of Homeland Security reported that on the Southwest border, from the beginning of fiscal year 2015 through March 2021, the number of unaccompanied Central American and Mexican children encountered by U.S. Border Control totaled 335,662 (see table 2.1).

These surges of unaccompanied minors arriving at the southern border, including children seeking asylum or refugee status and those who are undocumented, has led to an increase of students in our schools.

When I first started working as an EL educator in Louisiana, the school district had fewer than one hundred ELs. Today we have over seven hundred ELs, and the number is growing daily. My teaching philosophy is to do no harm and accept children as they are when they come into my classroom. I firmly believe that a teacher should capitalize on the strengths that children bring and promote their holistic development. Unfortunately, deficit-

TABLE 2.1 Unaccompanied children encounters by country

Country	2015	2016	2017	2018	2019	2020	2021 (March)	Total
El Salvador	9,389	17,512	9,143	4,949	12,021	2,189	3,755	58,958
Guatemala	13,589	18,913	14,827	22,327	30,329	8,390	18,372	126,747
Honduras	5,409	10,468	7,784	10,913	20,398	4,454	11,949	71,375
Mexico	11,012	11,926	8,877	10,136	10,487	14,359	11,785	78,582
Total	39,399	58,819	40,631	48,325	73,235	29,392	45,861	335,662

Source: U.S. Customs and Border Protection (2020).
Note: All years refer to fiscal years. Beginning in March of fiscal year 2020, statistics include both Title 8 apprehensions and Title 42 expulsions.

oriented thinking and exclusionary policies affect the successful outcomes of ELs; this is an ongoing challenge within our community. For example, in 2018 the Louisiana High School Athletics Association created a state-wide policy requiring all athletes to have Social Security numbers. Alanah Odoms Hebert, executive director of the American Civil Liberties Union of Louisiana, challenged the association's policy, stating that "requiring student athletes to provide their social security numbers is a discriminatory practice that may prevent undocumented children from participating" (Clark 2018). This policy precluded many undocumented students from participating in sports. Despite the fact that this rule was eventually overturned, the damage had been done: many students were unable to play sports.

In 2019 Jefferson Parish Schools officials reported that five hundred children from Central America were enrolled in their schools. "The superintendent, James Meza, has called the influx of Hispanic children a 'major, major shift' from what the system saw before Hurricane Katrina. When it comes to English Language Learners, 'we are growing exponentially'" (*Times Picayune* 2019).

According to NYU Steinhardt School of Culture, Education, and Human Development, by 2025 English language learners will make up 25 percent of the U.S. student population (Counseling@NYU 2018). Samson and Collins (2012) indicate that English language learners score the lowest in standardized reading and math exams. The National Center for Education Statistics reports that students between the ages of sixteen and twenty-four who have limited English proficiency or are foreign born are less likely to have a high school diploma than their English-speaking peers (NCES 1995). These data indicate that we must provide educators with the knowledge and expertise necessary to address the learning needs of ELs now and in the future. Because research has been slow to keep up with this fast-growing student population, schools, teachers, and administrators fall short of knowing how to best help ELs and achieve optimal learning outcomes.

Drawing on my personal experiences as a teacher in a school district in Louisiana, I will share parts of the life stories of my students, describe my evolving relationship with their families, and highlight discussions with educators and administrators regarding pedagogy and educational policies as well as challenges that EL educators encounter in meeting the educational needs of EL students. I use pseudonyms to protect my students, their parents, and my colleagues while sharing specific examples of classroom interactions that will crystallize the challenges EL teachers and students face and conclude with recommendations for successful educational and social outcomes. This chapter is dedicated to my EL students, who are the future leaders of this country, and to EL teachers that make a difference every day in their students' lives.

Crossing Borders

Oxford Languages defines a border as "a line separating two political or geographical areas." Sounds simple enough: just a line, a man-made perimeter, but once it is crossed, it is followed by another, and another, and another. Whether it is a physical barrier, an interaction with government officials, or a border designated by the cartels, these "borders" are all too familiar to my students. By the time my courageous students reach my classroom, they have survived crossing many international and state borders only to be confronted again with linguistic, cultural, emotional, educational, and political barriers.

There are many challenges to working with a vulnerable population. In many cases our students live in the shadows, having to lie, be discrete, or not share information because they are undocumented or have an undocumented family member. This causes a lot of anxiety within our EL community (Aranda 2016). Lack of formal education, unique living arrangements, financial obligations back in their home country, limited English proficiency, and poverty are a few of the hindrances ELs face while learning. Two students, one from Guatemala and the other from Honduras, had never previously attended school and had no formal education. The student from Guatemala did not speak Spanish. Both of these students dropped out and are working in construction sites. In addition, students that have gaps in their education are classified as students with interrupted formal education (SIFEs), a small but growing subgroup in the United States. Due to violence in their home countries and their migration trajectories, some students have been out of school for months or, in some cases, years. These students are also most likely to drop out if we do not put interventions in place (Potochnick 2018). In my personal experience, the majority of these students indicate that they are here to work to send money home. Immigration officials or immigration policy requirements obligate them to attend school even when they are not academically or socially ready, compared to their peers, to begin their lives as high school students. Having gaps in their education compounds their inability to achieve academically. In their home country, many were living as adults, and attending school was not an option (Peña 2020).

Dealing with Trauma

Another factor we must take into consideration is trauma, which EL students are more likely to encounter than their nonimmigrant, nonrefugee peers (Schmidt 2019). Physicians for Human Rights, the American Medical Association, the American Academy of Pediatrics, the American Psychiatric Association, the National Association of Pediatric Nurse Practitioners—all these organizations have one thing in common: they agree that refugee/immigrant children are suffering from extreme trauma, having left their home countries, endured the arduous journey to the United States, and experienced further trauma by being separated from their parents and living in detention centers (Artiga and Ubri 2017). The kinds of trauma that EL students face are multiple: poverty, family turmoil, hunger, and migration, as well as the trauma of witnessing violent acts or running to cross borders only to end up in detention centers all alone. Five years ago I had one or two students out of a group of sixty who had experienced trauma, but today trauma has become the norm, and new students with trauma arrive almost daily.

School districts cannot provide bilingual counselors or trauma therapists because of a lack of funding or availability. Our school counselors are required to spend much of their time testing rather than counseling. Counselors receive accolades based on ACT scores, graduation rates, and WorkKeys, an assessment that measures students' workplace skills.

When children arrive in our schools, they often have dealt with heartache and hardships. In my classroom students ask how other students' relatives were killed; most have had at least one family member murdered at the hands of gangs. One student, Gloria, shared that her father was murdered and that, due to fear of others meeting the same fate, her remaining family left Honduras abruptly. Unfortunately, it is common to find that a student has experienced the loss of a loved one to violence and has not dealt with the resulting grief because of the family's imminent departure. Most of my students come from Honduras, El Salvador, and Guatemala, which in 2010 had the highest homicide rates in the world, largely due to the escalation of gang activity, which increased after the Central American conflict; illegal activities such as kidnapping, murders, robberies, and extortion grew alongside the rapid rise in the number of gang members (Shifter 2012).

When Gloria described how her father had been shot and killed in front of the family store, her EL peers were not surprised: they each began recounting their own personal losses due to violence. Ignacio and Juan had both lost their fathers to gang violence, and Elena had lost her brother. As an educator, I listened, creating a safe space for them to share their stories; however, there were neither tears nor emotion. They just shared their stories factually, and then class continued.

At age sixteen Edgar came from Honduras; his father had left for the United States years prior but was no longer communicating with him or sending money home. Edgar was detained at the United States–Mexico border and was in detention for six months in San Antonio, Texas. While he was in detention, U.S. government officials found his father living and working in a nearby state. Edgar was furious and hurt. He thought his father had been detained or was, even worse, dead, only to find him living the American dream with a new family. Edgar was angry, but he also was suffering from guilt. Once he was out of detention and living with his father, he had a roof over his head, air conditioning, food, and a safe place to live, while his mom was struggling to survive in Honduras.

Edgar received some help after threatening to kill himself. He was required to go to the emergency room and was held for observation, and he later received counseling. He graduated in 2020.

Another source of trauma and stress for EL students is the concern that they will be rendered deportable or that their asylum cases will be denied. When a student in my classroom has an immigration hearing, everyone is concerned and anxiously waits to hear the outcome. Some students do not come back because they have been deported, or they are put back in detention because their asylum case was denied. When there is a positive outcome, we have a collective celebration and a sigh of relief. It is important to note that during the Trump administration, many students refused to attend their immigration hearings because there were rumors that people were being deported without due process. Unfortunately, once students have missed a hearing, it is inevitable that they will be deported once the authorities catch up with them.

Educators in Louisiana complete online SafeSchools training. We complete modules to meet our professional training requirements regarding students' drug and alcohol abuse, the responsibility involved in being a mandated reporter, bullying, cyberbullying, blood-borne pathogens, domestic violence, dating violence, child abuse, and youth suicide. It is a good start, but it is not enough to create truly trauma-informed classrooms. I fear that an entire generation of ELs who are immigrants, undocumented, refugees, and asylum seekers as well as survivors of insurmountable trauma face hardships for which they do not have adequate resources and mental health support, leaving them more vulnerable.

Challenges in the Classroom

Marcos arrived in the United States in 2018, at the age of sixteen. He had left Honduras to help provide for his parents. Marcos came to the United States with his cousins with an understanding that he would need to pay them for bringing him. Marcos had no intentions of attending school. After spending several months in a United States Immigration and Customs Enforcement (ICE) detention center, he and his cousins were finally released. The U.S. government gave his oldest cousin custody and mandated that Marcos attend school. Marcos did not have any memory of having ever gone to school. He had toiled in the fields with his family his entire life. One day, when I was drinking a cup of coffee, he shared his life experiences as a coffee bean processor. He was an expert and was able to tell the quality of the coffee beans by the smell of my coffee. He told me that school was not his priority. He knew he could never catch up to his peers, but for two years he tried. After failing every state-mandated test, he came to summer school. Over the summer we spent weeks together reading countless texts for literary analysis, narrative writing, and research simulation tasks—all of this while he was learning to read in Spanish. He did not want to be in school; he had a debt to pay, and his family was expecting and needing money.

While reviewing for his third attempt to pass the state English test, he whispered, "Miss, ¿puedes enseñarme mis números?" (Miss, could you teach me my numbers?). He was working as a roofer on the weekends to help pay his debt, but he did not know how much he was being paid or how quickly he was paying his debt off. He knew he must learn how to add and subtract so he would know how much he was paying. We began reviewing his numbers, adding and subtracting and preparing for the next school year. After turning eighteen, Marcos left school to go work full-time. I found him on social media. We keep in touch, and he is working and providing for his family back home. He is also on the path to becoming a legal resident. Marcos's story is not unique; it is not the exception in relation to SIFE learners. The dropout rate of students in the SIFE category is 70 percent of those who enroll. Pew Research Center (2005) reports that SIFE characteristics, "especially for males, suggest that many of them are labor migrants: Their purpose in migrating was probably to seek employment in the labor market, and they may have never enrolled in U.S. schools."

As a teacher, I ask myself, What are some of the solutions to working with students that have never attended a school before or who have had their schooling interrupted by violence, poverty, and migration? These challenges are insurmountable with the current tools at our disposal, and policy makers in their ivory towers have done very little to address these current issues facing the EL population in education. This does not affect only students in the SIFE category; EL students are lower achieving than their English-speaking counterparts overall.

Multiple Roles of an Educator

The multiple roles of EL educators include serving as community/school liaisons, communicators, on-campus parents, social coordinators, resource finders, language acquisition experts, sociologists, psychologists, teacher-coaches, administrators, legal advisers, immigration rights advocates, and conflict-resolution mediators (between students, between teachers and administrators, between counselors and administrators, and between counselors, parents, and students). Educators need to be aware of what EL students face regarding immigration, poverty, exclusion, and trauma. Additionally, they need to understand how these issues affect learning, and they need the support and resources to provide trauma-informed learning environments so that teachers and students are successful.

ELs have a 43 percent graduation rate in Louisiana; some factors affecting graduation attainment have been attributed to a lack of linguistic support services, which increases the Hispanic-white achievement gap (Dondero and Muller 2012). Research shows that ELs are more likely to drop out compared to their English-speaking minority peers. The report *The English Learner Dropout Dilemma: Multiple Risks and Multiple Resources* (Callahan 2013) explored the causes, solutions, and consequences of the dropout rate among EL students and found that it has consequences not only for individual dropouts but also for their communities, in which it has negative economic and civic impacts.

Given the aforementioned statistics, let us grasp the enormousness of the tasks an EL educator must accomplish. Educators must consider each student's unique background, assess their language proficiency (if the student speaks an Indigenous language, sometimes this is not possible), and provide equitable access to content while meeting district pacing schedules. Teachers strive to ensure that EL students obtain a passing score on the state exam required to graduate from high school. Additionally, EL educators must train general education teachers, be advocates for students, and make sure teachers and administrators comply with federal and state policies.

Interactions with Families

A student from a high school in our district did not come to school for over a week. This student had never missed school before, is a rule follower, and does not like to miss class. My colleague contacted her parents to find out why their daughter had not been to school. They said she had run away. When my colleague asked whether they were going to file a police report, they said, "No, she is married!" They asked whether they could return their daughter's laptop and have her dropped from school. Janet, my colleague, had to explain to them that they could not have her dropped from school and had them meet with the school resource officer to discuss their daughter's whereabouts. Culturally, to this family, since their daughter was with a boy, she was now married, and she was now his responsibility. The authorities were contacted, and a report was filed with child protective services. An investigation is ongoing, and the child is now in foster care and back in school.

Some situations raise complex intercultural issues. Are parents within their rights to discipline kids as they did in their home country? In Honduras corporal punishment is an accepted form of child discipline (Humanium, n.d.). Previously, I rarely had to report a family to child protective services—maybe once every five years—but in the last three years, these reports have increased exponentially.

Lazaro's story provides an example of the dilemmas educators face. I received a phone call from Lazaro's mom early one morning, prior to the beginning of school. She informed me that Lazaro was going to miss school for a couple of days. When Lazaro returned, he could barely move. He would wince every time his back hit the backrest of his chair. I asked him whether he was OK, and he said he was in pain. I asked him what had happened. He said his father had gotten angry because Lazaro had the gay pride flag on his screensaver. He had been punished, which was why he hadn't been to school. I called home and spoke to his mom. She said that for cultural and religious reasons, they had every right to discipline their son how they saw fit. After contacting the school resource officer, I filed a report with child protective services. There is a lot of gray in this area and not enough information specific to the EL population with whom I work regarding how to handle these situations. If I believe it is egregious, does that mean it is illegal? In my district, when working with increasing numbers of ELs, we have seen an influx of legal issues concerning our student population. We sometimes question whether reporting will hinder the students' ability to receive legal status.

Administrators will call me prior to reporting to seek counsel about whether students' status will be affected. Honestly, I cannot answer these types of questions because I am not an immigration attorney. So we keep asking hypothetical questions as we seek answers, but there is much uncertainty as we move forward.

Achieving Success in the Classroom

Natalia, a newcomer from Honduras, arrived to Mrs. Tevert's English II class. She was beginning school in the United States in December because the school year ends in November in Honduras. Natalia was screened for EL services, and it was determined that she qualified for EL accommodations. Accommodations used by Mrs. Tevert include bilingual dictionaries and electronic translators, which are allowed at all times; cooperative learning and peer assistance; extended time for tests and assignments; modified or shortened tests; provision of English or native-language word-to-word dictionaries; repeated directions; and shortened, modified, fewer, or taped assignments. All of these accommodations were arming Natalia with tools to help her access the content based on her language proficiency level. Natalia was making progress in Mrs. Tevert's class. There was a lot of language growth, but in April, when Natalia took the state-mandated English II test, the only support she received was extra time and a word-to-word dictionary. State policies dictate that the other tools cannot be made available during testing. Subsequently, Natalia did not pass her exam, which is a requirement for her to graduate from high school.

I ask policy makers responsible for these decisions the following: Why can we not use the same accommodations during state testing that are used in the classroom to help maximize the possibility of success?

"My" Students Versus "Our" Students

The rapid growth of the EL population has not been matched by sufficient growth in teachers' understanding of how best to educate these students. As a result many districts are buckling under the weight of having to meet the needs of EL students who are not demonstrating proficiency in academic areas such as reading, writing, and math (Samson and Collins 2012). A lack of professional development and training and minimal EL instruction in college education programs have left many educators feeling unprepared to enter the classroom. Inundated general education teachers cannot keep up with the current needs of their students. I often hear teachers refer to ELs as "your students," "your kids," and so on. I, too, am guilty of being territorial about "my" students. As EL teachers, we need to learn to share the responsibility for and accountability of teaching EL students between all stakeholders. We must be careful not to use language that shows otherness; it presents a negation of identity. Administrators and school leaders must be mindful of using the language of inclusivity. Language creates worlds. Once we address "our" students or "our" parents, we can include EL stakeholders in planning EL programs (Samson and Collins 2012).

Mr. West, an algebra teacher, stopped me in the hallway. "Miss Marissa, I need you to tell Wilman that he cannot wear a hoodie in class." My response was, "Did you tell him not to wear it in class?" He responded, "No, I figured he was one of yours, so you should tell him!" I have learned to use these opportunities as teachable moments. It takes a lot of finesse, patience, and restraint to work around this type of language. Sarcasm and shaming colleagues will not promote positive change. I, too, have had to reflect on some of my own unconscious biases in working with educators who I assume do not want to help my students. Mr. West and I have had our share of issues concerning EL students. Now I call on him to share his experiences during professional development workshops. We turn these issues into lessons for our colleagues to learn from.

Administrators and EL Teachers

In light of the challenges that I have described throughout the text, as educators, we are evaluated and observed in our classrooms. It is difficult to be evaluated by someone who does not understand EL instruction, cannot understand another language, and has no experience in language acquisition. Most administrators have a low self-rating of their knowledge of evaluating EL teachers (Gonzalez-Herrera 2017). As Figueroa Murphy and Torff argue,

> most administrators' educational experiences are remote from ESL instruction; few administrators are former ESL teachers, and supervisory training routinely fails to encompass ESL pedagogy. Hence, it remains unclear whether the administrators who supervise ESL teachers feel competent to do so. It seems plausible that the increasing ESL population is causing a supervision problem in modern schools: more and more ESL teachers whom administrators feel unprepared to supervise. (2012, 1)

If administrators lack confidence in assessing EL educators and these assessments affect teacher efficacy, how does that impact students? Administrators occasionally make uninformed decisions that affect curriculum and staffing. EL students come from diverse backgrounds and have different learning styles and needs that should be addressed, sometimes individually. A one-size-fits-all curriculum or program, while it may be convenient for the school district, is not effective. In my experience this has been the most significant disconnect and disservice to EL communities, educators, and students. When the administration focuses on purchasing a quick-fix curriculum or language program without considering feedback from EL educators and students, EL programs suffer. The "we know better than you" approach is disheartening and demoralizing to EL teachers who are the experts in the field. It would behoove administrators to consult and include EL teachers, students, parents, and all other stakeholders when making curricular and program decisions.

They All Speak Data

Communication is key, and it starts from the top. Administrators have a role in shaping EL programming at schools. They want to help, but like most people in education, our administrators are overwhelmed and do not necessarily have time to focus on a small percentage of the overall student population.

My advice to teachers is to not wait for school administrators to give instructions on how to work with English language learners. I realized quickly that my administrators relied on my expertise and recommendations to implement an action plan suitable for our school environment. I suggest doing the groundwork by researching student scores and identifying teachers who work well with students and those who do not. Complete a SWOT (strengths, weaknesses, opportunities, and threats) analysis concerning ELs on campus. These data are essential in painting a picture not only for administrators but also for faculty. The weaknesses in my district were a lack of school participation and a higher number of ELs who dropped out when compared to their peers.

Administrators may not speak students' native language, but they all speak data; they want to see the numbers. Once administrators are aware of the data, it is their job to present teachers with real-life strategies and solutions that they can implement in their classrooms immediately. Start small, and celebrate teachers who are meeting these expectations. Allow people to make mistakes and to share their fears and concerns about teaching EL students. Administrators should put themselves in the place of an educator: it is scary and quite daunting, and sometimes teachers are not properly equipped. Some decision makers need to be reminded that meeting the needs of English language learners is a work in progress and that we are all doing our best to figure it out. It is important to give educators a safe space during professional development where they can openly discuss any biases or fears they feel will preclude their success as educators. Once fears are publicly expressed, others will feel they have permission to voice concerns. This has been the most productive part of my professional development workshops. Amid the COVID-19 pandemic, professional development has taken a back seat. I am no longer able to provide in-person training or continue professional development workshops. I create short videos of a minute or less via TikTok or Screencastify. I provide a useful strategy while keeping the communication brief. I have found that using Canva and free editing software to create educational content for professional development is a good challenge during these unprecedented times.

Best Practices and Solutions

At my high school, we host an annual day-long consortium where parents, teachers, law enforcement officers, and local business owners participate in looking at school data while asking hard questions of school officials, who, in turn, provide answers. "Why are the majority of students receiving suspensions African American students?" "Could our implicit bias affect our approach to disciplining students of color?" "What is the best way to communicate with parents?" For my school this consortium is a work in progress. It was initiated after a number of student suicides. Our students were voicing the loneliness they felt, the stress, and demanded action from our administrators. In the first year the consortium was held, administrators were more reserved in their approach to opening up our school. Schools are like families in that way: they do not want to talk about the bad; they do not want to assign blame or be blamed. So opening this consortium to our community was a big step in being vulnerable as a school community/family. Despite the initial concerns, as a school we have come to realize that the more transparent we are, the better the feedback we receive and the better the solutions we can create as a community.

One thing I have learned through this process is that it is best to get feedback from former students. They have nothing to lose by being honest. An African American student held back tears as she discussed how lonely she felt being the only person of color in her advanced classes. She wanted to know why these classes were not being made available to other students of color. A former EL student discussed how he had witnessed teammates making derogatory remarks about Hispanic students at practice, yelling "run like you run for the border" to the Hispanic players on the team. He said he felt guilty for not saying anything at the time because he did not want to start problems but that he wanted to say something now. Mr. Moreno, a parent of two EL students, stood up and said in accented English that the school needs to do better to communicate with Spanish-speaking parents, who get information too late or not at all.

Administrators can hear these same grievances from teachers, but hearing them from former students and parents makes them real, which is why we invite former and current EL students and parents to participate in this event. Administrators' seeing and listening to our parents and students in this light has been empowering. The voices of the parents have a profound impact on administrators, especially when the contributions are meaningful and insightful. In turn, parents feel confident in sharing their wishes and desires along with their suggestions for improvement and for enhancing the quality of education for their children.

See Through the Eyes of Your ELs' Families

It's worth repeating that communication is key, and communication means nothing if you do not include EL students' parents. Imagine a family from

Honduras arriving at your school. How are they greeted? What is their experience from the time they arrive to the minute they leave? This is by far the most important part of the educational journey for EL students' families. Go through the experience as a newcomer arriving at your school. It is amazing how much we assume is understood that is in reality lost in translation. From my experience I learned that the school is difficult to enter: there are no signs in any languages other than English, and if you are not an English speaker, the experience is quite intimidating. During the intake process, we take the time to learn as much as we can about the family's prior education, expectations, passions, and goals. We discuss the home environment: Is there a place for their child to study? Do their children have chores? We emphasize the importance of completing schoolwork at home and give parents resources in the beginning so they are equipped to support their child. Providing parents with pertinent information at the beginning of the school year helped keep students in school and improved EL student success. Something to keep in mind as middle-class educators is that it is not easy for people to take time off from work. Transportation, gas money, and access to childcare can all be barriers.

It is vital that we make the intake process efficient and provide families with useful information, directions, instructions, and resources. Parents also need to understand how to communicate grievances or concerns at any given time. Parents should leave the intake meeting with a sense of self-empowerment and the feeling that their child is receiving the best attention, education, and care. They should know who to call and how to document events pertaining to their child's welfare and education. If you are an educator who works with EL students' families, I cannot stress enough how important it is to go through the process yourself, from going to the school to completing the intake process and going to get vaccinations and uniforms, scheduling bus pickup and drop-off, and setting up parent accounts and lunch applications. Investing more time into planning how to provide your EL students' parents and guardians with tools to help them in the long term will save so much time for everyone involved.

Creating a positive line of communication between myself and our EL students and their parents has been key to student success on my campus. After hosting a parent night that only one parent and daughter attended for a district-wide high school and its feeder schools, we realized that we were not communicating effectively with our community, so we decided to call parents and ask them why they do not participate. The main response given was that they did not think it was important or they felt it did not matter whether they went to the event or not. Our parents need an invitation. It takes a couple of minutes to call a parent and enthusiastically invite them to our event, but hearing from us personally lets them know we need their participation. You want the parents to come and to have their children participate in presenting information. This is not only a valuable experience for our students to share in building our community; it also empowers their parents to see their children advocating on their own behalf. Another thing we learned was that most of our EL students' families prefer to communicate via social media. So we listened to their advice, and our district created a special Facebook page specifically for the families of EL students in our district. This has been a great way to communicate events, announce important deadlines, and share opportunities. Parents are able to share the information on their Facebook pages, and it has increased student participation at my schools (see figures 2.1, 2.2, and 2.3).

Parents' phone numbers often change and are not updated in the school's system. Using social media to message a parent has been one way to reach our parents. Social media is also useful in finding and locating students who stop attending school, which does, unfortunately, happen among our students due to various circumstances. Whether students are deported or moved to another state, as educators, we should attempt to find them to make sure they are safe.

My EL students' community is accustomed to receiving calls, emails, and Facebook messages. The more you call parents, the easier it gets. Reaching out also lowers parents'

FIGURE 2.1 EL students' parents on campus.

FIGURE 2.2 EL students' parents listening to a presentation.

FIGURE 2.3 Parent night: Brenda (a student) presenting "Moises in Math" to our EL students' parents.

personal anxiety about contacting me if they have issues, doubts, or concerns. I honestly believe our active parent participation is due to having an open line of communication.

Student Success Story

During scheduling, I inevitably get the question, "Why? Why should I even take a college prep class if I can't go to college?" It's a good question: some English language learners do not see the point in taking classes if they do not have the status or means to attend school. This is my advice to students who really do want to pursue higher education: do not let a piece of paper determine your future. If you want to go to college to be a doctor, nurse, or educator, then you prepare yourself to be accepted into those programs. We never know what opportunities will be available to students when the time comes. It is better to be prepared than not. We do not have a lot of control over what happens outside of our classroom, but we can prepare students to beat as many odds as possible.

Franklin arrived in the United States from the Dominican Republic in his freshman year. "Look, Miss Marissa—I do not want to waste my time taking classes. That won't help my future. My neighbor said that I can't go to college because I'm not a U.S. citizen."

My response: "Is your neighbor a school counselor? An expert on college admissions? An immigration lawyer? Who is this man who knows this information?"

Franklin responded with certainty of his neighbor's credibility: *"Mira, mira, es hombre de negocios!"* (Look, look, he is a businessman). It is not only his neighbor; it is also the lady at church, a friend from work, the guy who fixes that guy's car who works for a lawyer: the list of self-appointed experts could go on and on. It frustrates me to no end how self-appointed experts stomp on a dream before a student can even begin. I do not think people's intentions are cruel, but within the EL community, I work with kids that are afraid to dream because these experts give their unsolicited expertise. What happened to Franklin? He's in college! (See figures 2.4 and 2.5.)

There are many students not aware of their own legal status. Some are afraid to ask; other times their parents have not had this conversation yet. This is an issue that I have encountered with families from different countries and socioeconomic backgrounds. With immigration laws more confusing

FIGURE 2.4 Franklin showing his diploma.

FIGURE 2.5 Franklin at his college campus.

than tax laws and lots of "experts" giving unsolicited advice, people are making long-term decisions on misinformation. My response to most questions is, "I do not know, but let's figure it out." I also model and teach our students how to do the research and to always ask about their options. The problem is not only outside of school; the lack of expertise in our schools about these issues raises many concerns, especially in regard to completing college applications and completing the FAFSA (Free Application for Federal Student Aid) form: Should parents complete the form if they are not in the United States legally? What if the kid was born in the USA? What if the parents did not pay taxes? Should they file for taxes if they are not documented? Will the financial aid office report them to immigration officials? I know some of these questions seem silly, but they are real concerns. Career coaches and school counselors are not aware of how to help students complete these forms. I once was instructed by a school counselor to advise students not to complete the form but to do a waiver, because it could get our families into trouble. Always direct students to call the Federal Student Aid Information Center and get the technical help they need to complete the forms. If parents do not feel comfortable doing so, schedule a call with them to help guide them through the process. This does not mean all EL students are going to college, but if they are capable and that is what they want to do, our duty is to prepare them and remove as many obstacles in their pathway to success as possible.

Be "the What?"

Since ninth grade Carlos had been trying to drop out to work in construction. We had the same conversation about staying in school, weighing the pros and cons, and each year he would agree to keep going. We called Carlos "El Bufalo!" I'm a fan of quotes: I have them everywhere in my classroom. We read, discuss, and look for quotes to inspire us when needed as a class. One of the quotes we reviewed was by Donna Brazile (2010):

> Wilma Mankiller, the first female principal chief of the Cherokee nation, once told me how the cow runs away from the storm while the **buffalo** charges directly toward it—and gets through it quicker.
>
> Whenever I'm confronted with a tough challenge, I do not prolong the torment. I become the **buffalo**. (emphasis mine)

Carlos became the buffalo. Every year he would inch closer to graduation. He made it to twelfth grade, which he had sworn was never going to happen, but his twelfth-grade year was going to be a challenge. As Carlos would say, *"La ley de Murphy estaba a cien!"* (Murphy's law was at a hundred!). Everything that could go wrong did. He did not pass the state-mandated exam, and he missed his welding exam due to not knowing at which campus he needed to take it. He had to pass all of his current classes and exams, plus retake two others, and a week prior to graduation, we were informed that he needed the welding credential to graduate. Welding is a credential that can potentially provide him with future job opportunities; however, welding is precise. The test administrator has to send the welded piece to have the work x-rayed. Prior to his state-mandated retake exams, Carlos began missing school. He was ready to give up. He believed he was going to fail, so why even try? His counselor, his teachers, myself, his peers—everyone was pushing him to do the retakes. He finally came back to school and passed all his exams. However, his welding test was still being processed and had to be sent away. We did not know whether he was going to get the results in time. The day prior to graduation, we received the good news. Carlos would graduate! (See figure 2.6.)

When he crossed the stage, the crowd screamed, "*El Bufalo!*" His resolve would inspire so many. When my EL students decided to turn our after-school program into a club, they named it "Be the Buffalo Cafe."

Be the Buffalo Cafe was originally just after-school tutoring. If you are an EL teacher, you know that keeping up with schoolwork is a challenge. I decided I would stay after school a couple of days a week to help students catch up, and it was more than I could handle. So many kids wanted help, so I began asking other students to come and help me with tutoring. This time after school became sacred. It gave people an opportunity to share issues that needed voicing while providing them an opportunity to work together to problem solve. It was their favorite part of the day, and I enjoyed watching this community blossom. We have coffee and snacks, talk about the highs and lows of school, do homework, and encourage one another to get out of our comfort zones. School participation has gone way up! They build one another's confidence and try things they otherwise would never have the courage to do alone. ELs are participating more than ever before, even during the COVID-19 pandemic, which I feel would never have happened without

FIGURE 2.6 Carlos at his graduation ceremony.

our little club. DonorsChoose helps us receive funding for our coffee, snacks, and books. Teachers use the Be the Buffalo quotes in their classes, and one teacher gives students extra credit points for finding out why we are called Be the Buffalo Cafe. It's made all of us feel more included at our school. Parents are participating too: they help us with cultural events on campus, like Día de los Muertos and the cultural exchange festivity we host at the beginning of the school year (see figure 2.7). This time with my students has really made the most difference in creating a strong academic community, but more than anything else, students know that they add value to our school, their culture is honored, and they are improving and growing linguistically and academically. My advice to you when you are feeling overwhelmed as an educator and want to give up: *be the buffalo!*

Concluding Comments

Nobody is coming with solutions. Administrators, neither the federal nor state departments of education are prepared or able to give us real-life solutions. We cannot wait for someone to fix us, save us, or give us anything. We

FIGURE 2.7 Día de los Muertos.

have to approach our EL programs much like a grassroots organization tackles community issues. We have to do what works for us with the resources we currently have available while waiting on policy change and hoping for more support staff and research that identifies best practices, knowing these are not going to happen overnight, if ever.

The COVID-19 pandemic has only magnified the current challenges our EL students are facing daily. As an educator, I am angry that in this day and age, in the United States, disparities and inequity exist for so many children. Despite these issues burdening the EL student population, our program has managed to make gains in learning: over the past five years, we have increased our graduation rates, though we have lost a few students in the process.

My students and their families are some of the most courageous people I know. Our EL students and their families are the most valuable resource we have as educators. It is important to take the time to get to know them. Hosting events outside of school has also been beneficial to our school program.

Creating opportunities for parents to engage with EL teachers, their children, and one another helps break down barriers, creates bonds outside of school, and gets our parents out of their comfort zone. It costs nothing to host a meet and greet at a local park or at school. The parents enjoy seeing their kids socialize, and it gives them a chance to discuss their shared dreams for their children, to problem solve, and to give suggestions and advice in an informal, laid-back environment. We lower the affective filter for students; such activities do the same for our parents.

My advice to parents, students, and colleagues is to be the person they wish they had when they arrived at school. I think of that of-

FIGURE 2.8 Sharon and Paloma, brain-break fun at Be the Buffalo after-school program.

ten. I try to be the person who puts students at ease as they embark on their new educational journey. In the process I advocate for their success, promote change in educational policies, and rejoice in their achievements (see figure 2.8).

References

Aranda, Roy. 2016. "Living in the Shadows: Plight of the Undocumented." *Journal of Clinical Psychology* 72 (8): 795–806. https://doi.org/10.1002/jclp.22361.

Artiga, Samantha, and Petry Ubri. 2017. "Living in an Immigrant Family in America: How Fear and Toxic Stress are Affecting Daily Life, Well-Being, and Health." Kaiser Family Foundation. Issue brief, December 2017. http://files.kff.org/attachment/Issue-Brief-Living-in-an-Immigrant-Family-in-America.

Brazile, Donna. 2010. "Donna Brazile's Rules to Live By." CNN, July 19, 2010. http://edition.cnn.com/2010/LIVING/07/19/o.smartest.advice/index.html.

Callahan, Rebecca M. 2013. *The English Learner Dropout Dilemma: Multiple Risks and Multiple Resources.* California Dropout Research Project. Research report, February 2013. Santa Barbara: University of California. https://cdrpsb.org/research report19.pdf.

Clark, Maria. 2018. "LHSAA Asks for Athletes' Social Security Numbers, Preventing Some New Orleans Students from Playing." *New Orleans Advocate,* November 15, 2018. https://www.nola.com/news/article_156e6773-14cd-5b1e-9a8c-aa0ad889 10fb.html.

Counseling@NYU. 2018. "1 in 4 Students is an English Language Learner: Are We Leaving Them Behind?" *Counseling@NYU Blog.* NYU Steinhardt, May 1, 2018. https://counseling.steinhardt.nyu.edu/blog/english-language-learners/.

Dondero, M., and C. L. Muller. 2012. "School Stratification in New and Established Latino Destinations." *Social Forces* 91, no. 2 (December): 477–502. https://doi.org/10.1093/sf/sos127.

Figueroa Murphy, Audrey, and Bruce Torff. 2012. "Administrators' Sense of Self-efficacy in Supervision of Teachers of English as a Second Language." *Journal of International Education and Leadership* 2 (3): 1–12. https://files.eric.ed.gov/full text/EJ1139404.pdf.

Gonzalez-Herrera, Maria. 2017. "ESL and ELL Program Effectiveness: Providing Academic Success for Students." Master's thesis, California State University Monterey Bay. https://digitalcommons.csumb.edu/cgi/viewcontent.cgi?article=1200& context=caps_thes_all.

Grimm, Andy. 2019. "Hispanic Immigration Post-Katrina Finding Permanent Roots in Metro New Orleans." *New Orleans Advocate,* July 18, 2019. https://www.nola.com/news/article_ddb9794b-8bd7-5be8-8d55-6669024d3cb3.html.

Humanium. n.d. "Children of Honduras: Realizing Children's Rights in Honduras." Accessed September 2, 2021. https://www.humanium.org/en/honduras/.

NCES (National Center for Educational Statistics). 1995. "Immigration, Participation in U.S. Schools, and High School Dropout Rates." https://nces.ed.gov/pubs/dp95/97473-4.asp.

Peña, Maria. 2020. "Absent Students, Murdered Teachers: Gang Violence Permeates Honduras' Schools." NBC News, March 8, 2020. https://www.nbcnews.com/news/latino/absent-students-murdered-teachers-gang-violence-permeates-honduras-schools-n1144951.

Pew Research Center. 2005. "The Higher Drop-Out Rate of Foreign-Born Teens." Research report, November 1, 2005. https://www.pewresearch.org/hispanic/2005/11/01/the-higher-drop-out-rate-of-foreign-born-teens/.

Potochnick, Stephanie. 2018. "The Academic Adaptation of Immigrant Students with Interrupted Schooling." *American Educational Research Journal* 55, no. 4 (August): 859–92. https://doi.org/10.3102/0002831218761026.

Samson, Jennifer F., and Brian A. Collins. 2012. *Preparing All Teachers to Meet the Needs of English Language Learners: Applying Research to Policy and Practice for Teacher Effectiveness.* April 2012. Washington, D.C.: Center for American Progress. https://files.eric.ed.gov/fulltext/ED535608.pdf.

Schmidt, Lauren M. 2019. "Trauma in English Learners: Examining the Influence of Previous Trauma and PTSD on English Learners and Within the Classroom." *TESOL Journal* 10 (1): 1–10. https://doi.org/10.1002/tesj.412.

Shifter, Michael. 2012. *Countering Criminal Violence in Central America.* Special report no. 64, April 2012. New York: Council on Foreign Relations. https://cdn.cfr.org/sites/default/files/pdf/2012/03/Criminal_Violence_CSR64.pdf.

SPLC (Southern Poverty Law Center). 2012. "M.V. vs Jefferson Parish Public School System." Published August 22, 2012. https://www.splcenter.org/seeking-justice/case-docket/mv-vs-jefferson-parish-public-school-system.

Times Picayune. 2019. "Spike in Central American Immigrant Students Posing Challenges in Jefferson Parish." July 19, 2019. https://www.nola.com/news/education/article_90a2f6be-7891-5d8f-a79b-8b97404be683.html.

U.S. Customs and Border Protection. 2020. "U.S. Border Patrol Southwest Border Apprehensions by Sector." U.S. Department of Homeland Security. https://www.cbp.gov/newsroom/stats/southwest-land-border-encounters/usbp-sw-border-apprehensions.

CHAPTER 3

Mobility, Racism, and Cultural Borders

Immigrant and Returned Children from the
United States in the Schools of Oaxaca, Mexico

MARTA RODRÍGUEZ-CRUZ

Introduction

During his administration (2017–21), President Donald Trump gave continuity to the policy of forced return, which has had notable repercussions for Mexican migrants in the United States. Accompanied by an anti-immigrant discourse sustained on the rhetoric of hate (Hernández 2019), this recrudescence of U.S. immigration policy was intended not only to prevent the entry of new migrants into the United States but also to expel those who were already there. As a consequence of these events, there has been an increase in the return of Mexican nationals to their country of origin—some through direct deportation for being in a situation of documentary irregularity, others as a result of the policy of fear of deportation managed by Trump. This policy of fear is built on the conditions of social, economic, political, and cultural coercion in which Mexican migrants live in the United States.

Located in the southwest of Mexico, the state of Oaxaca has been one of the states that has received the most returnees during the Trump administration. Of the 763,404 deportations of Mexicans by the United States from January 2017 through December 2020, 68,509 deportations were of Oaxacan migrants. This has placed Oaxaca in one of the top positions in terms of the number of migrants deported from the United States (Unidad de Política Migratoria [Migration Policy Unit, MPU] 2017, 2018, 2019, 2020). To these forced returns one must add others that have also been involuntary in nature, insofar as the returning individuals respond to the situation of social, cultural, political, and economic coercion mentioned earlier, as well as those that occur on a truly voluntary basis, including those carried out for reasons of family reunification. In their return process from the United States to Oaxaca, adult migrants have arrived accompanied by their children, some born in the United States, now immigrants to Mexico, and others born in Mexico and now returning. The predominant presence of children[1] in this return process has turned this diaspora into a different kind of diaspora from previous ones, in which the presence of the adult population was predominant (Valdéz et al. 2018; Valdéz 2019; Zúñiga and Giorguli Saucedo 2019). Therefore, the arrival in Mexico of this large school-age population, which, according to recent figures, already includes more than nine hundred thousand children (Barros 2019), constitutes a great challenge, not only for the Mexican education system but also for migrant children, who face (re) insertion into school in a system that is not prepared to receive them.

After spending the first part of their lives in the United States, in order to initiate and develop their process of (re)insertion into the new society, these children enrolled in Oaxacan educational institutions, where they encountered a social, cultural, and linguistic universe they had never known before. Although these children have already crossed the geographical borders that separate the United States from Mexico to reach their new geographical destination, they must now cross other social, cultural, and linguistic borders to (re)insert themselves in their new sociocultural destination, despite being Mexicans by right of blood, for those born in the United States, or by right of soil, for those born in Mexico (Cámara de Diputados del H. Congreso de la Unión 2021, Article 30). At this juncture it is important to study the processes of frontierization and racialization that take place in the school, as a place where difference is encountered, and the consequences thereof. Thus, the purpose of this chapter is, on the one hand, to analyze which elements integrate the cultural boundaries between subjects with and without migratory experience and how they are constructed and operate in the school institution, as a space of intercultural encounter, and, on the other hand, and related to the previously discussed, how cultural racism is constructed in regard to the immigrant otherness and toward the returnee as well as the relation it has with those cultural boundaries.

In order to respond to this, and once the object of study has been contextualized, I will now analyze the theoretical and conceptual categories on which the research is based. Next, I present the methodology developed, analyze the results obtained, and finalize with the respective conclusions.

Migration, Racism, and Cultural Boundaries

In opposition to traditional biological racism, since the 1980s there has been a discussion on cultural racism as one of the ways of naming the new racism (Barker 1981; Wieviorka 2006, 2014). Cultural racism replaces the category of race with that of cultural belonging and conceives culture as an essentialist trait (Balibar and Wallerstein 1991; Grosfoguel 1999). Thus, within the logic of racism, one of its forms of operation resides in "the way in which culture can be used with segregationist and exclusionary strategies" (Aguerre 2011). When speaking of how racism uses culture, Balibar expresses that "culture can also function as nature, especially as a way of enclosing *a priori* individuals and groups in a genealogy" (Balibar and Wallerstein 1991, 38).

The uses that racism makes of culture have also led to talk of differentialist racism (Taguieff 1987) or racism without races (Balibar 1991; Martínez 2001). The term "differentialist racism," coined by Taguieff (1987), refers to racism sustained on the basis of two main arguments: "(1) that the suppression of cultural distances endangers the survival of cultures" and "(2) that since cultural difference is the natural environment of man, the disappearance of these differences will eventually lead to inter-ethnic conflicts" (Aguerre 2011, 24). For his part, Balibar (1991) speaks of a neoracism based on racism without races that "does not focus on biological difference, typical of the racism of colonization, but on cultural difference, a 'differentiating racism,' that promotes the idea of 'racism without races,' going through processes of ethnification without biological basis" (Salazar 2020, 48).

As pointed out by Riedmann and Stefoni (2015, 195), one of the nuclear elements on which the transition from biological racism to cultural racism rests is that the foundation of the former is based on the idea of the existence of human races recognizable through phenotypic and biological elements, and the latter moves away from this biologicist approach to look toward cultural differences. This cultural racism can also be understood in the sense of Cruz (2011, 142): as a "system of differentiation oriented by representations expressed in practices that exclude, inferiorize and belittle the 'other,'" since "in the cultural field, racism hegemonizes and reproduces aspects but not phenotypes." Similarly, when Balibar (1991, 3) distinguishes between biological racism and cultural racism, he hypothesizes that "both types of racism in practice produce the same effects (forms of violence, contempt, exploitation) that are articulated around stigmas of otherness," but "in the second case, the notion of race is replaced by that of culture." According to anthropologist Alicia Barabas (2001), a recognized expert in the study and analysis of Oaxacan society and cultures, the cultural configurations built from migration and transnationalism are constituted as borders and not as hybrid elements in the case of Oaxaca, whose singularity contradicts theses such as that of cultural hybridization (Canclini 1989) and others that defend the questioning of the meanings usually associated with the notion of border. This case is made by Pujadas (1999, 2001), who stresses the need to replace the notion of border as a limit between separated and contrasting units with that of border as a space of contact and crossbreeding. I am not questioning the relevance of these approaches in other cases in which these borders may act as spaces of crossbreeding and cultural hybridization and not as boundaries between clearly contrasting cultural groups, nor am I questioning the porosity of cultural borders. On the contrary, what I want to emphasize is the particularity of the case study, widely observed in the educational institutions analyzed, where the cultural boundaries between subjects with and without migratory experience allow us to define very clearly the social, cultural, symbolic, and linguistic universes that they limit. Children arriving from the United States and children without migratory experience interact from these differentiated universes. This has been corroborated, even among those who are not recent immigrants or returnees but who, on the contrary, have been in Mexico for several years but were born or grew up in the United States, or both.

In relation to the previous discussion, I agree with authors who emphasize the reciprocal tension between inside and outside that marks cultural boundaries (Barei 2013; Castellanos 2004; Cuberos, Martín, and Padilla 2014; Moreno 2014; Rizo and Romeu 2006). These can serve as theoretical-methodological tools to understand how the sense of self and other is constructed and how the "us" is constructed and distinguished from the "others" (Rizo and Romeu 2006, 38); some migrant "others" are discriminated against and inferiorized for belonging to a world that is considered "cultural outside" (Barei 2013, 115) from the nonimmigrant "us." In relation to the inside-outside cultural binomial, it is worth mentioning here the approach of De Genova (2007) on how racialization through migration cannot be only a process of hierarchization from the top down but must also be from the inside out: my culture versus the other culture; the migrant is not inside my culture but outside of it. Along the same lines, Alicia Castellanos (2004) examines the construction of foreignness based on the cultural racialization of the "other" in the logic of the constitution of cultural outsides and insides. In particular, the author emphasizes how "without being foreigners, that is, non-nationals, a type of foreignness, of exteriority, is invented to preserve the supposed privileges of origin" (Castellanos 2004, 111–12).

Hatred, fear, and rejection of these foreignized "others" as a result of migration and the cultural racialization of their distinctive characteristics can lead to the denaturalization of their differences and translate into aggression, violence, and exclusion. In this sense I agree with Castellanos (2004, 115) when she argues that pluriculturality is a phenomenon that deepens with migrations and that, concomitantly, brings with it the appearance of new exclusions in physical spaces and in relational spheres. In this case these new forms of exclusion take place in the school environment and in the relationships among its members.

As a space of socialization of the migratory phenomenon, the school represents a privileged locus to which the researcher's gaze can be directed in order to analyze the construction of borders and the cultural racialization of the "other." As a mirror of society, the school reflects its conflicts and tensions: "the racist reality of society is replicated in the school" (Velasco and Baronnet 2016, 4). But it must be recognized, as Van Dijk (2007) does, that, as a phenomenon of ideological nature, racisms are taught and learned. Education is a highly effective instrument for this purpose, and the school is a privileged space for racism's transmission and reproduction. Racist ideas are "wherever education manifests itself . . . they circulate in classrooms and recesses, in teaching materials, blackboards and electronic screens" (Velasco and Baronnet 2016, 4). Depending on the pedagogical models and strategies developed, the school may have the potential to combat racism or, on the contrary, to reproduce it.

The school institution is a meeting place for diversity embodied in concrete subjects who are inscribed in different universes—social, cultural, linguistic— and who have different origins—geographical, ethnic, sex, gender, class. For this reason it is necessary to study what happens in these institutions and, more specifically, in the intercultural relations established between the individuals who are part of them. While recognizing the value of childhood per se, as a living category, understood and valued in its own present, and not as a transition to adulthood from an interpretation of incompleteness, it must also be recognized that today's generations will be the society of the future. Therefore, the analysis of these intercultural relations will allow us to explore and analyze the tensions, gaps, and distances that occur between diverse subjects within this living laboratory called school in order to seek scientific analyses that allow the promotion of social cohesion.

Methodology

The results presented here were obtained through anthropological fieldwork that involved the development of a qualitative, ethnographic, and descriptive methodology. Particularly, this study, developed during 2018, 2019, and 2020, falls within the framework of school ethnography (Velasco and Diaz 1997), understood as a form of representation based on a set of research strategies, methods, and techniques (Velasco and Diaz 1997, 73).

The ethnographic research was developed in four schools, two of them middle schools and two high schools. They are located in different communities and municipalities in the Valles Centrales and Sierra Norte regions of Oaxaca, cataloged as places where high numbers of migrants to the United States returned during the Trump administration. For this reason they were selected for the research.

Access to the schools was provided through the Oaxacan Institute for Attention to Migrants and through snowball sampling. First, the institute put me in touch with a teacher at Technical High School 48 in Tlacolula de Matamoros, in Valles Centrales, whose director put me in contact with the principal of another educational institution, and so on. Once I was inside the institutions, the respective directors and administrators located the children from the United States, with whom the research was carried out with the prior authorization of their parents.

The data were obtained through the application of the following techniques: observation with and without participation, semistructured interviews, and informal conversations. The observation was based on a script. This was also aimed at recording the constitutive elements of cultural boundaries between students with and without migratory experience, as well as practices of cultural racism. On the other hand, the interviews have sought to understand and analyze how the subjects—immigrants, returnees, and nonmigrants—live and explain their own experiences of borderization and cultural racism from their own discourses. This technique was applied to sixty-four students, twenty-two of them with no immigration experience and forty-two of them who had emigrated or returned from the United States

TABLE 3.1 Educational institutions selected for research: Level, area, and location

Name	Educational level	Area (rural/urban)	Location
Technical High School 40	High school	Rural	Ixtlán de Juárez, Sierra Norte
Technical High School 48	High school	Urban	Tlacolula de Matamoros, Valles Centrales
Benito Juárez Middle School	Middle school	Rural	Teotitlán del Valle, Valles Centrales
Felipe Carrillo Puerto Middle School	Middle school	Rural	San Jerónimo Tlacochahuaya, Valles Centrales

between 2017 and 2020 and from Chicago, Illinois; Harvard, Massachusetts; Las Vegas, Nevada; Los Angeles, California; San Bernardino, California; Santa Monica, California; Nashville, Tennessee; Phoenix, Arizona; and Atlanta, Georgia. Since the ages recorded among the subjects with migration experience ranged from seven to fourteen years old, the sample of subjects without migration experience consisted of children in the same age range in order to ensure consistency in the sample and the research results. Finally, informal conversations were developed because of their flexible nature, allowing us to obtain information relevant to the research in situations where the interaction was spontaneous and unplanned. All names are fictitious in order to guarantee the anonymity of the subjects.

An analysis of the specialized bibliographic production has also been carried out, official sources have been consulted to obtain statistical data on migration and return, and data available in public media, such as local and national radio stations, have been collected.

Racialization and Frontierization in the School Environment

As Cuberos, Martín, and Padilla (2014, 903) point out, cultural boundaries organize relationships between individuals and groups on a daily basis. In the context of the school institutions studied in the state of Oaxaca, the main boundaries that organize the relationships between subjects with and without migratory experience have to do fundamentally with language and culture, elements that, in turn, are intimately linked to cultural racism, as we shall see.

In the context of this study, language acts as a boundary: English as the main language of migrant students and Spanish as the mother tongue of non-migrant students. It should be noted that, although there are children who speak Zapotec,[2] it is not operational in the cases studied, where Spanish is the exclusive language of communication and educational instruction and the students with international migratory experience do not know this Indigenous language. The ethnographic records show that in the educational institutions analyzed, the student body from the United States is composed of children who either were born in the United States and arrived in Mexico between the ages of seven and fourteen or were born in Mexico, migrated to the United States between the ages of zero and three, and returned to Mexico in the same age range—between seven and fourteen years of age. In addition to being born and/or raised in an English-speaking country, many of these children were not taught Spanish at home, so for all intents and purposes, English is their primary language, the only language they know when they arrive in Mexico.

This first border, that of language, has the following repercussions: First, the impossibility of establishing communication between students with and without migration experience, since there is no common language to do so. Second, for children from the United States, the lack of knowledge of Spanish prevents them from building new networks, an extremely important element in favoring their socio-school (re)insertion. These children have spent most of their lives in the United States, where they have woven their social networks.

And while a minority of these children have some relatives, such as cousins, who are similar in age to them and can facilitate the establishment of new networks (although this is not always the case), the vast majority must start from scratch to build relationships of companionship and friendship in the new destination with many limitations. Many of the immigrant and returnee students interviewed, in fact, express statements such as "I want to go back, because there are my friends, here I have no friends and I feel discriminated against" (A. Saavedra, November 7, 2018).

The reality observed has shown the great difficulty encountered by these children in progressing adequately in their formative process, given their lack of knowledge of speaking, reading, and writing skills in Spanish, the language of instruction, and the lack of programs available for teaching them. In this regard we should highlight what Velasco and Baronnet (2016) said when, in reference to the studies of Klein et al. (2014), they point out one of the ways in which inequality and educational racism in Mexico are concretized through the application of standardized Spanish tests to students in Indigenous Chiapas schools, which they qualify as "true factories of intelligence racism" (Velasco and Baronnet 2016, 4). Without downplaying the importance of what these authors denounce, it should be noted that the same procedure is used in Oaxacan schools where there are students from the United States who, without knowing Spanish, are subjected to the same standardized tests and to a constant process of linguistic subtraction in which they progressively lose English, their main language. This is a new form of school racism that originates as a result of the reversal of the migratory flow in United States–Mexico mobility—a consequence of the U.S. migratory contingency—and is directly related to the lack of preparation of the Mexican educational system to adequately attend to a large school-age population coming from that country.

On the other hand, in the field of culture, there are numerous records that have highlighted borderization. One of them was collected while attending a first-year physics and biology class in high school, where, in order to carry out a practical activity aimed at explaining the nervous system and the taste buds, the students prepared, under the direction of their teacher, a salad of jicama, banana, orange, and apple seasoned with chili, Tajín, and lime. It can be noted that the combination both of food and of flavors is typically Mexican, which was pleasing to the palates educated in this gastronomic style: those of the students present there who had no migratory experience. In contrast, the children from the United States preferred not to eat the salad because of the strong flavors it contained and to which they are not accustomed, and therefore they were placed by the rest of the students outside the culture of Mexicanity. However, later in the same class, a nonmigrant student refused to try the salad because she did not like lime, and the refusal was taken as a normal issue. This highlights not only the existence of cultural borders but also the construction of foreignness based on migratory situation, so that, even when similar facts are registered in a given scenario—as in this case, the rejection of characteristic elements of Mexican gastronomy— these are relativized according to the migratory condition and the social and cultural origin of the subjects.

Along the same lines, the discourses of children without international migratory experience are quite illustrative in terms of the delimitation between "us" and "the others," based on cultural elements constituted as border markers. Such is the case of the interview with a middle school student, in which he told me about the recent arrival of another student from Atlanta, Georgia: "It's just that he plays **basketball** and not **football**, and he dresses like this, with a **Lakers** basketball jersey, but he doesn't wear the **Pumas** jersey like **we** do"[3] (L. Sandoval, March 14, 2019).

As can be seen, the subject himself employs the notion of cultural inside-outside by establishing a comparison between the elements proper to "others" and "ours," using, in fact, the term "we" to delimit what is proper to the external. These borders present in schools are fed back by other communication spaces in which Mexicanness is reinforced through its markers and symbols. This is the case of radio, television, newspapers and magazines, movies, and websites as means of reproduction of a national identity that is enhanced at times of commemoration of relevant events in the country's history. For example, during the first weeks of November, radios throughout the republic broadcast messages aimed at enhancing this national identity to finally commemorate the anniversary of the revolution on the twentieth of the same month, highlighting the national symbols: "What are your national symbols? What things do you identify with to be Mexican? Your national soccer team! The revolution! Your flag! The tortillas! The chile!" (Radio Universidad 2019).[4]

These national symbols, markers of Mexicanness, are present in a prevailing manner in the school as an educational, social, and cultural space; in curricular and extracurricular content and activities; and in the interaction between students with and without migratory experience, demarcating the border between the cultural inside and outside and between Mexicanness and Americanness. This Americanness is integrated by other cultural markers that are carried by immigrant and returnee children from the United States and that converge with the Mexican ones in the school, as a space for social interaction and intercultural encounter. In this intercultural encounter, one of the most frequently recorded facts during the ethnographic fieldwork has been the pointing out of this Americanness through its verbalization, as a way of separating, creating foreignness, and constructing a border between Mexican and American identity, thus obscuring the existence of a shared nationality between subjects with and without migratory experience due to a common ancestry: Mexican.

Numerous records have registered the use of the term *American* to refer to students from the United States. The records have been common in the totality of the school institutions studied, where every time a student coming from the United States has to do some exercise on the blackboard, many of the classmates harangue him or her with "now you go, American" or "it's your turn, American" (nonparticipant observation, November 8, 2018). In fact, this term has become a marker with which the student arriving from the United States is identified by the rest of the educational community, which is made up not only of students but also of faculty, administrative and service personnel, and the management team.

Going further, in some educational institutions, immigrant and returnee students who arrived in Oaxaca when they were eight and nine years old were registered as American and, although they are now fourteen years old, they are still considered foreigners and called "Americans," which shows the strength of foreignness and frontierization despite the passing of time. That is to say, although the migratory condition could have been a distinctive element only at the moment of arrival in Oaxaca, diluted and eroded as such with the passing of time, it has rather ended up becoming a mark of external identification through which these students are recognized by the educational community, in intimate articulation with other elements of social, cultural, and linguistic identification. The combination of these elements gives rise, then, to the construction of these subjects as foreign and borderline (Simmel 1997): "the Americans."

Regarding cultural racism, one of the expressions widely registered among students without migration experience to refer to immigrant and returnee students has been to "become more *güero*"—that is, to become whiter. This expression highlights cultural whiteness, understood in the sense of Echeverría (2010), as an identity that incorporates cultural elements of white, Western, and capitalist society. This is an identity that does not denote "whiteness of race" but the acquisition of the social, cultural, linguistic, political, and economic characteristics of the white human being (Echeverría 2010, 62). Hence, "Black, Asian, or Latinx people who show signs of good behavior [cultural] in terms of U.S. capitalist modernity become part of whiteness" (Echeverría 2010, 65).[5]

The cultural whiteness of this childhood integrates linguistic, social, and cultural identity, elements typical of white American society, a foundation on which cultural racism toward these "other" immigrants and returnees, toward these "other" Mexicans, is built. This cultural racism shows how the existence of shared biological and phenotypic traits leads to highlighting the social, linguistic, and cultural "mismatch" of children from the United States. For this childhood, which possesses Mexican phenotypical traits, it would "correspond" to have Mexican linguistic, social, and cultural elements. In addition to the preceding, the records made through the application of different ethnographic techniques reveal that the expression "to become more *güero*" is commonly accompanied by another: "to be superior to others." This alludes to an ethnic hierarchy in which cultural whiteness is associated with higher social status.

The speech of a nonmigrant girl during an informal conversation in a middle school is very revealing in this regard: "Aah, is that they already think they are more because they speak English, because they dress differently . . . because, because they come from the United States, they already think highly of themselves—well, because they are not like us, they think they are *güeros*" (informal conversation, O.P., March 2019).

And in contrast to the previous speech, that of a student returning from Los Angeles, California, interviewed at the same middle school: "They don't talk to me because I come from the United States, and they have the opinion that I think highly of myself because of that. They think I'm going to make them feel less. That's why nobody wants to talk to me. And even though I try to talk, they stay away. That is why it is harder for me to integrate into this culture, because they don't give me the opportunity" (J. L. Santiago, March 18, 2019).

Participant and nonparticipant observation has shown that, in response to the cultural whiteness associated with migrant children, Mexicanness is a way of measuring and excluding "the white," embodied in these children and in their differential linguistic, social, and cultural characteristics, a practice that is not developed when there are nonmigrant students with distinctive characteristics. As an example, during a second-year language and literature class in a high school, a nonmigrant student with a darker skin color than the rest was jokingly introduced to me by his classmates this way: "He is from Africa, from Wakanda" (participant observation, November 15, 2018), an introduction at which everyone, including the student being referred to, openly laughed. This is an example of how a differential element such as skin color is used to label but not to construct a border from which to racialize, exclude, and place the subject on the cultural outside, because, despite the existence of a differentiating element, there is no migratory element or other element of cultural whiteness on which this is based.

This cultural whiteness is interpreted in some ways as cultural whitening, to the extent that, as we pointed out, a sort of social, cultural, and linguistic "mismatch" is perceived between the children from the United States and their phenotype. However, this cultural whitening does not exist, since these children were born and raised in the heart of American society and culture, where they developed their first and main process of socialization and enculturation. Therefore, these children were not previously within any other cultural orbit and thus have not been whitened. The whiteness of the culture is confused with cultural whitening.

Along with the previously discussed ethnographic records, other ethnographic records have also made it possible to identify the different practices of cultural racism, such as gestures of mockery and contempt, other verbal expressions—which can range from an alleged joke to an openly insulting expression and even to hurtful nicknames—and physical actions that imply aggression. For example, in terms of verbal expressions, among others, we can point to the case of a girl born in the United States who was going through a hard process of insertion into a secondary school, to which was added the pain of family separation as a result of migration. Because she was different, she was singled out and isolated at school. This led her to develop trauma, one symptom of which was that whenever someone spoke to her, she would respond by curling in on herself and hiding her head in her torso, a reaction that earned her the nickname "the turtle."

Finally, with regard to physical aggression, in all the educational institutions analyzed, without exception, there have been cases of bullying of children who have migration experience in the United States, which has led to mental health problems among these students: "They do bully me. Sometimes they hit me and tell me to go back to the United States. They ask what am I doing here and say that I am not Mexican, that I am American, that I am gringo and such. . . . and, well, I went to the psychologist, and they enrolled me in another activity, which is playing football, and that distracts me from everything" (M. C., March 4, 2019).

Conclusion

The racialization of the "other" can transcend the merely biological element and be based on differential linguistic and sociocultural elements associated with migration. In this research the intercultural encounter between the subjects of study at school has revealed, precisely, the construction of a racialization not from differential phenotypical elements—since they do not exist—but from distinctive social, cultural, and linguistic elements evidenced from the experience of international mobility. Therefore, although between the immigrant and returnee population, issues of binational membership (United States–Mexico) intersect with issues of ethnicity, the elements shared with the society of descent are inhibited in favor of migratory status and social differences, both cultural and linguistic.

In the school context, the language of children from the United States is characterized by speaking English, not speaking Spanish, speaking with an Anglo accent, and having other ways of expressing themselves; the body is marked by a different way of dressing; and conduct is characterized by another way of thinking, codifying the world, and behaving. These elements constitute the basis on which borders and cultural racism are built toward this immigrant and returnee otherness. Also, the use of the terms *American* and *Americans* reveal how verbalized identity creates foreignness and bordering between the cultural inside and the cultural outside, between "us" and "the others," between Mexicanness and Americanness. This sheds light on two main issues: first, that although the subjects coming from the United States are descendants of Mexicans, the migratory experience dissolves their Mexican national belonging so that, in order to be thought of and accepted as Mexicans, they must experience and internalize Mexicanness from an early age, which implies not developing any process of international mobility; second, that the phenotypical elements are understood as indistinguishable from the linguistic, social, and cultural elements that make up that Mexicanness.

The presence in Mexican schools, and particularly in Oaxaca, of students born in and returning from the United States, where they have spent most of their lives from an early age, is evidence that migration has altered the usual identity patterns, in which there was a correspondence between the phenotypical, social, cultural, and linguistic characteristics of the subjects.

Based on the results presented, I make two fundamental recommendations for public policy: the development of educational plans and programs built on intercultural perspective, where the interactions between subjects with and without migratory experience are especially addressed; and teacher training in intercultural pedagogy and attention to migrant students.

Notes

1. According to the Convention on the Rights of the Child (United Nations General Assembly, n.d.), children are persons under eighteen years of age.
2. Indigenous language of the people of the same name.
3. Emphasis mine.
4. As heard on the Universidad Autónoma Benito Juárez radio station in Oaxaca on November 14, 2019.
5. Translations are mine.

References

Aguerre, Lucía Alicia. 2011. *Desigualdades, racismo cultural y diferencia colonial.* DesiguALdades.net Working Paper Series no. 5. Berlin: DesiguALdades.net Research Network on Interdependent Inequalities in Latin America.

Balibar, Étienne. 1991. "¿Existe un neorracismo?" In *Raza, nación y clase,* edited by Étienne Balibar and Immanuel Wallerstein, 31–48. Madrid: IEPALA.

Balibar, Etienne, and Immanuel Wallerstein. 1991. *Raza, nación y clase.* Madrid: IEPALA.

Barabas, Alicia. 2001. "Traspasando fronteras: Los migrantes indígenas de México en Estados Unidos." *Amérique latine histoire et mémoire* 2:209–20.

Barei, Silvia. 2013. "Fronteras naturales / fronteras culturales: Nuevos problemas / nuevas teorías." *Tópicos del seminario* 29:109–25.

Barker, Martin. 1981. *The New Racism: Conservatives and the Ideology of the Tribe.* London: Junction Books.

Barros, Magdalena. 2019. "Las deportaciones y su efecto en la vida de los niños y niñas que forman parte de las familias migrantes: Casos de la costa central de California, Estados Unidos." Seminar presentation, March 13, 2019. Instituto de Investigaciones Antropológicas, Universidad Nacional Autónoma de México.

Cámara de Diputados del H. Congreso de la Unión. 2021. *Constitución Política de los Estados Unidos Mexicanos.* Digitized legislation, May 28, 2021. http://www.diputados.gob.mx/LeyesBiblio/pdf_mov/Constitucion_Politica.pdf.

Canclini, Néstor García. 1989. *Culturas híbridas: Estrategias para entrar y salir de la modernidad.* Mexico City: Grijalbo.

Castellanos, Alicia. 2004. "Racismo y xenofobia: Un recuento necesario." In *Leer y pensar el racismo,* edited by Mónica Inés Cejas, 102–21. Guadalajara: Petra Ediciones.

Cruz, Tania. 2011. "Racismo cultural y representaciones de inmigrantes centroamericanas en Chiapas." *Migraciones internacionales* 6 (21): 133–57.

Cuberos, Curro, Emma Martín, and Beatriz Padilla. 2014. "Repensando las fronteras culturales en la sociedades de la globalización." In *Periferias, fronteras y diálogos,* edited by Agustí Andreu Tomàs, Yolanda Bodoque, Dolors Comas, Joan Josep Pujadas, Jordi Roca, and Montserrat Soronellas, 902–32. Tarragona, Spain: Publicacions Universitat Rovira i Virgili.

De Genova, Nicholas. 2007. *Working the Boundaries: Race, Space, and "Illegality" in Mexican Chicago*. Durham, N.C.: Duke University Press.

Echeverría, Bolívar. 2010. *Modernidad y blanquitud*. Mexico City: ERA.

Grosfoguel, Ramón. 1999. "Introduction: 'Cultural Racism' and Colonial Caribbean Migrants in Core Zones of the Capitalist World-Economy." *Review* 22, no. 4: 409–34.

Hernández, Janeth. 2019. "Tecnologías necropolíticas en el acceso a la justicia de las mujeres migrantes víctimas de violencia de género en San Diego, California." Seminar presentation IIJ-UNAM, May 18, 2019.

Klein, Marc Georges, José Antonio Girón, Brenda Hernández Zavaleta, Martín López López, Sergio Iván Navarro Martínez, Bárbara Carolina Salazar Narváéz, Antonio Saldívar Moreno, and N. Elizabeth Santos Baca. 2014. "Desde Chiapas: Criterios básicos para la exigencia de pertinencia cultural y lingüística en la educación." In *Desenmascarar la discriminación: La violencia en el sistema educativo mexicano hacia los pueblos originarios y las personas con discapacidad*, edited by Incidencia Civil en la Educación, 69–117. Mexico City: ICE.

Martínez, Ubaldo. 2001. *El Ejido: Discriminación, exclusión social y racismo*. Madrid: Catarata.

Moreno, Isidoro. 2014. "Confrontación y fronteras entre lógicas culturales: Extractivismo desarrollista versus Sumak Kawsay en Ecuador." In *Periferias, fronteras y diálogos*, edited by Agustí Andreu Tomàs, Yolanda Bodoque, Dolors Comas, Joan Josep Pujadas, Jordi Roca, and Montserrat Soronellas, 1158–67. Tarragona, Spain: Publicacions Universitat Rovira i Virgili.

Pujadas, Joan Josep. 1999. "Lengua, identidad y frontera: El caso de la Franja catalano-aragonesa." In *Lenguas, identidades e ideologías: Los usos sociales y políticos de la diversidad cultural*, edited by Antonio Barrera, 129–42. Santiago: FAAEE/AGA.

Pujadas, Joan Josep. 2001. "Frontera, nación y ciudadanía: Los usos de la lengua en los confines e Aragón y Catalunya." In *Lengua, cultura y evolución humana*, edited by Fernando Represa and Inés Gómez, 21–40. Oiartzun: Sendoa Editores.

Riedmann, Andrea, and Carolina Stefoni. 2015. "Sobre el racismo, su negación, y las consecuencias para una educación anti-racista en la enseñanza secundaria chilena." *Polis* 14 (42): 191–216.

Rizo, Marta, and Vivian Romeu. 2006. "Hacia una propuesta teórica para el análisis de las fronteras simbólicas en situaciones de comunicación intercultural." *Estudios sobre las culturas contemporáneas* 12 (24): 35–54.

Salazar, Isabel. 2020. "La ambivalente afirmación de la identidad: Conversaciones entre Balivar y Mbembe." *Enfoques* 32 (1): 45–57.

Simmel, George. 1997. "Digresión sobre el extranjero." *Revista de Occidente* 2:716–22.

Taguieff, Pierre-André. 1987. *La forcé du préjugé: Essai sur le racism et ses doubles*. Paris: La Découverte.

Unidad de Política Migratoria (Migration Policy Unit, MPU). 2017. "Repatriación de mexicanos, 2017." Secretaría de la Gobernación. Statistical bulletin, accessed

January 18, 2021. http://portales.segob.gob.mx/es/PoliticaMigratoria/Cuadros BOLETIN?Anual=2017&Secc=5.

Unidad de Política Migratoria (Migration Policy Unit, MPU). 2018. "Repatriación de mexicanos, 2018." Secretaría de la Gobernación. Statistical bulletin, accessed January 18, 2021. http://portales.segob.gob.mx/es/PoliticaMigratoria/Cuadros BOLETIN?Anual=2018&Secc=5.

Unidad de Política Migratoria (Migration Policy Unit, MPU). 2019. "Repatriación de mexicanos, 2019." Secretaría de la Gobernación. Statistical bulletin, accessed January 18, 2021. http://portales.segob.gob.mx/es/PoliticaMigratoria/Cuadros BOLETIN?Anual=2019&Secc=5.

Unidad de Política Migratoria (Migration Policy Unit, MPU). 2020. "Repatriación de mexicanos, 2020." Secretaría de la Gobernación. Statistical bulletin, accessed January 18, 2021. http://www.politicamigratoria.gob.mx/es/PoliticaMigratoria /CuadrosBOLETIN?Anual=2020&Secc=5.

United Nations General Assembly. n.d. *Convention on the Rights of the Child*. United Nations Human Rights Office of the High Commissioner. Accessed May 29, 2021. https://www.ohchr.org/en/professionalinterest/pages/crc.aspx.

Valdéz, Gloria Ciria. 2019. "Migración de retorno: Desafíos de la Cuarta Transformación; Un enfoque Regional Transfronterizo." Seminar presentation, January 16, 2019. Instituto de Investigaciones Antropológicas, Universidad Nacional Autónoma de México.

Valdéz, Gloria Ciria, Liza Fabiola Ruiz, Óscar Bernardo Rivera, and Ramiro Antonio López. 2018. "Menores migrantes de retorno: Problemática académica y proceso administrativo en el sistema escolar sonorense." *Región y sociedad* 30 (72): 1–30.

Van Dijk, Teun A. 2007. *Racismo y discurso en América Latina*. Barcelona: Gedisa.

Velasco, Honorio, and Ángel Díaz. 1997. *La lógica de la investigación etnográfica: Un modelo de trabajo para etnógrafos de escuela*. Madrid: Trotta.

Velasco, Saúl, and Bruno Baronnet. 2016. "Racismo y escuela en México: Reconociendo la tragedia para intentar la salida." *Diálogos sobre educación* 7 (13): 1–17.

Wieviorka, Michel. 2006. "La mutación del racismo." *Migraciones* 19:151–63.

Wieviorka, Michel. 2014. "Les mutations du racisme contemporain." In *Identities on the Move*, edited by Flocel Sabaté, 503–15. Bern: Editions Flocel Sabaté.

Zúñiga, Víctor, and Silvia E. Giorguli Saucedo. 2019. *Niñas y niños en la migración de Estados Unidos a México: La generación 0.5*. Mexico City: El Colegio de México.

PART II

Children on the Border in Literature, Art, and Culture

The second part of this book comprises three chapters that focus on literature, art, and culture and how migration figures in different media in the Americas. Alejandra Josiowicz explores U.S. Latinx and Latin American children's and young adult literature on migration, looking at the way it can question stereotypes and may function as a tool to combat racism and xenophobia, addressing the topic of child migration empathetically and critically. Josiowicz develops tools and practices for teaching about migration and migrant children by exploring the concept of resilience.

Élisabeth Vallet and Nancie Bouchard highlight a project that intends to generate a teaching approach to border issues and migration. It develops a highly innovative approach to global education while intending to increase nonmigrant students' understanding of ethics and global literacy. Valentina Glockner develops a case study of a group of unaccompanied Mexican children who travel across the Sonoran Desert to understand how borders shape and affect the lives of migrant children. The fieldwork includes an art project in Nogales, Sonora, Mexico, in which children depict their understanding of migration through discussion, writing, and art. Glockner discusses the way in which children confront and challenge borders, contributing not only to their destabilization but to their reification as well.

In the intersection between cultural studies, education, and the anthropology/ethnography of migrant children, these chapters show the importance of studying the relationships between children and cultural discourses on children, borders, and borderlands, problematizing the role of borders as physical and symbolic realities as well as interrogating and destabilizing the ways in which borders produce children and culture, and children and culture, in time, produce borders.

CHAPTER 4

A Civil Rights Pedagogy on Children on the Borders

The Search to Belong in Latin American and Latinx Children's and Young Adult Literature

ALEJANDRA JOSIOWICZ

Introduction: Intersectional, Decolonial Latin American Children's and Young Adult Literature on Migration

Children's and young adult literatures reveal the symbolic dimension of migrant children's oppression, how cultural meanings have worked either to reinforce or to question systems of privilege, inequality, and power. For many years immigrant children and youths were either invisible or appeared—in communication, governmental policies, literature, visual arts, school textbooks, and, more recently, social media—through stereotyped images that combined racism, sexism, xenophobia, and imperialism. These cultural texts stigmatized difference and privileged normality, which was equated with white, middle-class, urban childhoods. Black, Indigenous, and mixed-race children and young people, as well as rural migrants, were associated with promiscuity, degradation, and uncleanliness (Rosemberg, Moura, and Silva 2009). Black nannies were frequently represented with nonhuman characteristics, not individualized, associated with bestiality, or ridiculed (Rosemberg 1984; Rosemberg, Moura, and Silva 2009). In textbooks, magazines, and films and in children's literature, Indigenous and Black children and migrants were stigmatized and seen as savages, as submissive, bestialized, degraded, corrupt, even promiscuous, never as protagonists or narrators but as passive objects of the actions of others (Artieda 2017; Lajolo and Zilberman 2017; Belmiro and Martins 2018). Furthermore, until the 1960s many school texts, magazines, and works of children's literature undervalued and under-represented girls, depicting them in stereotypical fashion: passive, obedient, weak, subservient (Rosemberg 2001). In school texts and some children's texts, even after the 1970s, women were rarely shown working outside the domestic environment (Rosemberg 2001). In this way textbooks ignored the educational needs of girls, Indigenous children, migrants, and Black children and reinforced gender hierarchies and traditional family models, together with racial, ethnic, and class inequalities (Rosemberg 2001).

Some of the central questions of this chapter are as follows: How have immigrant and refugee children been portrayed in Latin American and Latinx children's literature? In what ways has children's literature questioned stereotyped images of migrant children as they frequently appear in TV, newspapers, and other communication media? How can children's literature become a powerful tool to combat racism, nationalism, sexism, and xenophobia and to address the topic of child migration empathetically and critically? How can it become a meaningful tool to influence policy makers and generate emotional identification with child migrants? How is children's literature capable of pointing to the struggles of children on the border to create spaces of belonging?

During the last decades of the twentieth century, a children's and young adult literature that questioned structures of domination and subordination in relation to race, class, gender, and citizenship emerged, questioning differences of power and privilege. It had a role in the extension of civil and political rights to previously excluded groups and in the democratizing processes that took place in Latin America and among Latinxs, African Americans, and Native Americans from the 1960s until the present (Lajolo and Zilberman 2017). This happened at the same time as the expansion of education and the inclusion of an ever larger proportion of the population in different levels of education and civic life. Since the 1980s and 1990s, children's and young adult literature in Latin America started including nonconventional gender and family models, as well as new ways of thinking about masculinity and femininity, emphasizing the suffering of children and young people that do not fit gender conventions. During the last decades of the twentieth and the beginning of the twenty-first centuries, children and young adult literature has also explored racism and antiracism. This has been correlated with the emergence of political movements demanding rights for women and LGBTQ+ individuals, as well as the rights of people of color in Latin America, together with the expansion of bilingual education and public policies that require inclusion of ethnic-racial relations in school curricula (Lajolo and Zilberman 2017). Gender-diverse characters and people of color started appearing as protagonists and narrators, neither stereotyped nor submissive. In the late twentieth and early twenty-first centuries, the theme of migration and transnational citizenship appeared in children's and young adult literature in many Latin American countries and among Latinx writers in the United States, narrating in visual and written form the experience of children and young people as subjects of mobility. This literature questions xenophobic narratives of invasion and cultural pollution in which nonwhite, Hispanic, Black, Indigenous, and poor children appear as invaders, threats to national security and to the social order (Alexander 2018). Children's and young adult literature on refugees and migrants is a powerful tool for public intervention and for fighting for social change and justice, a way to create new social meanings regarding immigrants and refugees. These texts are capable of spreading new understandings and meanings about refugees and immigrant subjects and of persuading the general public of the justness of these individuals' cause and struggles (Alexander 2011). This literature can, by generating emotional identification with immigrants and refugees among the public of children and adults, mobilize public opinion in struggles to acquire rights and influence policy making and in the creation of laws and the construction of political power (Alexander 2011).

Because it deals with intersectional as well as decolonial questions, denouncing imperialism and xenophobia, this literature does not follow the way theories of traditional children's literature and classic texts in western Europe and the United States have considered space but instead deviates from those traditions and even questions them. In those classics, home tends to be associated with safety and constraint and journeys away from home with danger and freedom (Nodelman 2008). Perry Nodelman (2008, 223) has argued that the "home/away/home pattern is the most common story line in children's literature." This spatial dichotomy of home and away is related to ideas about childhood that emerged and became generalized in western Europe and the United States during the eighteenth and nineteenth centuries (Foucault 1978; Ariès 1962; Mintz 2004). In them white, middle-class children were associated with affection and considered physically, socially, and psychically innocent, pure creatures, apparently devoid of any marker of gender, class, race, ethnicity, or nationality (Higonnet 1998).

For these children home is the place to be safe and childlike, a controlled, limited, protective space to leave from and return to, while trips away from home are unfamiliar experiences, linked with defiance, excitement, freedom, and danger (Nodelman 2008). Many of these stories begin with the protagonists at home; then they go on a journey, and they return home at the end. These narrative patterns have been read as allegories of psychic journeys that reinforce binary oppositional worlds, of constraint and freedom, safety and uncertainty, knowledge and innocence, desire and possibility, childhood and adulthood (Nodelman 2008). However, in Latin American and Latinx literature for children and young adults, home (be it region, country of origin, or a precarious house) is a much more complex construction, frequently determined by social, economic, and political conflicts and by ethnic and racial hierarchies.

In Latin American and Latinx children's and young adult literature, depictions of both being at home and being away from home reveal migrant children's struggles to create spaces of belonging. Because home is not a safe space, or the origin of a stable identity, but a space of civil conflict, of economic hardships and social upheaval, and the journey away is not seen as (exclusively) dangerous but as a possibility of finding stability and employment opportunities, the dichotomy of home and away is questioned.[1] This way Latin American and Latinx literature reveals how space is the result of a sociocultural construction in which children and young adult characters are active protagonists in the search for a place to live, work, and learn. As will appear in the next sections, many of these stories begin with the lack of homes and the lack of stability—many characters are homeless or live in places where they are threatened or do not belong, and others feel at home in places that would not be socially classified as typical middle-class family homes. Furthermore, in the Latin American and Latinx children's texts I analyze, children and young adults appear as agents and protagonists, aware of the racial, gender, and social problems of their societies and communities, highly accultured, capable of acts of resistance against oppression and thus of shaping their own stories (Gubar 2011). Children are not completely autonomous, but they act collaboratively with others, and so they highlight the importance of social collaboration in effecting social change (Gubar 2011).

At this point it is important to distinguish children's literature on the topic of migration from children's literature destined for child migrants and refugees. While the purpose of the former is to make children, young adults, and their families aware of the experiences of migrants and refugees, combating racism, nationalism, sexism, and xenophobia, the objective of the latter is to help child migrants and refugees process their experiences and eventually find ways of empowerment, ways of expressing their feelings and perceptions. These two corpora of texts have very different implications and intended publics. However, they may overlap, as some texts that raise empathy among the general public for the tribulations of migrants and refugees may be used to help them deal with abuse, cruelty, and discrimination because of their status or condition, and some texts that are capable of stimulating resilience and creativity among refugee and immigrant children and young people might also be used to raise awareness about their status and the struggles for the recognition of their rights among the public.

Because of the scarcity of studies on this topic, this chapter intends to give a broad perspective on some of the most important texts in Latin American and U.S. Latinx children's literature on migrant children and children on the border, functioning as an abridged contemporary cultural history on children on the border in children's literature. It covers U.S. Latinx children's literature, including the most important publishing houses and books published, as well as the most relevant Latin American contemporary children's literature that deals with childhood migration. However, its panoramic nature does not prevent a closer examination of some of the texts under analysis, as it zooms in on some of the most relevant texts written on the topic, such as Gloria Anzaldúa's children's books. This way, it gives visibility to the ways in which the struggles and challenges of migrant children have appeared in children's literature: their search for belonging, as resilient and resourceful individuals. These texts have a threefold nature: they are aesthetically powerful, they stimulate empathy for those who migrate, and they denounce imperialism, xenophobia, and racial oppression. In short, these texts display a civil rights pedagogy on children on the borders, teaching empathy toward their sufferings, creating alliances, and bridging gender, national, citizenship-status, and racial differences.

The rest of the chapter is divided into three sections. The first one examines children's and young adult literature that deals with borders and migration in U.S. Latinx texts. The second one looks at Latin American children's literature on the topic. The third one offers some pedagogic tools and practices for teachers working on migration or with migrant children, elaborating on the concept of resilience in connection with children's literature. It presents activities and tools for discussing migration through a Puerto Rican children's text by Fernando Picó.

Latinx Children's and Young Adult Literature on Migration and Refuge

Since 1980, with the growth of the U.S. Hispanic population and its increasing access to education, a new public for children's and young adult literature emerged among Latinxs in the United States. The momentum of the civil rights movements and the interest in redefining school curricula to reflect intersectionality and multiculturalism have reaffirmed the place of this literature through the publication of bilingual texts, some of them in Spanglish. Themes central to this literature are identity, immigration, socioeconomic issues, unemployment, illegality, poverty, and linguistic, racial, and cultural differences. A pioneer in the field was the Puerto Rican writer, storyteller, puppeteer, and librarian Pura Belpré, who promoted children's and young adult literature among Hispanic communities in the United States, translating, adapting, and publishing various texts in which she rewrote Puerto Rican folk tales (Nuñez 2009). Her book *Santiago* (1971) tells the story of a Puerto Rican boy that has moved to New York and misses his little hen Selina, which he thinks he sees in his new school patio. In 1996 the Pura Belpré Award was established in Belpré's honor, with the purpose of recognizing Latinx authors and illustrators whose work represents Latinx experiences for children and young people (Nuñez 2009). A bilingual children's book, *The Storyteller's Candle / La velita de los cuentos* (2008), by Lucía González, depicts, through the story of Hildamar and Santiago, two Puerto Rican children newly arrived in the United States, Belpré's ability as a storyteller and her cultural work in the Hispanic community. Hildamar and Santiago, like many Puerto Rican children, find a place of refuge in the Spanish-language cultural dissemination activities that Belpré instituted in the New York Public Library.

During the second half of the twentieth century, different publishing houses created collections dedicated to Hispanic and Latinx children and young adults in the United States. Lectorum, founded in 1960 and still in existence, specializes in bilingual texts for children and young people, some of them dealing specifically with Latinx identity and Mexican cultural heritage, such as meals and celebrations. The collection Cuando los grandes eran pequeños (When the great ones where young), dedicated to re-creating the childhoods of important Latin American cultural figures, such as Gabriel García Márquez, Julia de Burgos, and José Martí, has gained enormous popularity, as has the 2008 anthology *Arco iris de poesía* (Rainbow of poetry), with poems by José Martí, Gabriela Mistral, Rubén Darío, and many others. In recent decades Lectorum has published numerous books on how migrations and borders affect children's lives. *My Diary from Here to There / Mi diario de aquí hasta allá* (2009), by Amanda Irma Pérez, tells the story of a girl's journey from Ciudad Juárez to Los Angeles in search of work for her parents. The girl's diary serves as a refuge and a tool for her to explore the transformations in her identity. *A Movie in My Pillow / Una película en mi almohada* (2007), by Jorge Argueta, is a book of poetry that narrates the poet's journey as he escapes civil war in El Salvador and arrives in San Francisco. *My Grandma / Mi abuelita* (2007), by Ginger Foglesong Guy, is a book that captures a baby boy's emotions when traveling abroad to see his grandma.

Another publishing house specializing in Latinx children's and young adult literature is Children's Book Press, founded in 1975, a multicultural publishing house dedicated to bilingual books, including those that present oral traditions and Indigenous legends as well as stories situated in the contemporary United States. At present the press is part of Lee & Low Books, specializing in diversity and multiculturalism. They have published *From the Bellybutton of the Moon and Other Summer Poems / Del ombligo de la luna y otros poemas de verano* (2005), by Francisco Alarcón, bilingual poems in which the narrator remembers his childhood trips to Mexico to visit his family in the town of Atoyac. Moreover, in *From North to South / Del Norte al Sur* (2013), by René Colato Laínez, the mother of the child protagonist is deported to Tijuana for not having the necessary documents, so the boy and his father travel to Mexico to find her.

Among the hugely diverse corpora of texts on children and migration which has only increased in recent years, I would like to call attention to Gloria Anzaldúa's children's texts not only because she is a pioneer in writing stories about child migrants but mostly because her texts avoid reifying or essentializing Hispanic children, as borders appear not as spaces of fixation but of negotiation and transformation of children's and young people's identities. Anzaldúa was a Chicana mestiza lesbian writer, professor, and theorist who pointed out the importance of giving voice and visibility to Third World women, children of color, and Black, Latinx, Asian, and Jewish individuals and their cultural heritage. Her famous book *Borderlands /*

La frontera (1987) is a poetic manifesto on hybrid identity in which a Latina Hispanic woman in the United States acquires voice on the border of different languages (Spanish, English, Spanglish, Nahuatl) and of different nationalities (Mexican, American, Chicano, Latina) as well as of gender identity and sexual choice (female, lesbian, homosexual) and in-between ethnicities (white, Indigenous, mestiza) while not belonging to any of these traditions completely (Anzaldúa 2012).

Gloria Anzaldúa: Hispanic Girl's Empowerment in Latinx Children's Literature

Anzaldúa wrote two bilingual texts for children, which were published by Children's Books Press: *Prietita and the Ghost Woman / Prietita y la Llorona* (1995) and *Friends from the Other Side / Amigos del otro lado* (1993). Both of them have a Hispanic girl, Prietita, as a protagonist. In *Prietita and the Ghost Woman / Prietita y la Llorona*, Prietita's mother is ill, and the girl asks a woman healer, Doña Lola, to make a remedy for her. However, there is one ingredient missing, a rue plant, and Prietita needs to look for it at the King Ranch, which is being heavily patrolled by private security. Prietita shows her courage and resourcefulness by going into the ranch alone to look for it. There, she follows different animals and gets in contact with different plants typical of southern Texas, asking them for help in finding the plant, without success. Many times Prietita feels lost or afraid and gets desperate and cries but says words of encouragement to herself and finds strength to resist and continue struggling. Finally, she encounters *la Llorona*, a ghost woman who, according to Mexican popular traditions, cried for her lost children and looked for other children to steal. However, instead of trying to steal or harm Prietita, *la Llorona*, a dark woman dressed in white, helps her find rue. Prietita, no longer afraid, is guided out of the ranch by the ghost woman, where she finds her family and Doña Lola, who are looking for her. Together, they make the remedy for Prietita's mother.

The text shows a Hispanic, Chicana girl living in South Texas who is strong, resourceful, and shrewd. Prietita lives in an all-female community composed of her sister, her mother, and Doña Lola, *la curandera*, her role model, who collaborates with her in curing her mother. However, there is no medical institution or money involved in the cure, and the consumer logic that would suggest buying a remedy in the pharmacy or contacting a doctor is replaced by alternative medicinal practices that connect women with Indigenous traditions as well as with natural and supernatural forces. Her mother's illness (referred to as "the old sickness" [Anzaldúa 1995, 8]), probably some kind of mental disturbance into which she is relapsing, points to Hispanic women's suffering and social degradation as they deal with unemployment, abuse, discrimination, and invisibility. The illness gives Prietita a central place as the protagonist and heroine of the story, the eldest daughter and acting head of her family, as men are absent in the text. Prietita turns to the healer, "*la curandera*" (7) (the Spanish word is used in the English version also, pointing to the specificity of Hispanic popular healing traditions), who is training her in the use of medicinal herbs, for help. However, Doña Lola does not give the girl a clear solution for where the plant is to be found: she mentions it is present on the King Ranch (one of the biggest ranches in the United States, a center of agricultural production,[2] well known in Chicanx popular culture) but advises against going there because "it is not safe for a little girl" (6). Prietita's bravery is revealed as she defies the image of female defenselessness and vulnerability and dares to go into the dangerous zone by herself. The place that is not "for a little girl," the forbidden space, the space of violence and possible death ("I've heard that they shoot trespassers" [6], warns *la curandera*) is also Prietita's place of initiation, where she leaves the world of girlhood and becomes a woman.

As the sun goes down, Prietita wanders into the King Ranch, where she encounters natural and supernatural forces. First, she sees different animals—a deer, a salamander, a dove, a jaguar, lightning bugs—all of which make strange sounds and try to guide Prietita to the rue plant, with no results. But Prietita continues and sees the *Llorona*, a "dark woman" (Anzaldúa 1995, 26). Initially, she feels scared, but then she "force[s] herself to walk" (21) toward her and asks the woman for help. *La Llorona* helps her find rue, guides her from the King Ranch, and disappears.

During her trip inside the ranch, which is an experience of discovery and initiation, Prietita finds the power of her own womanhood and of collaboration with other women that suffer, that are in pain. She also finds an alternative view of Hispanic traditions, which helps her question the representation of women's suffering ("Perhaps she is not what others think she is" [Anzaldúa 1995, 28], says Doña Lola). *La Llorona* is not a revengeful, bestial, hysterical, or irrational woman but instead is someone wise, calm, reasonable, and helpful. As a substitute for Prietita's absent mother—herself a woman that

suffers, that is mentally ill—and for her own adult self in the painful process of growing up, *la Llorona* shows how Hispanic girls' suffering should
not be regarded with fear or prejudice, as it can lead to wisdom, autonomy,
rationality, and activism and therefore make these girls powerful citizens
and members of their civic communities. As she returns home with Prietita,
Doña Lola promises they will make the remedy for her mother together and
tells her, "I am very proud of you. You have grown up this night" (29). This
encounter with *la Llorona* puts Prietita in contact with her strength as a
woman, teaching her the power of collaboration and resilience.

Prietita and the Ghost Woman rewrites the spatial dichotomy that, according to many critics, is a central element of classical children's literature,
according to which the child's home tends to be associated with safety and
constraint and journeys away from home are associated with adulthood,
danger, and freedom (Nodelman 2008). However, like other children's texts
on migration, *Prietita and the Ghost Woman* goes beyond this dichotomy,
emphasizing not the safety and constraint of the child's home—in this case
a place of suffering and instability—or the freedom or threat of the outside
but instead the girl's resilience, her resourcefulness in helping her mother,
even when she feels disoriented and frightened.

Prietita is not a vulnerable, innocent girl in need of adults' protection,
who leaves home in search for adventures and is under threat, but instead a
responsible, independent being that is aware of adults' suffering and needs
and is able to find resources and collaborate with others. When she is alone
and feels frightened, she gives herself words of encouragement and continues struggling: "She wiped her tears, straightened her shoulders and looked
up" (Anzaldúa 1995, 15). After many failed attempts, she finally finds the
remedy for her mother. Prietita's courage is shown in her continuous resistance, her ability to overcome fear, to avoid external threats and obstacles
and start again even when she thinks all is lost. This way, the text questions
stereotypical images of girls' vulnerability and defenselessness, as well as of
adult, white, male power. *Prietita and the Ghost Woman* is a journey of self-
discovery of the wisdom, activism, and power of Hispanic and Latina girls,
even—and perhaps more so—in times of suffering. It questions prejudices
and reinterprets Hispanic, Chicanx myths and popular cultural traditions in
a feminist, nonconsumerist way, emphasizing the relation with natural and
communal forces. It is also a story about Hispanic girls' resistance in the face

of adversity, in which children learn that only by believing in themselves and the justness of their causes will they overcome.

Gloria Anzaldúa II: Prietita Struggles for the Rights of Latinx Migrant Children

In *Friends from the Other Side / Amigos del otro lado* (1993), Anzaldúa includes a foreword in which she narrates having seen, as a child, many women and children crossing the border toward Texas, in search of employment, and how many of them were called wetbacks or *mojados* because they got wet crossing the river. The story makes reference to many typical elements of Chicanx cultural life, not only the natural environment but also the specific words (some of them in Spanglish) that refer to the daily life of Mexican immigrant communities in South Texas. In this text Prietita befriends Joaquín, a Mexican boy "from the other side," and notices that he speaks Spanish differently, seems hurt or ashamed, and tries to hide the sores he has on his arms. When other kids bully Joaquín, calling him *mojadito* (wetback), telling him "why don't you go back where you belong?" (Anzaldúa 1993, 8), and threatening to beat him with some rocks, Prietita defends him. Instead of being afraid, she openly defies them and denounces their gang-like behavior, saying, "What's the matter with you guys? How brave you are, a bunch of machos against one small boy. You should be ashamed of yourselves!" (10). Prietita's cousin Tete and his (probably Hispanic) friends from the neighborhood deride the boy, treat him as a foreigner, an outsider who does not belong and therefore deserves to be kicked out. Prietita confronts the boys, defying their performance of masculine aggressiveness, and successfully sends them away. Then Joaquín invites her to the shack where he lives, where he and his mother tell her about their lack of employment and their migration. Slowly, Joaquín and Prietita become friends, and Joaquín starts feeling less ashamed of himself in front of her.

One day someone warns them that the border patrol, *la migra*, is coming to the area, so Prietita helps Joaquín and his mother hide. They wait as border patrol passes by. "While the white patrolman stayed in the van, the Chicano *migra* got out and asked 'Does anyone know of any illegals living in this area?'" (Anzaldúa 1993, 25). The text reveals not only subtle racial hierarchies between officers but also the complicity of the Chicano border patrol agent (himself a migrant or son of migrants) with the incarceration of illegals. Everyone in the area avoids answering them, and instead a woman says, "Yes, I saw some over there," and points "to the *gringo* side of town—the white side," at which everybody laughs, "even the Chicano *migra*" (25). The text uncovers subtle acts of resistance by the Hispanic community. Instead of betraying the illegal migrants, a woman denounces the illegal status of the white, gringo side, referring to the United States' annexation of Texas in 1845, which resulted in the Mexican-American War and the United States' acquisition of Mexican territory. The text denounces, through the fresh, humorous perspective of popular culture, the injustices of imperialism, questioning the legitimacy of the United States' military hegemony and subverting the idea of illegality. Instead of referring to the Hispanic immigrants who have traveled to the United States in search of employment and live in the poorest neighborhoods, she refers to the illegal status of imperialist military conquest and of the oppression of Hispanics and particularly Mexicans. The text points to how official language and history tend to cover up imperialist domination, calling those who are defenseless and oppressed *illegals* and legitimizing economic and political power. Even the complicit Chicano border patrol agent laughs at the joke, implicitly agreeing with the woman's denunciation of injustice and oppression. After the border patrol agents leave, Prietita and Joaquín gather some herbs to heal Joaquín's sores as Doña Lola affirms that Prietita has finished her training and will be able to cure him, as she has become a healing woman herself.

Friends from the Other Side is another story of initiation, another process of growth and learning for Prietita. Throughout this story Prietita enters into contact with the suffering of children who are oppressed, marginalized, who are the object of racism and xenophobia because of their status as illegal migrants. At the beginning Prietita notes the marks of Joaquín's strangeness: his accent is different, as he is "from the other side," and his shame, poverty, bodily gestures, and scars show that he has been through tremendous suffering and violence. However, instead of acting from a place of superiority, Prietita has enormous empathy for him and not only defends him in the face of other children, questioning their performance of sexism, racism, and xenophobia, calling them "a bunch of machos against a small boy," but also hides Joaquín and his mother from immigration police. This way Prietita and Joaquín establish an alliance despite their differences, one formed from empathy and collaboration instead of exclusion and fear. Central to this alliance is the children's common cultural heritage: Mexican, Chicanx, Hispanic language and culture. By showing their friendship despite their differences—in accent, in racial characteristics (Joaquín has "a chunk of limp blue-black hair falling over his forehead and his face" [Anzaldúa 1993, 5], which is a mark of Indigenous origin), in citizenship status (Joaquín is undocumented, while Prietita is not), in socioeconomic level, and in geopolitical origin—the text actively fights prejudice, xenophobia, and racism.

Joaquín and his mother are not portrayed as lazy criminals who want to break the law but instead as good-natured, hardworking people in search of better opportunities. Although they live in precarious conditions, fighting poverty, hunger, and unemployment, they appear dignified, as honest, generous, transparent, courteous people. The text questions the stereotypes that continue today to surround undocumented Hispanic (as well as many other nonwhite) immigrants in the United States and other parts of the world, portraying them as irrational, uncooperative, lazy, dishonest beings (Alexander 2013). In opposition to these stereotypes, *Friends from the Other Side* represents migrants as civil people in search of fair employment opportunities and the right to have a dignified life. The fact that Prietita consistently avoids shaming Joaquín means that instead of disparaging poverty, associating it with a lack of morality, the text shows that immigrants are honorable, dignified people for whom the scarcity of economic resources does not result from deficient morality but instead from a disadvantaged position. These revelations of Prietita's empathy toward what Joaquín feels, her ability to listen to him and his mother and gain Joaquín's trust, and her determination to defend them against injustices all qualify her as a community benefactor, a healer. This is the reason why the healing woman in the end tells her, "You are ready now" (Anzaldúa 1993, 29). Here, there is no dichotomy between home and away, as Joaquín and his mother are metaphorically homeless, in search of a place of belonging: they are under threat in the public space, which is heavily policed, and have no access to adequate living conditions in their precarious house, so Prietita offers them the alternative space of the healers' house, where they find refuge and a cure, symbolizing the protection of the Hispanic community.

The text displays a civil rights pedagogy for children—for Hispanic children of color as well as for white American children—teaching them that instead of shaming and bullying the most oppressed, those who lack the privileges of citizenship, they should empathize with their suffering. Instead of reinforcing divisions and exclusions, they should create alliances, bridging gender, nationality, class, citizenship status, and racial differences, as "friends from the other side." It is these friendships and these alliances that would help immigrants and refugees in the path toward becoming full members of the civic community.

Migration, Borders, and Refuge in Latin American Children's and Young Adult Literature

Since the beginning of the 1980s, children's and young adult literature in Latin America has reactivated the decades-old tradition of social and political critique, presenting a plural social reality and reflecting on ethnic, racial, economic, national, and gender injustices. Texts depict children's misery and suffering, and some emphasize the difficulties of those children who migrate to other countries or regions, with their families or by themselves, in search of better living conditions.

The search for a home also appears in Colombian writer Jairo Buitrago's 2012 illustrated book *Eloísa y los bichos* (Eloísa and the bugs), which narrates the impressions of a girl following her arrival in a big city, where the inhabitants are represented as insects. Central to this text is the subversion, through visual prompts, of the stereotyping and stigmas related to immigrants. Eloísa is overwhelmed by a feeling of strangeness, of not belonging, of being a stranger to school, friends, physical characteristics, city life, education, and culture. However, instead of portraying Eloísa and her father as different, the illustrations portray them as human figures, while all the city dwellers are represented as giant bugs, repulsive and threatening. The text subverts the stigmas surrounding immigrants and shows how natives' habits, physical appearance, clothing, customs, and institutions can also be considered in the light of alterity, difference, and even fear and threat.

With time, Eloísa starts adapting to the new circumstances, and the text recounts her process of familiarization with the new place, with the people, with cultural and educational institutions, as she finds a path toward belonging without losing her identity and memory. School is a central place in Eloísa's life: it is where she feels strangeness, loneliness, awkwardness, as a "strange bug," (Buitrago 2012, 12) during the first part, but it is also the place where she "learns to live" (38) in the new society. School functions as the new home, the place of belonging that Eloísa has found. In the end Eloísa appears as a schoolteacher, having succeeded in her incorporation as a rightful citizen, in which role she helps racially, physically, and culturally different children on the same path. In the last illustration, one of her students is also represented as a "bug," a stranger, a migrant "other," and Eloísa is helping in his or her process of adaptation to the new society. In this text, differently from Anzaldúa's, school, as a public state institution, is considered a possible space of belonging and identity for immigrant children, in which people are respected for who they are and they do not need to relinquish their identities to become a part.

Pedagogic Tools and Practices for Teachers Working with Migrant and Refugee Children: Resilience in Children's Literature

Different projects that concern children's and young adult literature may stimulate immigrant children's feeling of selfhood and self-worth, helping them to recognize difficulties and suggest solutions. I will term this a "resilient" Latin American and Latinx literature, that which consists of texts that, instead of helping readers resist psychological pain, stimulate reparatory psychic impulses (Cyrulnik 2010). The psychological concept of resilience emphasizes, instead of social success or invulnerability to suffering or loss, the ability to work intensely at the metamorphosis of a scar generated by the psychic impact of a painful event, which can lead to healing (Cyrulnik 2010).

A resilient literature for Latin American and Latinx children is one that enables them to transform their suffering into strategies of empowerment. It endows their lives with more meaning, stimulates their imaginations, helps them develop their intellects, clarifies their emotions, and suggests solutions to their problems (Bettelheim 2010). Instead of diverting children's attention from what troubles them most—their anxieties, their chaotic experiences, their feelings of anger and desperation in the face of social, racial, ethnic, and gender injustices; migration and displacement; poverty, unemployment, marginalization, loneliness, isolation, and loss—this literature shows them the value of resistance. Instead of presenting exclusively pleasant wish-fulfilling images, this literature shows them that only by struggling courageously against overwhelming odds can they master obstacles and find self-determination and freedom (Bettelheim 2010). Stories that model struggles against difficulties as intrinsic parts of human existence, in which individuals do not shy away but meet unjust hardships and master obstacles, following their inner confidence, can have an enormous impact in children's and young people's psychic lives (Bettelheim 2010).

It is important to choose texts that, instead of avoiding conflicts and problems, state dilemmas and conflicts that help children come to grips with problems by identifying with the protagonists' sufferings and tribulations (Bettelheim 2010). The category of refugee or even immigrant can be stigmatizing, so it is important to choose a varied range of topics and histories from a varied range of cultures, societies, and historic periods instead of those that deal exclusively with refuge or that focus on one specific cultural heritage, even though these topics are important and will definitely appear.

The Red Comb, or Stimulating Resilience Among Migrant Children

As an example of what I term resilient Latin American and Latinx literature, consider *La peineta colorada* (*The Red Comb*) (1991) by Puerto Rican writer Fernando Picó. Vitita, the protagonist, a girl from Puerto Rico, finds a fugitive enslaved woman in her basement and, instead of betraying her to the slave hunters, asks the village healer, Siña Rosa, for help to hide her. Siña Rosa openly opposes slave hunting, supports the freeing of fugitive slaves, and argues that they should be united in struggling for the rights of Black people. Vitita, who works all day long helping her widowed father, cooking and cleaning, has heard Siña Rosa in her conversations, so she does not get frightened when she sees the young enslaved woman. Instead, she asks for help to save the woman, giving her food and a place to hide. Vitita even gives her a red comb she received as a gift from her godmother. When Vitita's father tries to help the slave hunters, Vitita and Siña Rosa succeed in frightening them and making them run away. Weeks later Siña Rosa declares that her niece, Carmela, has arrived in town, and she presents her to everyone. She is a Black woman, very beautiful, who carries a red comb. Carmela falls in love and forms a family, and they become the town's musicians.

The story highlights Vitita's agency, her resistance and subversion of social, gender, and racial hierarchies, when she collaborates with another woman to help the enslaved woman. Vitita is not passive or obedient; she is aware of social, racial, and gender injustices and seeks other women's help to fight for the cause of enslaved migrants. By giving her comb to the enslaved woman, Vitita acknowledges her human, feminine nature instead of bestializing and dehumanizing her, as a slave hunter would do. She opens the woman's path to citizenship, to rights, and to belonging to the community. This is a story that very powerfully, and with a lot of humor, deals with race, gender, and social and economic inequalities as well as migration and citizenship. Non-immigrant as well as immigrant children can identify with Vitita and her understanding of the human condition of those oppressed, their right to belong and participate on equal grounds in the civil sphere. Vitita feels proud when she sees Carmela with her comb and, many years later, tells the story to her grandchildren. Readers can empathize with Vitita's actions and her resistance of social, racial, and gender injustice, feeling the power of resilience in the face of adversities and the pride of struggling for their beliefs, in their own skins.

Considering *La peineta colorada* in terms of activities, before reading the text, the teacher or facilitator might help students analyze the materiality, visual elements, and presentation of the book—the cover, the title, the illustrations—and ask questions that stimulate student's reflections. For example, students might speak about people they know (such as those within their own family histories) that have migrated or escaped unfair working conditions, as Carmela has, as well as about news, films, and music on slavery or migration throughout history and in different parts of the world (Brazil, Europe, the United States, Africa, the Caribbean). Students might use their previous knowledge on the topic of slavery or migration to formulate hypotheses and predictions about the text, pose questions or advance reflections, and say whether they feel like reading it or not.

During the first reading, which can be silent and individual, the students will become familiarized with the content and may start to test their hypotheses and answer their questions. During a second, collective reading, the teacher or facilitator may ask them to reflect on Vitita's emotions and point of view, as well as to think about how other characters might feel: Rosa, Carmela, the slave hunter, Vitita's father. Students can make a map of keywords with which they approach the most important emotions that appear in the story. They can also formulate new questions regarding points they consider ambiguous, such as the ending, for example. They can try to synthesize the global sense of the text in an abstract and can also look for more information on the topic of human slavery or migrations in the Caribbean.

After reading the book, students can carry out different activities that help them reflect critically on the text, such as writing the story from another character's point of view or looking for more information on the topic in newspapers, music, film, and television. They can also develop different creative activities, such as making a video—either nonfictional or fictional—on the topic, carrying out interviews, writing other stories, organizing playlists, and so on.

Conclusion: The Mission of Children's and Young Adult Literature

This chapter has provided theoretical and practical tools to better understand the way in which children's and young adult literature in Latin America and among Latinxs in the United States has portrayed the experience of children as subjects of mobility. This literature faces the enormous challenge of making children of all racial, ethnic, and national origins aware of the experience of migrants, combating racism, nationalism, and xenophobia. There is a second mission, equal in importance, that these literary texts have, which is to help migrant children process their experiences by acting as tools for psychological resilience and empowerment. These two monumental missions should not be faced solely by the literary text but also by governmental and educational policies, as other chapters in this volume illustrate. However, in this case, publishing houses, teachers, school officials, parents, and families have a specific responsibility in accomplishing this objective. Distributing the books at low prices and including them in the libraries of public and private schools as well as communities, thus making them available not only to well-to-do families but also to families with diverse socioeconomic backgrounds, is crucial for this mission. Real, effective educational democratization is a basic precondition to raising children that are empathic to the suffering of others as well as resilient and creative when they face challenges.

The COVID-19 pandemic has shown how not only migrant and refugee children need to be resilient; children from all social classes, economic backgrounds, and racial and ethnic origins are vulnerable to loss, trauma, death. The world crisis that COVID-19 spurred has only given more relevance to children's and young adult literary texts as tools for survival, resilience, and empowerment, as children have read at home and outside, to find solace, to cry, to express their feelings, to find joy, and to have fun. More than ever, humanity showed that tales can function as tools of resistance and resilience to deal with suffering. More than ever, children and young people in the world understand what it is to suffer from spatial and temporal instability, the lack of adequate spaces, the complexities of home and away. They know what it is to lose or be distant from relatives, to be subjected to measures and policies that they do not control. They understand why home is a complex construction, as its stability has become less and less guaranteed at the same time as journeys away from home have become more and more challenging. This crisis, however, has intensified extreme feelings of fear, threat, anger, and hate and with them racism, xenophobia, violence, and intolerance. As educators, writers, and academics, we need to make sure that books help children deal with their fears and understand that only by struggling together, with and not against others who are different in national, ethnic, and racial origin, will we be able to get along and find our place again as human beings.

Notes

1. This is due to the structural economic and social inequalities that shape the lives of many children in Latin America (Rizzini and Kaufman 2009; Zapiola 2019).
2. For the history of the King Ranch, see Leach (2017).

References

Alexander, Jeffrey. 2011. *Performance and Power*. Cambridge, Mass.: Polity.

Alexander, Jeffrey. 2013. "Struggling over the Mode of Incorporation: Backlash Against Multiculturalism in Europe." *Ethnic and Racial Studies* 36 (4): 531–56. https://doi.org/10.1080/01419870.2012.752515.

Alexander, Jeffrey. 2018. "Frontlash/Backlash: The Crisis of Solidarity and the Threat to Civil Institutions." *Contemporary Sociology* 48 (1): 5–11. https://journals.sagepub.com/doi/pdf/10.1177/0094306118815497.

Anzaldúa, Gloria. 1993. *Friends from the Other Side / Amigos del otro lado*. San Francisco: Children's Book Press.

Anzaldúa, Gloria. 1995. *Prietita and the Ghost Woman / Prietita y la Llorona*. San Francisco: Children's Book Press.

Anzaldúa, Gloria. 2012. *Borderlands/La Frontera: The New Mestiza*. San Francisco: Aunt Lute Books.

Ariès, Philippe. 1962. *Centuries of Childhood*. New York: Vintage Books.

Artieda, Teresa. 2017. *La alteridad indígena en libros de lectura de Argentina (1885–1940)*. Madrid: Consejo Superior de Investigaciones Científicas.

Belmiro, Celia Abicail, and Aracy Alves Martins. 2018. "Ethnic-Racial Relations in Literature for Children and Young People in Brazil." In *The Routledge Companion to International Children's Literature*, edited by John Stephens, 181–91. New York: Routledge.

Bettelheim, Bruno. 2010. *The Uses of Enchantment: The Meaning and Importance of Fairy Tales*. New York: Vintage Books.

Buitrago, Jairo. 2012. *Eloisa y los bichos. Ilustrado por Rafael Yockteng*. Bogotá: Babel Libros.

Cyrulnik, Boris. 2010. *Los patitos feos, la resiliencia: Uma infância infeliz no determina la vida*. Barcelona: Gedisa.

Foucault, Michel. 1978. *The History of Sexuality*. Vol. 1, *An Introduction*. New York: Pantheon.

Gubar, Marah. 2011. "On Not Defining Children's Literature." *PMLA* 126 (1): 209–16. https://doi.org/10.1632/pmla.2011.126.1.209.

Higonnet, Anne. 1998. *Pictures of Innocence: The History and Crisis of Ideal Childhood*. London: Thames and Hudson.

Lajolo, Marisa, and Regina Zilberman. 2017. *Literatura infantil brasileira: Uma nova outra história*. Curitiba, Brazil: Editoria Universitária Champagnat.

Leach, Duane M. 2017. *Caesar Kleberg and the King Ranch*. College Station: Texas A&M University Press.

Mintz, Steven. 2004. *Huck's Raft: A History of American Childhood*. Cambridge, Mass.: Harvard University Press.

Nodelman, Perry. 2008. *The Hidden Adult: Defining Children's Literature*. Baltimore: Johns Hopkins University Press.

Nuñez, Victoria. 2009. "Remembering Pura Belpré's Early Career at the 135th Street New York Public Library: Interracial Cooperation and Puerto Rican Settlement During the Harlem Renaissance." *Centro Journal* 21 (1): 53–77. https://www.redalyc.org/pdf/377/37721248003.pdf

Rizzini, Irene, and Natalie Kaufman. 2009. "Closing the Gap Between Rights and the Realities of Children's Lives." In *The Palgrave Handbook of Childhood Studies*, edited by Jens Qvortrup, William A. Corsaro, and Michael-Sebastian Honig, 422–34. New York: Palgrave Macmillan.

Rosemberg, Fúlvia. 1984. *Literatura infantil e ideologia*. São Paulo: Global.

Rosemberg, Fúlvia. 2001. "Caminhos cruzados: Educação e gênero na produção acadêmica." *Educação e pesquisa* 27 (1): 43–51.

Rosemberg, Fúlvia, Neide Cardoso de Moura, and Paulo Vinícius Baptista Silva. 2009. "Combate ao sexismo em livros didáticos: Construção da agenda e sua crítica." *Cadernos de pesquisa* 39 (137): 489–519. https://www.scielo.br/j/cp/a/XcmMtsQ76cwrJvXL43rR65d/?lang=pt&format=pdf.

Zapiola, María Carolina. 2019. *Excluidos de la niñez: Menores, tutela estatal e instituciones de reforma; Buenos Aires, 1890–1930*. Buenos Aires: Ediciones UNGS.

CHAPTER 5

The Border as a Pedagogical Object in an Integrative and Multidisciplinary Learning Approach

ÉLISABETH VALLET AND NANCIE BOUCHARD

The "antiseparation wall" project originated in a series of conferences on borders, conducted over several years at the request of teachers from École Lanaudière (Lanaudière primary school), with Professor Vallet and her team of researchers from the Center for Geopolitics at the University of Quebec at Montreal,[1] for student groups ranging from first to sixth grade. This series of lectures, which was the preamble to the project that Nancie Bouchard and her colleagues[2] then set up in 2015–16, showed that the evolution of border practices has an impact on the language students use to name the border and their experience of border crossing. Indeed, geographically, the island of Montreal is located in the borderland of the United States (see Deleixhe, Dembinska, and Danero Iglesias 2019). It is therefore these elements that have been mobilized to generate an integrated multidisciplinary teaching approach through an artistic project based on the geopolitical interpretation of a piece of children's literature.

Indeed, in a global world, mobilities and obstacles to mobility have evolved substantially over the last three decades. And despite the acceleration and intensification of trade, globalization and the fragmentation of the world have not become antinomic. Moreover, the reinforced marking of borders has become a corollary to globalization, of which it is now an essential component (Brown 2010). The Canada–United States relationship has therefore not been exempted from this process of securitization, a process that has contributed to redefining borders, now mobile, thick, reticular (Amilhat Szary 2015), and impacting the bodies crossing them as well as the very

Cristina Del Biaggio
@CDB_77   •••

#Walls are transparent and colourful in Montréal! Artwork
done by primary school children #BorderWalls

5:39 PM · Jun 2, 2016 from Montréal, Québec · Twitter Web Client

FIGURE 5.1 Screenshot of a tweet posted by Professor Cristina Del Biaggio during
the conference held in Montreal.

perceptions of mobility and immobility. Thus, over two centuries of shared
border history, the experience of Canada–United States border crossing
has been constantly transformed and has evolved through national political
practices and international events (Heath-Rawlings 2020). While the border
will necessarily be redefined in a post-COVID world, since the combination
of a pandemic and the lack of health coordination at the continental level
defined national borders as health ramparts at the expense of states' international obligations to asylum seekers and refugees, this project is situated
upstream of the pandemic: it therefore does not take into account the sub-
sequent border closure and recharacterization.

However, the evolution of the prepandemic frontier was already a major
element in the lives and bodies of those who live near it or cross it. This im-

pact, which is increasingly and better documented, is also having an effect on the lives of the children who experience it—as evidenced by scientific work (e.g., Griffin, Son, and Shapleigh 2014). The North American literature most logically focuses on migrant children, accompanied or unaccompanied, on immigrant children in a cross-border or extraborder context (see Spyrou and Christou 2014; Chavez and Menjívar 2010).

An Integrative Educational Project

It should be noted that this project took place in a middle-class-to-privileged, predominantly white neighborhood, as shown by the school's location on the disparity map compiled by the Comité de la gestion de la taxe scolaire de l'île de Montréal (Montreal school tax commission) (CGTSIM 2018).[3] However, École Lanaudière is located forty-two minutes (a sixty-eight-kilometer drive) from the closest border crossing, Champlain–Saint-Bernard-de-Lacolle, which is a customs post at the border between Canada and the United States, between the province of Quebec and New York State, as well as the sixth-largest border crossing between the two countries.

In this case the intuitive perception of the border by children who are seemingly privileged—since their mobility is not altered by their migratory status or their citizenship—remains that of a tense, stressful process. The school groups with whom the interactions (with the team of researchers from the University of Quebec at Montreal; see note 1) took place over several years consistently characterized the border somewhat in terms of tension, displaying a certain degree of stress—their own as well as their parents'. They thus empirically attested to the fact that while the border did not represent a major barrier for them, it had an impact on their mobility, and its practice affected their experience of the border—regardless of their status (Pickering and Weber 2006).

On this basis, primary school teacher Nancie Bouchard set up an integrative project for the first and second grades of École Lanaudière to incorporate and mobilize this knowledge and experience within a multidisciplinary learning approach. The method used was to mobilize children's literature and art in an integrative pedagogical approach in order to reach several subjects; doing so, by combining children's literature / art creation / border scholars, helps develop literacy (Myre-Bisaillon, Rodrigue, and Beaudoin 2017) as well as an understanding of history, geography, and global culture

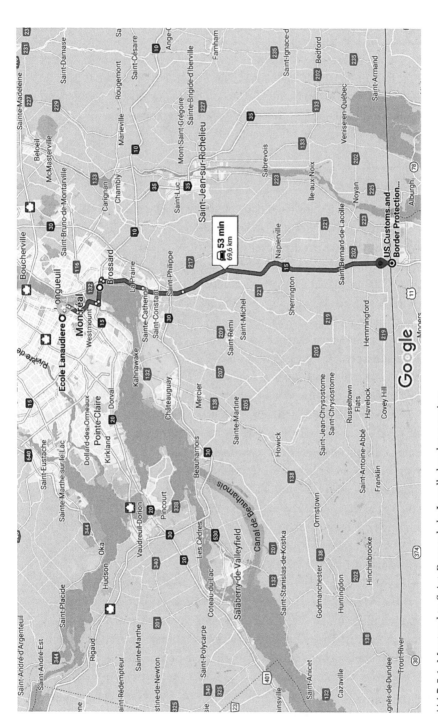

MAP 5.1 Montreal to Saint-Bernard-de-Lacolle border crossing.

(Diakiw 1990; Martens et al. 2016). This educational tool (Schall 2017) thus makes it possible to use additional instruments beyond the classic toolbox available in classrooms to promote literacy learning as well as "global education" (Pike 1991). The goal is to enable students to explore "the moral and social issues of the different regions of the world without feeling threatened" (Duguay 1996; see also Ferrer and Gamble 1990). By linking works of children's literature, general knowledge, and artistic experience, this approach makes it possible to construct learning (Dupin de Saint-André, Montésinos-Gelet, and Bourdeau 2015) within a broader perspective (Martens et al. 2016; Schall 2017).

The Border Wall as a Literature Background

The children's literature book that served as a foundation and a catalyst for the work is *Le mur* (The wall) by Angèle Delaunois and Pierre Houde, published in Quebec by Isatis in 2008, which presents a thinly veiled allegory of the Israeli-Palestinian conflict and the separation wall erected in the West Bank.

Le mur depicts a conflict leading to the erection of a dividing wall between two brothers who, when they finally knock it down, find out that the wall actually remains in their heads, as the following book description shows:

> Ian and Jean grew up in an idyllic meadow, lulled by the murmur of the creek and the songs of the birds. Their friendship comes to an abrupt end when the sheep belonging to Jean, who is now a shepherd, graze on the leaves of the wild cherry trees that Ian lovingly cares for as if they were his own. Jean doesn't take his friend's anger seriously, but he starts digging a ditch in the meadow to prevent the animals from devouring "his" trees. Faced with the inconclusive results of his attempt, Ian even goes so far as to build a wire fence, then a stone wall, which this time definitively separates the meadow into two. The two young men realize, too late, the proportions of their quarrel, and it will take a terrible drought, which kills both the trees and the animals, for them to unite their efforts and demolish the wall that stands between them. But they both know that nothing will ever be quite the same again: traces will remain in their hearts. . . . Watercolors bathed in a warm twilight light accompany this touching story, which echoes not only the wars that are tearing the planet apart but also the daily quarrels that often take on an unsuspected magnitude. (CSP, n.d.)

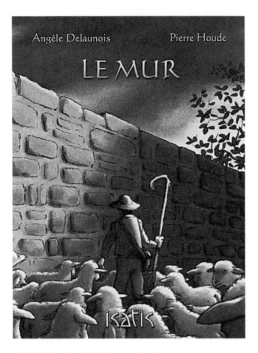

Angèle Delaunois   Pierre Houde

LE MUR

ଲଟ୍ଟ

FIGURE 5.2 The *Le mur* book cover.

Preliminary discussions with the students focused on the very idea of borders and the presentation of the many border walls that scarify the globe (Vallet 2014, 2020) in order to differentiate the elements that divide from those that simply dissociate and from those that unite. The main educational goals were reading, literary appreciation, writing, civic education, the practice of dialogue, reflection on ethical issues, and understanding of global culture. The resulting art project is part of the current of engaged art (see Kester 2005); socially engaged art practice is frequently mobilized in education to "encourage students by promoting creativity, a sense of citizen responsibility, critical thinking, reflection, an interest in social justice, and consideration of people living in the local community, and ultimately contributing significantly to character education" (Hyungsook 2014).

Constructing an "Antiseparation Wall"

The teachers involved in the project led their students to explore the terms that separate and distinguish them from those that bring people together. With the involvement of the multidisciplinary artist Anouk Looten (see Looten, n.d.), students were asked to create an "antiseparation wall" using the antonyms of the terms *wall* and *separation* as a counterpoint to the dividing line, the scarifying wall. Having identified the appropriate terms, the students wrote them down and assembled them into lexical groups. Under the direction of the artist, these collages were mounted in the form of plastic stained glass. Anouk Looten borrowed from the artistic approach of stained glass, referring to the stained glass work of Marc Chagall, which by definition lives by the light that shines through it, positioning it as an antonym of

FIGURE 5.3 Choosing words, writing words, and mosaic work (at École Lanaudière, 2015–16).

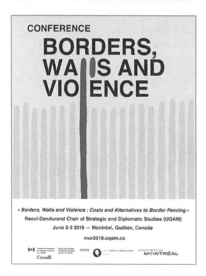

FIGURE 5.4 Building the antiseparation wall and hanging it. Mathieu Brouillard, from École Lanaudière, had to set up a particularly heavy structure for the work's exhibition at the University of Quebec at Montreal's Sherbrooke Pavilion, May 2016.

opacity, wall, and *separation* (Centre Pompidou-Metz 2020). Chagall referred to stained glass as a "transparent partition between my heart and the heart of the world," a "living, ultra-sensitive and intensely vibrating membrane" (Jover 2020). The artwork thus created by the artist Anouk Looten with the students also refers to the mosaic work of Antoni Gaudí, who also creates juxtapositions, exploring spaces, walls, and light, leading to "a true metaphorical meaning" (Raventos-Pons 2002). Thus, after having carried out lexical research around the theme of borders, the students elaborated mosaics with antonyms of the words *separation* and *wall.*

These words embedded with other forms and colors made up the plastic stained glass windows that were then assembled into a wall exhibited on the site of the fourth biennial Borders, Walls and Violence conference (held in Montreal) in May 2016 (see Gauvreau 2016).

The students knew that they would get some feedback from the panelists and were looking forward to it. This approach also aimed at incorporating different practices and a multidisciplinary perspective at the conference organized by Professor Élisabeth Vallet in May 2016.

FIGURE 5.5 The antiseparation wall up close. The stained glass tiles allow for transparency—hence, nonopaque separation—and can carry light as well as antonyms of the lexicon of separation.

FIGURE 5.6 Increasing multidirectional interaction. Professor Coronado signing the *livre d'or* (in French, a guest book is a "golden book").

The students submitted a guest book to collect testimonials from attendees—in this case, a vast majority were border scholars—and were able to read the comments and later map the attendees' various places of origin.

The outcome of the exercise was clearly positive for the primary school teachers involved in the implementation of the project because of the diversity, relevance, and richness of the learning experiences, which went far beyond the curriculum to encompass human and global dimensions. This also led to an evening discussion during the conference with Professors Cristina Del Biaggio, Irasema Coronado, and Élisabeth Vallet on the topic of border violence, particularly against children. And the physical presence of the students' antiseparation wall generated alternative types of discussion and fostered new practices for academic conferences.

Notes

1. Élisabeth Vallet and Zoé Barry, Andréanne Bissonnette, Mathilde Bourgeon, Thalia D'Aragon-Giguère, Josselyn Guillarmou Mylène de Repentigny-Corbeil.
2. Marie Désormeaux, Julie Chevrette, and Annie Dufresne.
3. Please note that the documents and quotations referred to in this chapter and originally published in French have been systematically translated by the authors.

References

Amilhat Szary, Anne-Laure. 2015. *Qu'est-ce qu'une frontière aujourd'hui?* Paris: Presses Universitaires de France.

Brown, Wendy. 2010. *Walled States, Waning Sovereignty*. New York: Zone Books.

Centre Pompidou-Metz. 2020. "Chagall Le Passeur de lumière." Exhibited November 20, 2020, to March 15, 2021, at Centre Pompidou-Metz, Metz, France. https://www.centrepompidou-metz.fr/chagall-le-passeur-de-lumi-re.

CGTSIM (Comité de gestion de la taxe scolaire de l'île de Montréal). 2018. *Carte et Guide d'accompagnement de la carte de défavorisation*. Montréal: Comité de gestion de la taxe scolaire de l'île de Montréal online. https://www.cgtsim.qc.ca/wp-content/uploads/2021/06/Guide_carte_defavorisation_2018_FR.pdf.

Chavez, Lilian, and Cecilia Menjívar. 2010. "Children Without Borders: A Mapping of the Literature on Unaccompanied Migrant Children to the United States." *Migraciones Internacionales* 5 (3): 71–111.

CSP (Centre de services scolaire des Phares). n.d. "TRP 0080 Au menu: Des auteurs québécois." Centre de ressources pédagogiques. Bibliographic record, accessed December 22, 2020. https://ressourcespedagogiques.csphares.qc.ca/trp-0080-au-menu-des-auteurs-quebecois/.

Deleixhe Martin, Magdalena Dembinska, and Julien Danero Iglesias. 2019. "Securitized Borderlands." *Journal of Borderlands Studies* 34 (5): 639–47.

Diakiw, Jerry. 1990. "Children's Literature and Global Education: Understanding the Developing World." *The Reading Teacher* 43 (January): 296–301.

Duguay, Rose Marie. 1996. "Possibilités pédagogiques de la littérature de jeunesse, la littérature de jeunesse et son pouvoir pédagogique." *Éducation et francophonie* 24, nos. 1–2. https://collections.banq.qc.ca/ark:/52327/bs61553.

Dupin de Saint-André, Marie, Isabelle Montésinos-Gelet, and Robert Bourdeau. 2015. "Intégrer la littérature jeunesse en classe à l'aide de réseaux littéraires." *Documentation et bibliothèques* 61, no. 1 (January–March): 22–31.

Ferrer, Catalina, and Joan Gamble. 1990. "Dès le niveau préscolaire, éduquer pour les droits humains, la paix et la solidarité international." *Revue de l'Université de Moncton* 23 (1–2): 3–28.

Gauvreau, Claude. 2016. "Les frontières se durcissent." *Actualités UQAM*, May 31, 2016. https://www.actualites.uqam.ca/2016/frontieres-murs-violence-colloque -chaire-raoul-dandurand.

Griffin, Marsha, Minnette Son, and Eliot Shapleigh. 2014. "Children's Lives on the Border." *Pediatrics* 133 (5): 1118–20.

Heath-Rawlings, Jordan. 2020. "What does the future of the U.S.-Canada border look like?" *The Big Story*, June 16, 2020. Podcast, 32:38. https://thebigstorypodcast.ca /2020/06/16/what-does-the-future-of-the-u-s-canada-border-look-like/.

Hyungsook, Kim. 2014. "Socially Engaged Art Practice and Character Education: Understanding Others Through Visual Art." *International Journal of Education Through Art* 10, no. 1 (March): 55–69.

Jover, Manuel. 2020. "Peinture de lumière: l'Art du vitrail selon Chagall." *Connaissance des arts*, October 28, 2020. https://www.connaissancedesarts.com/arts-expo sitions/peinture-de-lumiere-lart-du-vitrail-selon-chagall-11147781/.

Kester, Grant. 2005. "Conversation Pieces: The Role of Dialogue in Socially-Engaged Art." In *Theory in Contemporary Art Since 1985*, edited by Zoya Kucor and Simon Leung, 153–65. New York: Blackwell.

Looten, Anouk. n.d. "À Propos." Anouk Looten—Accueil. Accessed December 22, 2020. https://www.anouklooten.com/agrave-propos.html.

Martens, Prisca, Ray Martens, Michelle Hassay Doyle, Jenna Loomis, Laura Fuhrman, Elizabeth Soper, Robbie Stout, and Christie Furnari. 2016. "The Importance of Global Literature Experiences for Young Children." In *Teaching Globally: Reading the World Through Literature*, edited by Kathy Short, Deanna Day, and Jean Schroeder, 273–94. Portland, Maine: Stenhouse.

Myre-Bisaillon, Julie, Anne Rodrigue, and Carl Beaudoin. 2017. "Situations d'enseignement-apprentissage multidisciplinaires à partir d'albums de littérature jeunesse: une pratique littératiée contextualisée." *Éducation et francophonie* 45, no. 2: 151–71.

Pickering, Sharon, and Leanne Weber, eds. 2006. *Borders, Mobility and Technologies of Control*. Dordrecht, Netherlands: Springer.

Pike, Kathryn. 1991. "A Fantasy Flying Journey Through Literature." *Language Arts* 68, no. 7 (November): 568–756.

Raventos-Pons, Esther. 2002. "Gaudí's Architecture: A Poetic Form." *Mosaic: An Interdisciplinary Critical Journal* 35, no. 4 (December): 199–212.

Schall, Janine. 2017. "Crossing Borders with Children's Literature." Worlds of Words, University of Arizona, April 3, 2017. https://wowlit.org/blog/2017/04/03/crossing-borders/.

Spyrou, Spyros, and Miranda Christou, eds. 2014. *Children and Borders*. Studies in Childhood and Youth. London: Palgrave Macmillan UK.

Vallet, Élisabeth, ed. 2014. *Borders, Fences and Walls: State of Insecurity*. London: Ashgate.

Vallet, Élisabeth. 2020. "State of Border Walls in a Globalized World." In *Borders and Border Walls: In-security, Symbolism, Vulnerabilities*, edited by Andréanne Bissonnette and Élisabeth Vallet, 7–24. London: Routledge.

CHAPTER 6

"If They Catch Me Today, I'll Come Back Tomorrow"

Young Border Crossers' Experiences and Embodied Knowledge in the Sonora-Arizona Borderlands

VALENTINA GLOCKNER

> As the Tigres del Norte song says: if they catch me today, I'll be back to-
> morrow. And if they catch me again, I will be back the day after tomorrow.
> Wherever you go, do not fear, for you shall die where you must.
>
> —*Written testimony, seventeen-year-old*

Introduction

Every year thousands of Mexican young people are driven out of their rural and urban home communities by pressing inequality, poverty, a lack of jobs, and the failure of education to function as an engine for social mobility (Torres and Carte 2016). For many, fleeing their homes is the result of growing violence and the expansion of the activities of drug-trafficking cartels. This is particularly the case in states such as Sinaloa, Michoacán, Guerrero, Chihuahua, and Sonora, which have witnessed increasing rates of homicides and gun violence, according to official data (INEGI, n.d.; IEP 2020).[1]

Driven by these urgent economic and safety needs, the search for a different future for themselves and their families, and/or the desire to reunite with family members in the United States, many Mexican children try crossing the border before coming of age. A recent report from Amnesty International (AI 2021) has shown that "one in every three migrants and asylum-seekers from Central America and Mexico is a child, and half of them are unaccompanied by family members or other adults." A significant proportion of these cases would be eligible for asylum and international protection; however, this report has shown that most applications for asylum or protection are rejected and children/youths are immediately returned to the countries they have fled from, even though "more than 80 percent of them ... are hoping to reunify with family members who are already residing in the USA, according to the US Department of Homeland Security" (AI 2021).

A 2014 report from the United Nations High Commissioner for Refugees (UNHCR) on unaccompanied (UnAc) migrant children on the Mexico–United States border revealed that 64 percent of the Mexican children interviewed raised potential international protection needs; 32 percent of them spoke of violence in society, 17 percent spoke of violence in the home, and 12 percent spoke of both as reasons for leaving (UNHCR 2014). Data from the National Immigration Forum have shown that an estimated 75 to 80 percent of unaccompanied children of any nationality attempting to cross the border have traveled with smugglers at some point on the route (Zak 2020).

In addition to not having safe alternatives to travel, migrant children must face the threat of "systematic pushbacks and forced returns by US and Mexican authorities" and the routine denial of their right to asylum and international protection (AI 2021). According to Amnesty International's report, from November 2020 to April 2021, the Department of Homeland Security swiftly returned approximately 95 percent of Mexican children, often in a matter of hours, due to a bilateral agreement with Mexico[2] that, as Amnesty International has put it, pushes children into "harm's way." This also meant that "unaccompanied Mexican children were returned to Mexico more than 22 times as often as they were transferred to the Office of Refugee Resettlement (ORR) after being apprehended by the US Border Patrol," and that "those systematic forced returns of Mexican children by US authorities often happened without the legally required screenings of the children for fear of return to Mexico" (AI 2021). This already complex scenario has been further complicated by the summary and express deportations ordered under Title 42 because of the COVID-19 pandemic,[3] which has deepened a situation of helplessness and vulnerability for unaccompanied children.

Therefore, in the face of this context of systematic violation of migrant children's human rights, it is essential to understand the ways in which borders—conceived as regimes of power and classification—affect and disrupt the lives of migrant children. I posit that young people's experiences of border crossing constitute an "embodied knowledge" that helps us understand the way contemporary borderization regimes produce social as well as individual suffering.

The Border as Method

In this chapter I address the clandestine Mexico–United States border crossing of a group of unaccompanied Mexican young people, specifically teenagers between fifteen and eighteen years of age, who attempted to cross into the United States at the Sonora-Arizona borderland. The main purpose of this work is to contribute to what Spyrou and Christou (2014, 2) pose as the understanding of "the role and significance of borders in children's everyday lives while also recognizing the constitutive role of children in the social lives of borders and borderlands." The arguments developed here are situated at the intersection between the anthropology/ethnography of migrant children and the studies on the Mexico–United States border. Through this approach, I argue for the importance of studying children's relationships with borders, borderlands, and borderization processes (Glockner Fagetti 2019, 2021; Glockner and Colares 2020), not only as ways of problematizing the role of borders as physical—and symbolic—realities in children's lives (Spyrou and Christou 2014) but also as a way of interrogating and destabilizing the ways borders produce children and children produce borders.

Referring to the work of Sandro Mezzadra and Brett Neilson (2013) on the border as method, I intend to put the anthropology of child (im)migration into dialogue with the study of the Mexico–United States border. By doing this I seek to contribute to our understanding of not only the ways in which borders mold, affect, "cut across," and "break through" the lives of migrant children but also the ways in which borders are produced by children, both as intimate experiences and ethnographic categories, thus informing the ways in which children also "cut across" and "break through" national borders, immigration policies, and the physical, legal, and symbolic violence stemming from border and borderization regimes. By confronting and challenging borders, children and teenagers contribute not only to the permeability and destabilization of borders but also to their materialization and reification. This can be understood, as we will see, by the ways in which children understand and comply with the border as a physical and a legal demarcation while knowing that, as minors, they have certain advantages in these border encounters. This is something that has not escaped the notice of criminal groups and drug cartels, who have transformed this advantage into a strategy for border crossing and smuggling, as children are unimputable by the legal regime.

By understanding the border as method, Mezzadra and Neilson (2013) and Cordero, Mezzadra, and Varela (2019) have reflected on how borders understood as processes and phenomena play an important "world-shaping function" (Mezzadra and Neilson 2013), claiming it is crucial to historicize the existence and development of borders, to ethnographically situate the evolution of their functions of demarcation and territorialization, as well as their purposes of exclusion, securitization, and production of value. Such historicizing should also pay attention to how the emergence of past and present *luchas migrantes*, that is, collective migrant struggles, rebel against, resist, destabilize, and transform (im)migration policies and structures of violence (Cordero, Mezzadra, and Varela 2019).

Here, I aim for what can be called an "anthropological turn" on Mezzadra and Neilson's proposal, to reflect on the Mexico–United States border and unaccompanied young people's border crossings as what I call "embodied experiences of the border." I state that the border as a regime and the experience of border crossing produce new individual and collective agencies, life trajectories, and meanings deeply felt and ingrained within the bodies, identities, and subjectivities of young crossers. Hence, posing the border as method, and as an "anthropological tool," allows us to interrogate the ways in which the border and border crossing are crucial sites for the production of individual and collective experiences and knowledge.

Such experiences can be extreme, pushing the limits of life and the endurance of the body[4] and even producing close encounters with death while individuals attempt to cross through the desert. Being kidnapped while waiting for the opportunity to cross, deported by U.S. authorities, blocked by Mexican officials, or abducted by the very people that were supposed to provide help in crossing is also part of the challenging dynamics that push young border crossers' minds and bodies to their limits. Such happenings drive teenagers to question how they perceive themselves and their place in the world as well as within their own families, communities, and legal systems. These occurrences leave deep emotional traces and have significant social, family, and community impacts, inciting teenagers to question whether their own country—its authorities and government—recognizes their needs, desires, and claims, as well as the very value it places on their lives.

According to Mezzadra and Neilson, the border as method "is above all a question of politics" (2013, 17). That means looking at the intersections between individual and collective agency and different regimes of knowledge and power, and how they interact and come into conflict, to throw light on the subjectivities that come into being through such conflicts. This allows us to understand the deep and complex interrelations between the border as a physical and material existence, as a legal and political apparatus, and as a subjective experience of what can be understood as an "embodied liminality" (Mezzadra and Neilson 2013).

According to Presley (2020, 95), we can interpret liminality as "the detachment of a subject from their stabilized environment" and a "period of transfer and transition from one site to the next." But following the postcolonial turn, liminality is often referenced "not as a transitionary event, but rather a structural condition; a resonant metaphor for perpetual precarity" (95). Therefore, by "embodied liminality" I would like to refer not only to the experience of transition and detachment that border crossing might produce but also to those intersectional experiences of subjection and oppression (Viveros Vigoya 2016) stemming from lived interactions of gender, race, class, ethnicity, nationality, language, belonging, and legal status—to name a few—that are being transformed, amplified, and/or (re)produced by the border and the borderization regimes and that, more often than not, constitute a structural condition of power inequality not easily escapable by individuals.

Such experiences, their effects, responses, and processes of (re)production, should be analyzed and understood not only in relation to age as an intersectional category as well but in relation to childhood as a historical and sociocultural category, and as the result of specific minorization regimes.[5] The concept of "perpetual precarity" used by Presley (2020) is perhaps one of the most significant experiences of embodied liminality wrought by the border and young border crossers. It captures the structural violence, domination, exclusion, and disposability imposed by the border and border regimes of securitization and punishment on children's and young people's bodies and subjectivities.

Therefore, the main aim of this work is to document, recognize, and value the ways in which young border crossers' bodies are individually and collectively informed by both everyday and extraordinary events (Fassin 2002), but also how the memories and experiences resulting from such events are intimately related to the ways they, as "minorized subjects," recall, narrate, and challenge as well as help reify the border and the borderization regime.

Embodied knowledge, and especially that which derives from children's experiences, hasn't been sufficiently recognized and valued as the basis for social theory (Ignatow 2007). Nevertheless, the narratives of the body and its suffering matter as fundamental sources of individual and collective sociopolitical knowledge, in this case by informing new understandings of how children and young people respond to contemporary border regimes and their (re)production of violence and exclusion.

Methodological Overview

The ethnographic work presented here derives from four phases of fieldwork carried out between April 2019 and February 2020 for the collective multimedia and ethnographic project *Children on the Move in the Americas*.[6] The first three phases were conducted in the city of Nogales, Sonora, with unaccompanied Mexican teenagers who had been apprehended by the U.S. Border Patrol on the Sonora-Arizona border while crossing or attempting to cross. After this, they were repatriated/deported to Mexico and accommodated in state shelters. These provided the settings for the research workshops. At the time of fieldwork, all the teenagers participating in the workshops—a number fluctuating between eight and fifteen—were male; thus, it was not possible to ascertain the perspectives and experiences of girls. Most of the participants came from the southern states of Oaxaca, Chiapas, and Guerrero, while a minority came from the states of Morelos, Sinaloa, Sonora, and Veracruz.

Testimonies were produced through several participatory workshops employing ethnographic self-representation methods and using graphic, oral, and written tools and platforms. The purpose was to collectively explore young people's experiences and *saberes* (knowledge) about border crossing and its complexities, as well as to share, discuss, and disseminate information on the rights of "unaccompanied" migrant children/adolescents on both sides of the border. This goal was conceived given that many repatriated Mexican adolescents have been denied the right to seek refuge in the United States and a significant number of them have been recruited by organized criminal gangs operating at the border, as discussed in the following.

Since the young border crossers had recently been apprehended and deported, many saw workshops as an opportunity to discuss concerns about their future and issues of having to cover the debt they had already incurred with a coyote (guide) or family member that had lent them money to pay for the crossing. Others used workshops as a public and collective platform to process their harsh experiences of crossing the border. Still others used them as safe spaces to express their anger against the immigration system and its policies, especially through mockery and insults directed at Donald Trump, who emerged as the most iconic and representative figure toward whom they directed all their distilled anger and frustration for not having been able to fulfill the dream of reaching "the other side."

This safe space also allowed them to share with each other previous episodes of their lives, including many life-changing events, some of which had directly influenced their decisions to migrate. During such occasions the possibility of a private space for sharing and dialogue among them was always privileged. It is important to mention that, as it follows a mainly ethnographic approach, this work does not attempt to offer a generalizable analysis but rather to reflect on the importance and value of embodied knowledge for young border crossers and therefore for our understanding of child/youth (im)migration processes.

Young Mexican Border Crossers at the Sonora-Arizona Border

> I wanted to cross to fulfill my dreams and raise my family, but it's a pity they had to catch me.
>
> —*Seventeen-year-old (see figure 6.1)*

According to U.S. Border Patrol records, between fiscal years 2013 and 2018, a total of 70,840 apprehensions of Mexican unaccompanied children (UnAc) under the age of eighteen were registered on the southwest border. During this five-year period, Mexican children were the second-largest group of UnAc children to be apprehended, after Guatemalans and followed by Salvadorans and Hondurans. Within this same period, 2014[7] was the year with the highest number registered of UnAc child apprehensions of any nationality and the year in which the humanitarian crisis of unaccompanied children at the US Southern border was declared by then President Barack Obama (Cowan 2014, Swanson et al. 2015). Also in 2014 the number of Mexican UnAc children apprehended reached 15,634—that is, 23 percent of the total number across all nationalities. However, 2013 was the year with the highest

FIGURE 6.1 I wanted to cross to fulfill my dreams and raise my family, but it's a pity they had to catch me.

number of UnAc Mexican children detained by Border Patrol, with 17,240 cases, representing 45 percent of the total number of unaccompanied migrant children apprehended that year (CBP 2018). After a slight decrease in the number of arrests of UnAc Mexican children during 2017 (8,877) and 2018 (10,136), in 2020 UnAc Mexican children represented the largest group of children detained at the border, with 12,364 cases. That is 48 percent of total apprehensions (CBP 2020).

There are several explanations for the fluctuation in the percentage of Mexican UnAc children apprehended by Border Patrol over the past seven years. On one hand aggressive policies have been implemented by both Mexican and U.S. governments during the past couple of years, which could account for the significant decrease in the numbers of UnAc children coming from the so-called Northern Triangle of Central America (Guatemala,

Honduras, and El Salvador) during 2020.[8] These policies include the implementation of the Migrant Protection Protocols in January 2019,[9] the closure of the United States–Mexico border due to the COVID-19 pandemic, and the aggressive detention and deterrence operations implemented by Mexico between 2018 and 2020 in response to the "migrant exodus," or arrival of the massive migrant caravans.

However, there is a phenomenon particular to UnAc Mexican children that must be considered to understand the differences between apprehensions of Mexican children and children from other nationalities, which is central to explaining the increase in numbers of Mexican UnAc children at the border during 2020. According to a 2014 report from the Pew Research Center, a significant proportion of the UnAc Mexican children are apprehended multiple times, while most Central American children are apprehended a single time (Gonzalez-Barrera, Krogstad, and Lopez 2014). As stated by Gonzalez-Barrera, Krogstad, and Lopez (2014), only 24 percent of the UnAc Mexican children reported having been apprehended for the first time in their lives, while the remaining 76 percent reported that they had been apprehended multiple times before, and 15 percent of those children had been apprehended at least six times.

This means that "the total number of child migrants from Mexico is lower compared with the Central American nations" (Gonzalez-Barrera, Krogstad, and Lopez 2014). In other words there is a completely different migratory dynamic for the UnAc Mexican children happening at the border. For the UnAc Mexican children, the proximity of the border and a well-established migratory tradition (Gonzalez-Barrera, Krogstad, and Lopez 2014) means they have abundant and more diversified resources, networks, and personal/ family contacts with which to attempt the clandestine crossing. It also means the possibility that they will have multiple attempts to cross with the same *pollero* or coyote after being deported.

The high incidence of multiple crossings per individual is also an indicator that for many UnAc Mexican children and young people, and especially those between the ages of fifteen and eighteen, clandestine border crossing has become a socioeconomic survival strategy. The complexity of the phenomenon does not end there, as the data on multiple border crossings revealed by Gonzalez-Barrera, Krogstad, and Lopez (2014) is closely related to an extremely serious phenomenon that NGOs, researchers, and journalists have encountered at the border: the forced recruitment of young migrants to act as human smugglers and drug traffickers. A body of research on this topic has been developed during recent years, showing that this issue is present in various locations and cities along the border[10] (DHIA and UTEP 2017; Hernández-Hernández 2017, 2019; Hernández-Hernández and Segura 2018; Moreno Mena and Avendaño Millán 2015; Herrera and Venegas 2019; Pérez García 2019; Peña and García-Mendoza 2019).

In a 2014 UNHCR study of UnAc migrant children in need of international protection on the Mexico–United States border, 38 percent of the Mexican children reported being recruited and/or exploited by the criminal industry of human smuggling. The issue of forced recruitment and exploitation by drug cartels was so common among UnAc Mexican children that UNHCR recognized them as a unique category of children in need of international protection (UNHCR 2014). As discussed later, this dynamic is present on the Sonora-Arizona border, and some of the young border crossers participating in this study depicted themselves and/or other migrant people camouflaged in the customary military-like clothing provided by coyotes and transporting backpacks or packages across the border desert.

In what follows, I replace the category of unaccompanied child with that of the young border crosser. The first is a legal/migratory category created by the state to identify minors who travel without the company of a direct adult relative or who are in the company of an adult relative who has not been able to prove legal tutorship of the child with proper documentation. This category produces the child / young person as someone defined only by her/his minority condition, as well as by the status of being "defenseless" and "in need of protection," defined only by the absence of an adult who can legally represent and "protect" him. Instead, I prefer the term *young border crosser* for two reasons: in the first place, because it establishes a difference between being a child and being a young person or adolescent, a very important differentiation for young migrants who, for several years, have led lives with significant levels of autonomy and independence from the adults who care for them or used to care for them and, second, because this category intends to make visible the agency of young migrants and their capacity to make decisions and build their own strategies to deal with the border, border regimes, and their effects. To do so it is fundamental to transcend binary views of children and childhood/youth, where migrant children are often perceived as either victims or criminals, in order to recognize the multiple ways and dimensions in which migrant children manifest their agency (Thompson et al. 2019).

Brincar el muro (Jumping the Wall)

[This is] the struggle of a young man in search of a dream.

To have everything he ever wanted. May I not lack money, food, or house.

—*Written testimony, seventeen-year-old (see figure 6.2)*

The recruitment of young migrants, especially teenagers, is a critical strategy for the drug cartels, as it allows them to move drugs and groups of people across the border (DHIA and UTEP 2017); cartels know that if detained, underage migrants will usually be released immediately and therefore can return to their activities soon after deportation. Teens in Nogales reported having crossed the border carrying drug loads several times a month, demonstrating an agile and efficient trafficking network. Others reported having been given the task of coordinating transport and delivery of drug shipments across the border and guiding groups of people through the desert or functioning as *coyotitos* (immigrant guides or facilitators), *burreros* (drug carriers), *brincadores* ("wall jumpers" who are in charge of helping people climb the border wall, often by hooking rope ladders to the top of the fence), temporary *halcones* (lookouts strategically placed in different spots at the border zone who use cell phones to communicate and to help others

FIGURE 6.2 [This is] the struggle of a young man in search of a dream. To have everything he ever wanted. May I not lack money, food, or house.

to cross), *agüeros/aguadores* ("water carriers" to provide for migrants and other cartel members), or *bases* (who guard meeting points in the desert for the reception of drug shipments before the pickup).

The knowledge and experience of young migrant border crossers shows the existence of a complex and extremely well-articulated division of labor, revealing a full range of tasks, from the simplest to the most complex. Their testimonies reveal that the least complicated tasks—yet ones that constitute serious violations of the law and risk harsh penalties for adults—are usually assigned to young people.

In addition to the careful division of tasks, I have also recognized what I call a *smuggling grammar*—that is, the naming, classification, and assignment of different tasks and responsibilities so that they lend themselves to a detailed division of labor. I pose this concept in dialogue with the work of Varela Huerta and McLean (2019) and their proposition of a "migratory grammar" that allows us to understand the regimes of governmentality seeking to organize, administer, and control immigrant populations and how these are confronted and resisted.

This typology for the division of labor and the smuggling grammar have been crucial for, as I will discuss, the conceptualization and articulation of a complex, highly malleable, and adaptable system of clandestine border crossing and smuggling formed by the chaining of different people and tasks. Such chaining of tasks is organized in a manner that means it is not endangered in its entirety when the authorities discover or arrest those who fulfill any of its fragmented functions. In this context being underage and being Mexican are certainly perceived as advantages in performing some tasks, such as the transportation of drugs across the border. This is due to two main reasons: First, most of the children/youths are immediately returned across the border due to the bilateral agreement signed between Mexico and the United States, meaning that the links between migrant children and the cartels are not identified by the authorities, nor are their needs for international protection, due to having been victims of forced recruitment, detected. Second, it is much more difficult to prosecute a minor child or youth for this type of crime than it is an adult.

For many migrant teenagers, working as a *burrero* is a valuable alternative when they lack the financial resources to pay for a coyote (human smuggler). This activity not only allows them to have a guide through the whole journey but offers them the safe conduct of the cartels controlling the area as well

as the much-needed supply of food and water during the multiple-day journey through the desert. Some of them receive a payment at the end of the
crossing, after handing over the shipment. This, however, in no way means
that crossing becomes easy or that young border crossers are exempt from
danger. In fact, some did mention that they had been abandoned in the desert after serving as *burreros* to cartels and they had to turn themselves in to
Border Patrol to save their lives.

> I can only tell [my fellow countrymen] to be very careful when attempting
> to cross, because they risk their lives a lot. They suffer from cold, hunger,
> heat, thirst. Freedom! No to racism. No more deaths. (Written testimony,
> sixteen-year-old; see figure 6.3)

During the workshops three main themes became prominent in young
people's narratives. First, the dangers and difficulties they faced while crossing, together with the importance of sharing the strategies, equipment, and
preparation that coyotes and smugglers had provided them with. For many,
the journey through the desert had been an impressive and life-changing
experience and a challenge whose difficulty and ordeals they did not foresee
and for which they found they were not prepared.

> Help end the wall and to make crossing easier for Mexicans. I do not rec-
> ommend that Mexicans cross to the American side, so that they don't have
> to risk their lives. I am a witness. I was on the verge of losing my life for not
> having been prepared and not having paid for a *pollero*. I thank God that I
> am alive. The only thing I want now is to go back to my city and never return
> to the U.S. (Written testimony, fifteen-year-old; see figure 6.4)

Second, they talked about the reasons that had led them to migrate and
how their intention to reach the other side responded to the urge of providing for their family and searching for a "better life." In some instances
it was almost like they had to prove to themselves and others that their
attempt to migrate was a legitimate one and that they were well-meant and
hardworking people. In the background of such narratives and justifica-
tions, the effects of the xenophobic and racist statements made by President
Trump against migrants and Mexicans during the previous months could
be perceived.

FIGURE 6.3 For Donald Trump: Freedom [*gua, gua, gua* (dog barking)]. No to racism. Remove the wall. No more deaths. No more surveillance.

FIGURE 6.4 Free transit. Help end the border wall, so crossing can be easier for Mexicans.

I came to help my family. I have suffered much. I've tried it five times, but I still don't give up. I have been kidnapped once, but I don't give up, I know I'm strong. My story is true. Have courage, life goes on! (Written testimony, seventeen-year-old)

Third, teenagers shared emotions of anger and frustration at not having succeeded in crossing the border. They tended to direct these emotions toward two stereotypical figures: the U.S. president, Donald Trump, and the "Central American migrant." President Trump was the authority they perceived as the most despotic and insensitive, and they confronted his authority with the tools at their disposal: insult and mockery. At the same time, they perceived him as the one with the capacity to almost immediately overturn and change immigration policy. Therefore, some young people also sent messages urging him to open the border and let them through.

The "Central American migrant," on the other hand, was turned into the culprit for the extremely violent and unequal circumstances they encountered at the border—for example, the necessity of passing through remote and dangerous territories and exacerbated border-securitization technologies. Therefore, the trope of the "Central American migrant" was used to blame those they perceived to be "the other," guilty of "taking advantage of the asylum system" and, consequently, responsible for the "hardening" of immigration policies and border reinforcement. The "other migrants" were found responsible for the fact that border crossing had become "too difficult for Mexicans," thus reproducing and strengthening the racial borderization discourses of which they themselves are victims.

During the conversations it became clear that most young border crossers possessed detailed knowledge about the camouflage, communication, and concealment strategies employed by guides and cartels but had virtually no information about their rights when being detained and repatriated. Therefore, these topics were also brought into the conversations to provide important information. During the discussions some young border crossers recounted having to transport backpacks containing "tightly sealed packages" across the border in exchange for the "free" services of the coyote, while others talked about not having been asked and having no other choice.

In one of the workshops, a specific methodology was proposed to the group: to pick up a printed picture of the border wall and intervene in it to express their ideas and thoughts about borders. It was an invitation to tell their story and/or to send a message to their fellow migrants or other people who they thought needed to know about the dangers they had to face while migrating in search of a better life.

Two young border crossers that we will call Antonio and Manuel,[11] who called each other paisanos (fellow countrymen), as they were both from the southern state of Guerrero, and who were repatriated together, shared a drawing showing their crossing experience (see figure 6.5). In this drawing a man appears to be guiding a group of people depicted in a smaller size. He's equipped with a radio and a water bottle and is dressed entirely in camouflage, wearing slippers made from carpet cutouts to avoid leaving footprints in the desert sand. The depiction shows three elements common to all the

FIGURE 6.5 Antonio and Manuel's representation of border crossing.

human figures: the iconic black gallon water jug, the camouflage cap, and the camouflage backpack.

The accounts of the physical exhaustion that Antonio and Manuel had to endure, and the level of mental preparedness and control they had to exert on their emotions during the border crossing and the journey through the desert, were interwoven with the detailed accounts of the surveillance strategies and the technology they had to elude, and this was something other young border crossers shared too. Each technology and security obstacle they had to evade corresponded to a specific emotion and/or physical capacity, along with a skill, trick, or tool developed by the coyotes or smugglers, such as the use of radios, cell phones, rope ladders, water hidden in strategic places in the desert, code signs, timers, camouflage clothing, and hidden meeting points and surveillance spots (see figure 6.6). They talked about the importance of "using your senses" to stay alert to every danger and hindrance and about how some individuals were given tasks to help those coming behind cross successfully (see figure 6.6) once they had passed through the stretch of desert land where cell phone signal has been blocked by Border Patrol devices.

> Migrants who have already managed to cross are helping those who have just entered, so that they can also get through much easier. My experience of the U.S. is not being able to cross. But at least I made the attempt. On the one hand it's fine, I just wanted to get to know the U.S., but now I just want to go back home and never come back to the U.S. (Written testimony, sixteen-year-old; see figure 6.6)

Some teenagers had tried to cross the border up to five or six times, either by their own means or with the assistance of a coyote paid by a relative. Many of them had been returned to their home communities after every deportation, which allowed them to rest, gather new resources, and develop new relationships that, far from interrupting or impeding their journey, opened new possibilities to continue through different routes and with new strategies. During their stay at the Mexican government shelters where they are hosted after being deported, teenagers coming from central and southern states meet peers from border states and cities. During this time they develop ties of trust, friendship, and solidarity, as well as of exchange and negotiation. Being more experienced, younger border crossers living in bor-

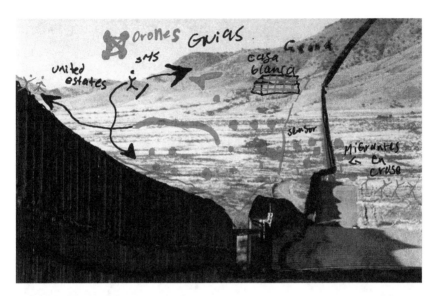

FIGURE 6.6 From left to right: united estates, drones, SMS, guides, white house, run, sensor, migrants crossing.

der cities and those who have attempted to cross multiple times share their contacts, knowledge, and advice with others. Some even offer to act as guides or coyotes once they get out from the shelters. Behind these bonds of solidarity lies a shared experience of the border as the only obstacle that prevents them from pursuing their dreams. Some stories compare the border, and the border wall, with the walls of a prison that encloses them within their own country and restricts their freedom of movement and to fulfill their most important needs and wishes (see figure 6.7). This closely resonates with the proposition of Angela Davis and Gina Dent (2001) that the prison and the border are not only increasingly similar systems but different manifestations of the same continuum of punishment.

What emerges from these encounters and practices of solidarity and identification are actions and strategies of resistance and rebellion against an extremely unequal and violent border regime that robs young border crossers of any possibility of fulfilling their wishes and seeking a different future. They constitute true efforts to confront the unequal relations of power and domination at play on the border, to help others to do the same, and thus to imagine new possibilities for the fight against, and the subversion of, such domination. One could say these constitute what Rita Segato (2018)

FIGURE 6.7 You must smile despite everything. I just want to feel the American dream. There is only one life; attempts, a thousand.

calls "counter-pedagogies of cruelty." By this I mean to signal the actions and strategies of resistance and confrontation that arise from embodied experiences and knowledge of a border that manifests itself, in a disproportionate and preponderant way, through the violence and cruelty that its materiality exerts on young border crossers' bodies, psyches, and subjectivities. Young border crossers' responses to the border regime can be thought of as ways of questioning and challenging the discourses and technologies that build "pedagogies" about desirable and undesirable bodies, and how they should be classified, processed, and filtered through borders. Following Segato's approach, we could say that the border regime constitutes one more element that has led to the emergence of contemporary pedagogies of cruelty and is itself a result of the confluence of the capitalist, patriarchal, and nation-centric order.

Final Remarks

This chapter has shown that young border crossers' experiences and knowledge constitute an important body of expertise and wisdom on the border as a space where new agencies, subjectivities, and processes of resistance are produced. Such experiences and sageness can be understood as embodied knowledge not only because it arises from intense bodily and sensorial experiences but because it allows us to understand the ways in which the border and the border regime are constantly reinstated and reinforced through the experiences of violence and vulnerability imposed on the body and subjectivity. Such experiences are central in the (re)production of technologies and rationalities that seek to discourage, punish, and control human mobility. Faced with this reality, young people respond by producing strategies and "counter-pedagogies" that question and confront the violence of a border regime that perceives them as dangerous, undesirable, and disposable. Even if these responses are merely symbolic and have little chance of transforming the border regime, they constitute practices and a *saberes*/knowledge that can be shared, taught, and transmitted to others, and that is where their greatest relevance and power lies.

These insights also allow us to understand the new strategies developed by cartels and coyotes in response to harsh immigration policies, which have turned the Sonoran Desert into deadly territory and have led migrant children and young border crossers to confront extreme conditions of risk and vulnerability. These must be thought of as emanating directly from the fragility of the body and its capacity to endure and resist the harshness of the journey but also from the deterrence strategies and technologies populating the border. Linked to this are the strategies that cartels have developed to take advantage of the minority status of children by using them as drug and people smugglers, thus transforming them and their bodies into a strategy for "border permeability." This occurs by incorporating teenagers into a well-ingrained division of labor and through the assignment of different tasks and responsibilities constituting what I call a specialized "smuggling grammar" in which, once again, the roles and tasks they must fulfill are linked to their minorization in terms of age, class, and status, to name a few. This minorization regime places children/youths at the bottom of a lucrative network for drug and human trafficking across the border that has not been sufficiently combated or understood.

It is in this context of increasing border securitization, which has imposed extreme violence and exploitation on the bodies of migrant people, that the border as method and as an ethnographic tool broadens our understanding of how children and young border crossers experience the effects of immigration policies. Here I have discussed how some of these experiences speak about fragility, inferiority, and disposability internalized through the body but also about young border crossers' ability to counteract and respond through "counter-pedagogies" that speak of agency, solidarity, and the importance of embodied knowledge. Therefore, it is crucial that we broaden our understanding of all such dynamics, not only because of the importance of recognizing and amplifying the voices and experiences of migrant and displaced children and youths, but because of the importance of creating effective policies and mechanisms to combat crimes such as exploitation, human trafficking, and forced recruitment, which keep growing amid the minorization and invisibilization of children and youths.

Notes

1.   In Mexico homicide is now the leading cause of death for people ages fifteen to forty-four and the fourth most common among children ages five to fourteen (IEP 2020).
2.   In 2008 the United States issued a law to prevent human trafficking and signed a bilateral agreement with the Mexican government to grant differential treatment to Mexican children. As a result children are expediently returned after detention, often without proper screening to identify whether they are potential victims of forced recruitment or human trafficking (Gonzalez-Barrera and Krogstad 2019). This has resulted in 95 percent of unaccompanied Mexican minors being deported immediately after detention. According to 2014 numbers, around 97 percent were adolescents. Among them only 8 percent were girls (Gonzalez-Barrera, Krogstad, and Lopez 2014).

3. "On March 21, 2020, the President, in accordance with Title 42 of the United States Code, Section 265, determined that by reason of existence of COVID-19 in Mexico and Canada, there is a serious danger of the further introduction of COVID-19 into the United States; that prohibition on the introduction of persons or property, in whole or in part, from Mexico and Canada is required in the interest of public health. Under this order, CBP is prohibiting the entry of certain persons who potentially pose a health risk, either by virtue of being subject to previously announced travel restrictions or because they unlawfully entered the country to bypass health screening measures. To help prevent the introduction of COVID-19 into border facilities and into the United States, persons subject to the order will not be held in congregate areas for processing and instead will immediately be expelled to their country of last transit" (CBP 2021).

4. These events are closely related to the evolution of the "prevention through deterrence" policy established by the U.S. government since 1994. "This was a policy designed to discourage undocumented migrants from attempting to cross the U.S./Mexico border near urban ports of entry. Closing off these historically frequented crossing points funneled individuals attempting to cross the border illegally through more remote and depopulated regions where the natural environment would act as a deterrent to movement. It was anticipated that the difficulties people would experience while traversing dozens of miles across what the Border Patrol deemed the 'hostile terrain' of places such as the Sonoran Desert of Arizona would ultimately discourage migrants from attempting the journey. This strategy failed to deter border crossers and instead, more than six million people have attempted to migrate through the Sonoran Desert of Southern Arizona since 2000. At least 3,200 people have died, largely from dehydration and hyperthermia, while attempting this journey through Arizona" (Hostile Terrain 94, n.d.).

5. I understand minorization regimes as "a social process occurring at local, regional, national and supranational levels that constructs minority groups with less political, economic, and social power than some dominant group" (Jaspers, Östman, and Verschueren 2010). In this case, migrant children and young border crossers minorization derives not only from experiences/positionalities of legal status, citizenship, class, gender, nationality but also age.

6. I am grateful to the National Geographic Society for funding this long-standing project, developed collectively by Colectiva Infancias, and which can be consulted at www.infanciasenmovimiento.org. However, the data and analysis contained here remain my sole responsibility. More about the project, including its main goals and findings, can be found in Glockner and Álvarez (2021).

7. This and all following years refer to fiscal year periods.

8. The number of Guatemalan unaccompanied children decreased from 30,329 in fiscal year 2019 to 7,540 in fiscal year 2020. The number of Honduran unaccompanied children went from 20,398 in fiscal year 2019 to 3,875 in fiscal year

2020, while the number of unaccompanied children from El Salvador dropped from 12,021 in fiscal year 2019 to 1,964 in fiscal year 2020 (CBP [2020?]).

9.   According to the U.S. Department of Homeland Security, the Migrant Protection Protocols are "a U.S. Government action whereby certain foreign individuals entering or seeking admission to the U.S. from Mexico—illegally or without proper documentation—may be returned to Mexico and wait outside of the U.S. for the duration of their immigration proceedings, where Mexico will provide them with all appropriate humanitarian protections for the duration of their stay" (USDHS 2019). However, a recently published joint report by Advocacy for Human Rights in the Americas and some of Mexico's most prestigious advocacy NGOs reveals the bleak picture of human rights violations, violence, and abandonment to which Central American migrants have been subjected through the Migrant Protection Protocols (Moncada and FJEDD 2020).

10. In some of these papers, recruited teenagers are called *menores de circuito* (circuit minors), a categorization that has been criticized for its emphasis on the illegal and criminal activities they are forced to perform and its strong revictimization effects.

11. Original names have been changed for privacy and security reasons.

References

AI (Amnesty International). 2021. *Pushed into Harm's Way: Forced Returns of Unaccompanied Migrant Children to Danger by the USA and Mexico.* London: Amnesty International.

CBP (U.S. Customs and Border Protection). 2018. "U.S. Border Patrol Southwest Border Apprehensions by Sector FY 2018." Department of Homeland Security. Last modified October 23, 2018. https://www.cbp.gov/newsroom/stats/usbp-sw-border-apprehensions.

CBP (U.S. Customs and Border Protection). 2020. "U.S. Border Patrol Southwest Border Apprehensions by Sector Fiscal Year 2020." Department of Homeland Security. Accessed January 18, 2021. https://www.cbp.gov/newsroom/stats/sw-border-migration/usbp-sw-border-apprehensions.

CBP (U.S. Customs and Border Protection). 2021. "Nationwide Enforcement Encounters: Title 8 Enforcement Actions and Title 42 Expulsions." Department of Homeland Security. Last modified October 25, 2021. https://www.cbp.gov/newsroom/stats/cbp-enforcement-statistics/title-8-and-title-42-statistics.

Cordero, Blanca, Sandro Mezzadra, and Amarela Varela, eds. 2019. *América Latina en movimiento: Migraciones, límites a la movilidad y sus desbordamientos.* Madrid: Traficantes de Sueños.

Cowan, Richard. 2014. "Waves of Immigrant Minors Present Crisis for Obama, Congress." Reuters, May 28, 2014. https://www.reuters.com/article/us-usa-immigration-children-idUSKBN0E814T20140528.

Davis, Angela, and Gina Dent. 2001. "Prison as a Border: A Conversation on Gender, Globalization, and Punishment." *Signs: Journal of Women in Culture and Society* 26 (4): 1235–41.

DHIA (Derechos Humanos Integrales en Acción) and UTEP (University of Texas El Paso). 2017. *Neither "Criminals" nor "Illegals": Children and Adolescents in the Migrant Smuggling Market on the US-MX Border.* Preliminary report, August 2017. https://cadmus.eui.eu/bitstream/handle/1814/50984/Sanchez_neither _criminals_2017.pdf?sequence=1.

Fassin, Didier. 2002. "Embodied History: Uniqueness and Exemplarity of South African AIDS." *African Journal of AIDS Research* 1 (1): 63–68.

Glockner, Valentina, and Soledad Álvarez. 2021. "Espacios de vida cotidiana y el continuum movilidad/inmovilidad: El protagonismo de niñxs y adolescentes migrantes en el continente americano; Un proyecto etnográfico multimedia." *Anales de antropología* 55 (1): 59–72.

Glockner, Valentina, and Elisa Sardão Colares. 2020. "Euphemisms of Violence: Child Migrants and the Mexican State." North American Council on Latin America, December 4, 2020. https://nacla.org/news/2021/04/23/euphemisms-violence-child -migrants-and-mexican-state-disponible-en-espa%C3%B1ol.

Glockner Fagetti, Valentina. 2019. "Gestionar y castigar a las poblaciones migrantes a través de las niñas, niños y adolescentes." *Revista común*, May 5, 2019. https:// www.revistacomun.com/blog/gestionar-y-castigar-a-las-poblaciones-migrantes -a-traves-de-las-ninas-ninos-y-adolescentes.

Glockner Fagetti, Valentina. 2021. "Régimen de frontera y la política de separación de familias: Racialización y castigo de la migración forzada a través de los cuerpos infantiles." In *#JovenesyMigración: El reto de converger; Agendas de investigación, políticas y participación*, edited by Mónica Valdez González and Juan Carlos Narváez. Mexico City: SIJ-SUDIMER, UNAM.

Gonzalez-Barrera, Ana, and Jens Manuel Krogstad. 2019. "What We Know About Illegal Immigration from Mexico." Pew Research Center, last updated June 28, 2019. https://www.pewresearch.org/fact-tank/2019/06/28/what-we-know-about -illegal-immigration-from-mexico/.

Gonzalez-Barrera, Ana, Jens Manuel Krogstad, and Mark Hugo Lopez. 2014. "Many Mexican Child Migrants Caught Multiple Times at Border." Pew Research Center, August 4, 2014. http://www.pewresearch.org/fact-tank/2014/08/04/many -mexican-child-migrants-caught-multiple-times-at-border/.

Hernández-Hernández, Óscar Misael. 2017. "Menores de circuito en Tamaulipas." El Colegio de la Frontera Norte (COLEF). https://s3-us-west-2.amazonaws.com /portalcolef/wp-content/uploads/2017/12/Menores-de-circuito-en-Tamaulipas.pdf.

Hernández-Hernández, Óscar Misael. 2019. "Menores de circuito y regímenes ilícitos en Tamaulipas, México." *Revista criminalidad* 62 (1): 87–100.

Hernández-Hernández, Óscar Misael, and Tamara Segura. 2018. "Coyotitos: Menores traficantes de migrantes en la frontera Tamaulipas-Texas." In *Cruces y retornos en la región del noreste mexicano en el alba del siglo XXI*, edited by Socorro Arzaluz and Efrén Sandoval, 69–100. Tijuana: COLEF.

Herrera, Tamara Segura, and Mara Rodríguez Venegas. 2019. "Jóvenes mexicanos en el umbral de la violencia." *Contraste regional* 7 (13): 23–42.

Hostile Terrain 94. n.d. "Background." Undocumented Migration Project. Accessed May 12, 2020. https://www.undocumentedmigrationproject.org/background.

IEP (Institute for Economics and Peace). 2020. *Índice de paz México 2020: Identificar y medir los factores que impulsan la paz*. Sidney: IEP.

Ignatow, Gabriel. 2007. "Theories of Embodied Knowledge: New Directions for Cultural and Cognitive Sociology?" *Journal for the Theory of Social Behaviour* 37 (2): 115–35.

INEGI (Instituto Nacional de Estadística, Geografía e Informática). n.d. "Tasa de incidencia delictiva por entidad federativa de ocurrencia por cada cien mil habitantes." Accessed May 12, 2020. https://www.inegi.org.mx/temas/incidencia/.

Jaspers, Jürgen, Jan-Ola Östman, and Jef Verschueren, eds. 2010. *Society and Language Use*. Vol. 7 of *Handbook of Pragmatics Highlights*, edited by Jef Verschueren and Jan-Ola Östman. Amsterdam: John Benjamins, 2009–11.

Mezzadra, Sandro, and Brett Neilson. 2013. *Border as Method, or the Multiplication of Labor*. Durham, N.C.: Duke University Press.

Moncada, Alicia, and FJEDD (Fundación para la Justicia y el Estado Democrático de Derecho). 2020. *En la boca del lobo: Contexto de riesgo y violaciones a los Derechos Humanos de personas sujetas al programa "Quédate en México."* Mexico City: FJEDD, Asylum Access, IMUMI, WOLA. https://imumi.org/attachments/2020/Informe-En-la-boca-del-lobo-Protocolo-Quedate-en-Mexico.pdf.

Moreno Mena, José A., and Rosa María Avendaño Millán. 2015. "Arrinconados por la realidad: Menores de circuito." *Estudios fronterizos* 16 (31): 207–38.

Peña, Jesús, and Enrique García-Mendoza. 2019. "Niños, niñas y adolescentes de circuito: Entre la precariedad y la frontera, México." *Revista latinoamericana de ciencias sociales, niñez y juventud* 17 (2): 1–21.

Pérez García, Juan Martín. 2019. "El Estado Mexicano continúa siendo negligente frente a la investigación y persecución contra la trata de niños, niñas y adolescentes." http://dererchosinfancia.org.mx/index.php?contenido=boletin&id=183&id_opcion=73. REDIM, Red Mexicana por los derechos de la Infancia en México.

Presley, Rachel. 2020. "Embodied Liminality and Gendered State Violence: Artivist Expressions in the MMIW Movement." *Journal of International Women's Studies* 21 (7): 91–109.

Segato, Rita. 2018. *Contra-pedagogías de la crueldad*. Buenos Aires: Prometeo.

Spyrou, Spyros, and Miranda Christou. 2014. *Children and Borders*. New York: Springer.

Swanson, Kate, Rebecca Torres, Amy Thompson, Sarah Blue, and Óscar Misael Hernández. 2015. "A Year after Obama Declared a 'Humanitarian Situation' at the Border, Child Migration Continues." North American Council on Latin America, August 27, 2015. https://nacla.org/news/2015/08/27/year-after-obama-declared-%E2%80%9Chumanitarian-situation%E2%80%9D-border-child-migration-continues.

Thompson, Amy, Rebecca Maria Torres, Kate Swanson, Sarah A. Blue, and Óscar Misael Hernández Hernández. 2019. "Re-conceptualising Agency in Migrant Children from Central America and Mexico." *Journal of Ethnic and Migration Studies* 45 (2): 235–52.

Torres, Rebecca M., and Lindsey Carte. 2016. "Migration and Development? The Gendered Costs of Migration on Mexico's Rural 'Left Behind.'" *Geographical Review* 106 (3): 399–420.

UNHCR (United Nations High Commissioner for Refugees). 2014. *Children on the Run: Unaccompanied Children Leaving Central America and Mexico and the Need for International Protection.* Washington, D.C.: UNHCR Regional Office for the United States and the Caribbean.

USDHS (U.S. Department of Homeland Security). 2019. "Migrant Protection Protocols." Official Website of the Department of Homeland Security. Last published January 24, 2019. https://www.dhs.gov/news/2019/01/24/migrant-protection-protocols.

Varela Huerta, Amarela, and Lisa McLean. 2019. "Caravanas de migrantes en México: Nueva forma de autodefensa y transmigración." *Revista CIDOB d'afers internacionals* 122 (September): 163–85.

Viveros Vigoya, Mara. 2016. "La interseccionalidad: Una aproximación situada a la dominación." *Debate feminista* 52: 1–17.

Zak, Danilo. 2020. "Fact Sheet: Unaccompanied Migrant Children (UACs)." National Immigration Forum, November 2, 2020. https://immigrationforum.org/article/fact-sheet-unaccompanied-migrant-children-uacs/.

PART III

Best Interests of the Child
Crossing Borders

The four articles in the third part of the book follow the unifying theme of the best interests of the child. Patrícia Nabuco Martuscelli addresses the specific needs and concerns around refugee children in Brazil while offering a review of relevant Brazilian legislation and policy on family reunification, as she interviews key informants in government and civil society. Martuscelli concludes that although the concept of "best interests of the child" is embodied in Brazilian law generally, it is not explicitly included in policy, which results in the violation of the rights of migrant and refugee children and youths.

Lina M. Caswell and Emily Ruehs-Navarro take a close-up view of the experiences of unaccompanied migrant children through the perspective of the child advocates who work with them. Caswell and Ruehs-Navarro discuss the role of the child advocate, offering a deep summary of how structural violence is at work in child detention and identifying ethical dilemmas and trauma that both children and their advocates face.

Irasema Coronado portrays the plight of U.S.-citizen children of deportees that reside in northern Mexico, arguing that the principle of the best interests of the child has been overlooked by both Mexico and the United States and concluding with public policy recommendations. Coronado incorporates qualitative interviews with families, including diverse situations and discussing the effects of family separation in legal status and citizenship for children who are at the margins of two nations.

María Inés Pacecca focuses on Bolivian teenagers' migrations in search for work in Argentine sweatshops, vegetable farms, retail stores, and the

domestic sphere. Pacecca offers insights into their independent migration—
that is, outside the parental context—as linked to a discussion of the charac-
terization of childhood among Bolivian migrants in Argentina.

The four chapters offer excellent summaries of legislation and policy on
migrant and refugee children and incorporate interviews and ground-level
views of the experiences of migrant children and those who work with them.
The four offer compelling approaches to the structural violence and trauma
children and their families suffer and include concrete policy recommendations to address the best interests of migrant and refugee children.

CHAPTER 7

Family Reunification and Childhoods

*Is Brazil Guaranteeing the Best Interests
of "Refugee" Children?*

PATRÍCIA NABUCO MARTUSCELLI

Introduction

Family, "as the fundamental group of society and the natural environment for the growth and well-being of all its members and particularly children, should be afforded the necessary protection" (UNTC, n.d.). Many human rights treaties, including the 1948 Universal Declaration of Human Rights, the 1966 International Covenant for Civil and Political Rights, and the 1989 Convention on the Rights of the Child, among others, guarantee rights to family and family life. Children, or people under eighteen years old, have a right to family in the sense that they should not be separated from their family against their will and best interests (UNTC, n.d., Article 9). However, when people are forcibly displaced, families are separated. To deal with this situation, the Convention on the Rights of the Child guarantees children's right to be reunited with their family members in "a positive, humane and expeditious manner" (UNTC, n.d., Article 10, paragraph 1).

Although the Committee on the Rights of the Child recommends that family should be defined in a broad way "provided these [definitions] are consistent with children's rights and best interests" (UNCRC 2006), many countries employ narrow definitions of family to limit to children the right to family reunification. Tapaninen, Halme-Tuomisaari, and Kankaanpää (2019) argue that Finland has enacted a strict family reunification policy to deter families from sending children alone as a migration strategy to obtain regularization for the rest of the family. This policy was implemented under the guise of protecting children, but it is instead meant to preclude future family migration. Most countries in Europe, North America, and Oceania adopt narrow definitions of a family (e.g., couples and minor children) to control family migration (Boehm 2017). This excludes other family configurations that are important for childcare, neglecting to take into account relationships with grandparents, uncles, and cousins as well as same-sex relationships, polygamous families, and extended families whose members are not relatives (King 2009). Different organizations, including the United Nations Committee on the Rights of the Child, recommend child-friendly family reunification procedures with the due assessment and determination of the best interests of the child.

Nevertheless, many countries put migration control before the best interests of the child (Kenny 2011). Reports show that children (especially unaccompanied children) have trouble navigating family reunification systems and bureaucracies (see, e.g., Connolly 2019; IJJO 2014; Haile 2015; Beswick 2015). Children also have a difficult time applying for and receiving visas in their countries of origin, especially in African and Asian countries, when they are alone.

In Latin America, the Inter-American Court of Human Rights recognized different provisions to protect and guarantee the rights of migrant children, including child-friendly procedures and consideration of children's best interests, in its Advisory Opinion 21/2014 on the Rights and Guarantees of Children in the Context of Migration and/or in Need of International Protection (IACHR 2014). In situations involving migrant children, the court held that the definition of family in the context of family reunification procedures should be extended to include even people who do not have blood ties. This perception is clear in paragraph 272 of the opinion:

> **The Court recalls that there is no single model for a family**. Accordingly, the definition of family should not be restricted by the traditional notion of a couple and their children, because other relatives may also be entitled to the right to family life, such as uncles and aunts, cousins, and grandparents, to name but a few of the possible members of the extended family, provided they have close personal ties. In addition, in many families, the person or persons in charge of the legal or habitual maintenance, care, and development of a child are not the biological parents. **Furthermore, in the migratory context, "family ties" may have been established between individuals who are not necessarily family members in a legal sense**, espe-

cially when children have not been accompanied by their parents in these processes. This is why the State has the obligation to determine, in each case, the composition of the child's family unit. (IACHR 2014; emphasis added)

Even countries that guarantee children's right to family reunification and expanded definitions of family may not consider the special needs and best interests of different types of refugee children. Brazil is a compelling case, as the country that received the sixth-most asylum seekers in the world in 2019 (UNHCR 2020). The Brazilian migration law, Law 13,445/2017, explicitly guarantees the right to family reunification to all immigrants in Brazil, including refugees (Câmara dos Deputados 2017b). The family unit is also one of the principles of the Brazilian migration policy. Brazil's asylum law, Law 9,474/1997, is also recognized as a progressive law (Jatobá and Martuscelli 2018) since it has an expanded definition of asylum, covering people that fled a situation of persecution due to their race, nationality, political opinion, religion, or membership in a particular social group or a situation of severe and generalized violation of human rights (Câmara dos Deputados 1997, Article 1). Moreover, it created a tripartite committee called the National Committee for Refugees (CONARE), composed of representatives of the federal government, civil society organizations, and the United Nations High Commissioner for Refugees (a nonvoting member). CONARE is responsible for recognizing people as refugees according to the definition in Law 9,474/1997 and creating and managing public policies for the refugee population in Brazil, including those regarding family reunification (Câmara dos Deputados 1997).

Brazil has, compared to other countries, a progressive family reunification policy with a broad definition of family and facilitated procedures (Martuscelli 2020). Article 2 of Law 9,474/1997 states that "the effects of the refugee condition will be extended to the spouse, the ascendants, and the descendants, as well as to the other members of the family group that depend economically on the refugee, as long as they are in the national territory"[1] (Câmara dos Deputados 1997). However, it is not clear if and how different categories of children affected by asylum situations are considered in the Brazilian family reunification policy. This chapter analyzes how the best interests of different categories of "refugee" children (left-behind children, children of refugees in Brazil, and unaccompanied and separated children in Brazil) are considered in family reunification procedures.

The best interests of the child should be understood as a substantive right, a principle, and a rule of procedure (UNCRC 2013). It is a right: "the right of the child to have his or her best interests assessed and taken as a primary consideration when different interests are being considered in order to reach a decision on the issue at stake, and the guarantee that this right will be implemented" (UNCRC 2013, 4). It is a rule of procedure: "Whenever a decision is to be made that will affect [children], the decision-making process must include an evaluation of the possible impact (positive or negative) of the decision on the child or children concerned. Assessing and determining the best interests of the child require procedural guarantees" (4). And it is a principle "for interpreting and implementing all the rights of the child" (1).

Besides this introduction, this chapter has four sections. The first section briefly explains the methodology of this chapter. The second section describes the family reunification procedure for refugees in Brazil and how different categories of refugee children engage with that. The third section discusses how the family reunification procedure in Brazil guarantees the best interests of different "refugee" children as an interpretative principle, a rule of procedure, and a substantive right. The final section highlights the main points of this analysis.

Methodology

This chapter is based on the summative content analysis of Brazilian laws and application forms involved in the family reunification procedure to assess whether the best interests of each one of the different categories of children involved in asylum situations are rightly considered in the family reunification procedure in Brazil and how (Hsieh and Shannon 2005). Summative content analysis "involves counting and comparisons, usually of keywords or content, followed by the interpretation of the underlying context" (Hsieh and Shannon 2005, 1277). I examined the following Brazilian legislation: Law 9,474/1997; Law 13,445/2017; Decree 9,199/2017; CONARE Normative Resolutions 4/1998, 16/2013, and 27/2018; Joint Resolution 1/2017; and Interministerial *Portaria* 12/2018. I employed the approach of the best interests of the child (substantive right, rule or procedure, and interpretive principle) to guide this summative content analysis.

The summative content analysis allows us to understand the design of the legislation. I use information from expert interviews and phenomenological interviews with refugees that applied for family reunification to complement the analysis and to understand whether the implementation of the Brazilian family reunification policy guarantees the best interests of the child. The names of refugees and experts were withheld for confidentiality. I conducted twenty-two semistructured expert interviews with representatives of CONARE, the Brazilian Ministry of Foreign Affairs (MRE), Defensoria Pública da União (DPU, or the Brazilian Federal Public Defenders), and representatives of civil society organizations that help refugees with their family reunification. "Experts may provide a unique source for 'inside' information about the policy-making process. In political science, experts 'code' information about policy processes and political actors" (Dorussen, Lenz, and Blavoukos 2005, 317). The selection of participants was through purposive sampling, in which the researcher chooses the participants based on their knowledge and involvement with the phenomenon (Tansey 2007). All the interviews were conducted in Portuguese between August and November 2018. The participants gave their oral consent to avoid risks of breaking confidentiality. I recorded, transcribed, and coded the interviews using ATLAS.ti 8. The results of expert interviews are employed in the third section to aid in understanding the implementation of the legislation previously analyzed and the problems faced by refugees applying for family reunification in Brazil.

I also conducted nineteen semistructured phenomenological interviews (Husserl 1962) with refugees from the Democratic Republic of the Congo, Syria, Mali, Cameroon, and Guyana who applied for family reunification in the city of São Paulo. All the interviews were conducted in São Paulo between August and November 2018 in person by the author with no need for interpreters. Most interviews were conducted in Portuguese, though one was conducted in English and two in French. They were recorded and transcribed with the oral consent of the interviewees, following the ethical considerations presented by Jacobsen and Landau (2003) to research forced displaced populations. I also coded the qualitative data using ATLAS.ti 8. I used snowball sampling to recruit participants because refugees living in Brazil are a hard-to-reach population (Tansey 2007). The interviews with refugees are employed in the second section to contribute to our understanding of how the different categories of children are involved in family reunification procedures for refugees. They also appear in the third section to explain the implementation of the examined legislations and the problems faced by refugees in family reunification procedures.

How Do Different Categories of "Refugee" Children in Brazil Engage in the Brazilian Family Reunification Procedure?

The family reunification procedure for refugees was created and changed by normative resolutions from CONARE. The first resolution was Normative Resolution 4, approved on December 1, 1998. However, this document had no clear steps on how to apply for family reunification. On September 20, 2013, CONARE revoked Resolution 4 with the approval of Normative Resolution 16. This normative resolution created a clear procedure in which refugees in Brazil were responsible for starting the process in Brazil, sending the forms and documents proving family ties and economic dependency (when it was necessary) to CONARE. CONARE was responsible for analyzing the documents and sending the request to MRE (Comitê Nacional para os Refugiados 2013). They, in turn, would ask the consulate abroad to grant the family members a visa. Although the system seems smooth, many refugees faced problems bringing their families to Brazil due to delays, lack of information, and loss of documents. On October 30, 2018, CONARE approved Normative Resolution 27, which transferred the entire family reunification procedure abroad. Now refugees in Brazil only send a form (the Form to Manifest the Will, or Formulário de manifestação da vontade) confirming that they authorize the family member's arrival. The family abroad is responsible for applying for the family reunification visa (Comitê Nacional para os Refugiados 2018). This normative resolution gives much power to diplomats abroad. Resolution 27/2018 was approved by CONARE to harmonize the family reunification procedure stated in Law 13,445/2017 and Interministerial *Portaria* number 12/2018 on family reunification visas in general (Ministério da Justiça and Gabinete do Ministro 2018).

Different children may be affected by family reunification procedures.[2] The first group is children left behind. These are foreign children that are relatives (mostly sons and daughters) of refugees that live in Brazil. These children were not able to come with their families (most of the time, parents) due to many reasons, and now their family members are trying to bring them to Brazil through family reunification. When the family separation is extended, these children can feel betrayed and not loved by their caregivers that left them behind (Dench 2006). In cases where the refugees have many children and they do not have the money to pay for documents, visas, and tickets for everybody to come together, refugees have to choose which children are coming first. That was the case of this Congolese refugee that was able to bring his small children and had to apply for family reunification a second time for the oldest daughter: "She says she has to come, you know. She misses us; she wants her mom. Then we tell her the problem is money. I was paying much debt that we had."

Until October 2018 adult refugees in Brazil were responsible for starting family reunification procedures to apply for visas for children left behind. However, now these children are responsible for doing the entire procedure abroad with no support from Brazilian organizations that used to help refugees in Brazil fill out the forms and put the documents together. Studies in the United States and the United Kingdom have shown that children face a harder time applying for family reunification visas, including encountering risks due to the distance of embassies and consulates, lack of understanding of the bureaucratic procedures, and denial of access to embassies and consulates (Haile 2015; Beswick 2015).

The second category is children in Brazil. In this category there are two groups: children with refugee status and Brazilian children with refugee parents. Children that were recognized as refugees in Brazil came accompanied by one or more adults that were legally responsible for them. In these cases the adult was the principal applicant in the asylum procedure (refugee status determination). In this same category are Brazilian children that were born in Brazil and have at least one parent who has been recognized as a refugee. Although these children are Brazilian according to Brazilian citizenship legislation, the fact that they have at least one refugee parent can mean that some family members do not live in Brazil and will need family reunification. In many cultures the entire family (grandparents, aunts, cousins) is responsible for the care and development of the children. Hence, other family members (besides the parents) are essential for taking care of children, including for allowing the parents to engage in the formal labor market. In their study of fourteen immigrant families in Canada, Bragg and Wong (2016) found that ten families wanted to bring a family member to look after their children.

During the interviews Congolese refugees explained that in their country, raising children is the responsibility of the whole family, not just the parents, unlike what they perceived was the prevailing logic in Brazil. Refugee women were applying for family reunification visas for their sisters or mothers to come and take care of children that were already in Brazil: Brazilian children and refugee children. A Congolese refugee woman reflected that her children do not live with her siblings and family members who stayed in the Democratic Republic of the Congo. According to her, living with uncles and cousins, just as she had while growing up, would be important for their development. On the other hand, another refugee reported that after bringing his mother and two brothers through family reunification, his Brazilian child was able to have contact with his grandmother and uncles, and this changed the family dynamics in Brazil. In regard to refugee children in Brazil, adults were responsible for applying for the family reunification procedure in Brazil until 2018. Currently, the family members abroad are responsible for starting the procedures in the Brazilian consulates. These children in Brazil can also be separated from their brothers and sisters, who can be left-behind children, as explained before.

The third group of refugee children consists of separated and unaccompanied children. These children arrive in Brazil mostly by land (as in the case of Venezuelans) and by sea (as in the case of Congolese children).[3] Joint Resolution 1 of CONANDA (the National Council on the Rights of Children and Adolescents),[4] CONARE,[5] CNIg[6] (the National Council of Immigration), and DPU,[7] approved on August 9, 2017,[8] defines *unaccompanied child* as a child that enters the national territory without an adult and *separated child* as a child that enters the national territory accompanied by an adult that is not her or his legal guardian (Ministério da Justiça e Segurança Pública, Secretaria Nacional de Justiça e Cidadania, and Departamento de Migrações Coordenação-Geral de Assuntos de Refugiados Comitê Nacional para os Refugiados 2017). This joint resolution created a procedure to guarantee the best interests and protection of unaccompanied and separated children that arrive in Brazil. Before it, there were no precise forms, procedures, or guidelines on how to grant these children access to asylum and other migration procedures, protection, and rights. One of the joint resolution's essential innovations is to grant DPU the power to represent separated and unaccompanied children in migration and asylum procedures and help them gain access to documents, rights, and protection. DPU is also responsible for conducting the initial protection assessment with children in a child-friendly manner and discussing their options with them (Ministério da Justiça e Segurança Pública, Secretaria Nacional de Justiça e Cidadania, and Departamento de Migrações Coordenação-Geral de Assuntos de Refugiados Comitê Nacional para os Refugiados 2017).

Unaccompanied and separated children have the same right to family reunification as other refugees. Before the joint resolution came into effect, these children were responsible for starting the family reunification procedure in Brazil by themselves. They received help from civil society organizations to do that. After this resolution and until 2018, DPU, as their representative, could start the process for them (Ministério da Justiça e Segurança Pública, Secretaria Nacional de Justiça e Cidadania, and Departamento de Migrações Coordenação-Geral de Assuntos de Refugiados Comitê Nacional para os Refugiados 2017).[9] Since Resolution 27 came into effect, children's family members abroad that are willing to be reunited with them in Brazil are responsible for starting the procedure in a Brazilian consulate. DPU can help the children fill out the Form to Manifest the Will.

There are three categories of "refugee" children that are affected by family reunification in Brazil: children left behind in their countries of origin, children in Brazil (Brazilian children with refugee parents and refugee children in Brazil), and unaccompanied and separated children. The next section discusses how the best interests of each of these categories of children are considered in the Brazilian family reunification procedures (in legislation and in practice).

Does the Family Reunification Policy for Refugees Guarantee the Best Interests of Different "Refugee" Children?

The best interests of children is not a principle in the Brazilian family reunification policy for refugees.[10] No CONARE normative resolution on family reunification considers children or their best interests as a principle. There is no mention of the best interests of the child in Law 9,494/1997 (Câmara dos Deputados 1997); CONARE Normative Resolutions 4/1998, 16/2013 (Comitê Nacional para os Refugiados 2013), and 27/2018 (Comitê Nacional para os Refugiados 2018); or Interministerial *Portaria* 12/2018 on family reunification visas in general (Ministério da Justiça / Gabinete do Ministro 2018a). However, the integral protection and attention of the best interests of the migrant child and refugee is a principle and guideline of the Brazilian migration policy, as stated in Article 3 XVII of the migration law (Law 13,445/2017) (Câmara dos Deputados 2017b). Although the best interests is a principle of Brazilian migration policy in general, it is not explicitly a principle in the family reunification policy, and this is the first barrier to adequately considering the different categories of refugee children that are separated from their family members in Brazil.

Considering the best interests of the child as a rule of procedure, Brazil has prioritization rules in the family reunification application forms. The family reunification form (Annex 1 of Resolution 16/2013 [Comitê Nacional para os Refugiados 2013]) and the Form to Manifest the Will (Annex of Resolution 27/2018 [Comitê Nacional para os Refugiados 2018]) have a blank space where applicants can demand prioritization in the analysis of their family reunification applications. The prioritization categories are children (people under eighteen years old), the elderly (people over sixty years old), people with special needs, and people facing security risks. However, there is no implementation of this prioritization of cases involving different refugee children. Representatives of civil society organizations have said that CONARE, MRE, and consulates abroad do not read the forms accurately and do not grant any prioritization for children (or other groups). When asked about the prioritization possibilities during an expert interview, a representative from CONARE explained, "We do it when there are unaccompanied children in Brazil and prioritization of the first instance (refugee status determination procedure): unaccompanied children who have a court order or unaccompanied elderly. Then we prioritize. Now we do not have an express rule regarding [any prioritization in family reunification procedures]" (representative of CONARE, Brasilia, September 2018).

There is also no prioritization in Brazilian embassies and consulates abroad for cases involving children. That is, children compete for the same scheduling times as people applying for any other visa in the Brazilian consular authorities. Additionally, interviews conducted with representatives of MRE confirmed that diplomats receive no specific training on asylum, humanitarian issues, and children's rights. That is, they treat family reunification visa applicants in cases involving asylum as they would treat any visa applicant, without considering specific protection needs connected with the forced displacement of one or more family members that are already in Brazil. Representatives of civil society organizations have said that diplomats are conducting lengthy interviews with family members (including children) applying for family reunification visas, asking questions about the asylum procedures (which are confidential, according to the asylum law): "They did interviews even with people under eighteen years old without the company of an adult, without defense, without anything" (representative of a civil society organization that helps refugees in family reunification procedures, São Paulo, September 2018).

The family reunification procedure is not child friendly in Brazil or in Brazilian consulates. There is no prioritization in practice for cases involving children, no explicit guidelines, and no training for diplomats or people from CONARE to do the assessment and determination of the best interests of children and their protection needs. The closest thing that Brazil has to considering the best interests of the child as a rule of procedure is Joint Resolution 1 for separated and unaccompanied children. Article 3 states that "the administrative procedures involving unaccompanied and separated children will have absolute priority and agility, considering the best interests of the child in the decision-making"[11] (Ministério da Justiça e Segurança Pública, Secretaria Nacional de Justiça e Cidadania, and Departamento de Migrações Coordenação-Geral de Assuntos de Refugiados Comitê Nacional para os Refugiados 2017). Article 6 states that children should be consulted and informed about the procedures, decisions, and rights in a proper manner considering their development (Ministério da Justiça e Segurança Pública, Secretaria Nacional de Justiça e Cidadania, and Departamento de Migrações Coordenação-Geral de Assuntos de Refugiados Comitê Nacional para os Refugiados 2017). These two articles are pointless because the family reunification procedure in Brazil for unaccompanied children does not consider their best interests. And the procedure abroad in which their families receive the visa to enter Brazil does not consider their best interests either. MRE officials are violating Joint Resolution 1 when they do not consider the best interests of separated and unaccompanied children in their family reunification visa procedures. This is even more complicated now that the diplomats abroad have more power in the family reunification process for refugees since the approval of CONARE Normative Resolution 27/2018 (Comitê Nacional para os Refugiados 2018).

Joint Resolution 1 also guarantees the best interests of unaccompanied and separated children as a rule of procedure in other administrative procedures in Brazil, such as registration and the DPU interview to assess the child's protection needs. The registration procedure of unaccompanied and refugee children in Brazil should be conducted in a safe manner considering age, gender identity, sexual orientation, special needs, and religious and cultural diversities. DPU should conduct interviews to determine the protection needs of unaccompanied and separated children adequate to their age, gender identity, language, and individual needs and considering measures of protection, including family reunification. "Unaccompanied and separated children should be consulted about their possibilities of residence and shelter assuring their protagonist role"[12] (Ministério da Justiça e Segurança Pública, Secretaria Nacional de Justiça e Cidadania, and Departamento de Migrações Coordenação-Geral de Assuntos de Refugiados Comitê Nacional para os Refugiados 2017, Article 13, single paragraph). The Annex of Joint Resolution 1 has the Protection Analysis form. This is used to determine and assess the best interests of unaccompanied and separated children who have just arrived in Brazil (Ministério da Justiça e Segurança Pública, Secretaria Nacional de Justiça e Cidadania, and Departamento de Migrações Coordenação-Geral de Assuntos de Refugiados Comitê Nacional para os Refugiados 2017). These child-friendly procedures could be expanded, allowing the family reunification policy to guarantee the best interests of different categories of refugee children (children left behind, children in Brazil, and unaccompanied and separated children). The assessment and determination of the best interests of the child should be considered in all administrative procedures involving children, including in family reunification.

Finally, the only explicit expression of best interests as a substantive right of children in Brazilian migration law is in Article 157 of Decree 9,199, which regulates Migration Law 13,445/2017. It says that "the residence permit may be granted to a child or adolescent who is a national of another country or a stateless person, unaccompanied or abandoned, who is in a point of migratory control on the Brazilian borders or in the national territory." According to paragraph 1, "the evaluation of the request for a residence permit based on the provision in the caput and the possibility of returning to family life should consider the best interests of the child or adolescent in making the decision"[13] (Câmara dos Deputados 2017a). Once more, the best interests as a substantive right is provided to only some categories of "refugee" children, not all of them.

Family reunification is a right for all documented migrants and refugees in Brazil. That is, Brazil also guarantees the right to family reunification to unaccompanied and separated children. However, refugees and experts interviewed in my research argued that refugees have a hard time accessing family reunification visas for their families, especially since 2018. One problem is that the Brazilian legislation has no explicit definition of what economic dependency means; this lack of definition opens space to the discretionary assessment of bureaucrats and diplomats. The law has no clear deadlines and allows no possibility for appeals when visas are denied or cases dismissed. Refugees and experts said that refugees lack information about their family reunification procedures with CONARE, MRE, and consulates. Since 2017 refugees have not received information regarding the outcome of family reunification visas denied in Brazilian consulates. Moreover, refugees and experts reported that diplomats were conducting long interviews with family members about the asylum process and that diplomats demanded additional documents that could put the lives of refugees' relatives in danger. Therefore, families are being separated for more extended periods.

If visas are not issued, children left behind cannot come to Brazil to be reunited with their families, children in Brazil are separated from family members important to their development and care, and unaccompanied and separated children are away from their main protection structure, their families. Problems in the family reunification procedures that lead to extended family separation and denial of family reunification visas separate families against children's will, hence there is a violation of the best interests as a substantive right to all refugee children (children left behind, children in Brazil, and unaccompanied and separated children).

Conclusion

There are different categories of "refugee" children that can be involved in family reunification in Brazil. This chapter analyzed how three different groups of refugee children (children left behind in the countries of origin whose family is in Brazil; children in Brazil, including children with refugee status and Brazilian children with refugee parents; and unaccompanied and separated children in Brazil) engage with the Brazilian family reunification policy. This is an important contribution because refugee children tend to be analyzed as a single category that makes invisible their particularities. These particularities originate different needs and challenges in the family reunification procedure.

This chapter also contributes to the discussions of family reunification policies for refugees outside Global North countries. Analyzing the Brazilian family reunification policy considering different categories of "refugee" children and through the lens of child's rights demonstrates how Brazil could improve its policy to end family separation and guarantee the rights of all refugee children in the country, as well as children that are not yet in the country whose family is already in Brazil. The Brazilian family reunification policy for refugees does not consider the best interests of different refugee children as a principle, as a substantive right, and as a rule of procedure. Problems in the family reunification process and denial of visas make extended or permanent refugee children's separation from family members that may be responsible for their care and development. The lack of consideration of the best interests of the child in the Brazilian family reunification policy (both normative and in its implementation) consists of a violation of the rights of the child set forth in the Convention on the Rights of the Child, which Brazil has accepted and internalized. There is a violation of children's right to family and family life, their right not to be separated from family against their will, their right to have their best interests considered, and their right to positive, humane, and expeditious family reunification.

In the case of unaccompanied and separated children, Brazil is also violating Joint Resolution 1, which guarantees the best interests of these children, child-friendly procedures, and absolute priority and agility in all administrative procedures involving them. Joint Resolution 1 creates a procedure for the assessment and determination of best interests through the interview with DPU to identify children's protection needs. These interviews considering their best interests should be replicated in the family reunification process. The different categories of "refugee" children, including children that are not in Brazil, must have their best interests considered in family reunification procedures. Although some categories of children, such as separated and unaccompanied children, have received more attention in the Brazilian migration policy, all categories of migrant and refugee children have rights that should be respected and guaranteed by the Brazilian government without any type of discrimination.

In that sense Brazil could learn from other countries that have adopted guidelines, procedures, and systems to assess and guarantee the best interests of refugee children considering the particular needs and situations of different children explained in this chapter. For example, a 2017 study by the European Migration Network showed that most countries in the European Union and Norway guaranteed in their laws and policies that the best interests of the child receive priority consideration from all institutions dealing with family reunification (EMN 2017). It is crucial to consider the best interests of different "refugee" children as a substantive right, a rule of procedure, and a principle of interpretation. Brazil is not doing this.

Notes

1. All quotes from Brazilian legislation in this chapter were translated from Brazilian Portuguese to English by the author. The original in Portuguese is "Art. 2° Os efeitos da condição dos refugiados serão extensivos ao cônjuge, aos ascendentes e descendentes, assim como aos demais membros do grupo familiar que do refugiado dependerem economicamente, desde que se encontrem em território nacional."

2. There is a growing literature on refugee children in Brazil discussing different aspects of protection, integration, and access to rights. See, for example, Martuscelli (2014), Santos (2015), and Viana (2016). There are also important master's theses and dissertations on the topics, such as those of Grajzer (2018), Lazarin (2019), and Cruz (2020).

3. See, for example, UNICEF (2019).

4. See Presidência da República (n.d.).

5. See Ministério da Justiça e Segurança Pública (n.d.-a.).

6. See Ministério da Justiça e Segurança Pública (n.d.-b.).

7. DPU provides support for vulnerable people (including migrants and refugees) to access their rights in federal legislation (cases involving the Brazilian federal government, or União). See Defensoria Pública da União (n.d.).

8. For a comprehensive analysis of this resolution, see Cruz and Friedrich (2018).

9. For a deep discussion of DPU work with refugee children, see de Oliveira Silva (2019).

10. Another interesting reflection on the best interests of unaccompanied refugee children is Conte and Mendonça (2019).

11. Original in Portuguese: "Art. 3° Os processos administrativos envolvendo criança ou adolescente desacompanhado ou separado tramitarão com absoluta prioridade e agilidade, devendo ser considerado o interesse superior da criança ou do adolescente na tomada de decisão."

12. Original in Portuguese: "Parágrafo único A criança e adolescente desacompanhados ou separados deverão ser consultados sobre as possibilidades de residência e acolhimento, assegurado o seu protagonismo."

13. Original in Portuguese: "Art. 157. A autorização de residência poderá ser concedida à criança ou ao adolescente nacional de outro país ou apátrida, desacompanhado ou abandonado, que se encontre em ponto de controle migratório nas fronteiras brasileiras ou no território nacional.

    "§ 1° A avaliação da solicitação de autorização de residência com fundamento no disposto no **caput** e da possibilidade de retorno à convivência familiar deverá considerar o interesse superior da criança ou do adolescente na tomada de decisão."

References

Beswick, Jacob. 2015. *Not So Straightforward: The Need for Qualified Legal Support in Refugee Family Reunion.* London: British Red Cross. https://www.redcross.org .uk/-/media/documents/about-us/research-publications/refugee-support/not-so -straightforward-refugee-family-reunion-report-2015.pdf.

Boehm, Deborah A. 2017. "Separated Families: Barriers to Family Reunification After Deportation." *Journal on Migration and Human Security* 5 (2): 401–16.

Bragg, Bronwyn, and Lloyd L. Wong. 2016. "'Cancelled Dreams': Family Reunification and Shifting Canadian Immigration Policy." *Journal of Immigrant and Refugee Studies* 14 (1): 46–65.

Câmara dos Deputados. 1997. "Lei nº 9.474, de 22 de julho de 1997." Digitized legislation, July 22, 1997. https://www2.camara.leg.br/legin/fed/lei/1997/lei-9474-22 -julho-1997-365390-publicacaooriginal-1-pl.html.

Câmara dos Deputados. 2017a. "Decreto nº 9.199, de 20 de novembro de 2017." Digitized legislation, November 20, 2017. https://www2.camara.leg.br/legin/fed /decret/2017/decreto-9199-20-novembro-2017-785772-norma-pe.html.

Câmara dos Deputados. 2017b. "Lei nº 13.445, de 24 de maio de 2017." Digitized legislation, May 24, 2017. https://www2.camara.leg.br/legin/fed/lei/2017/lei-13445 -24-maio-2017-784925-publicacaooriginal-152812-pl.html.

Comitê Nacional para os Refugiados. 2013. "Resolução Normativa nº 16, de 20 de setembro de 2013." Digitized legislation, September 20, 2013. https://dspace.mj .gov.br/bitstream/1/1662/1/REN_CONARE_2013_16.pdf.

Comitê Nacional para os Refugiados. 2018. "Resolução Normativa nº 27, de 30 de outubro de 2018." Digitized legislation, October 30, 2018. https://www.in.gov.br /materia/-/asset_publisher/Kujrw0TZC2Mb/content/id/48230094/do1-2018-11 -01-resolucao-normatina-n-27-de-30-de-outubro-de-2018-48229911.

Connolly, Helen. 2019. *Without My Family: The Impact of Family Separation on Child Refugees in the UK.* Edited by Judith Dennis, Lina Nicolli, Daniela Reale, and Lucy Wake. London: Amnesty International UK, the Refugee Council, and Save the Children. https://www.amnesty.org.uk/files/FAMILY%20REUNION/Without %20my%20family%20report/Without_my_family_report.pdf.

Conte, Mariana Silva, and Paulo Roberto Soares Mendonça. 2019. "O princípio do melhor interesse e a nova condição jurídica de crianças refugiadas separadas ou desacompanhadas: Uma abordagem sobre Brasil e Itália." *Revista de estudos e pesquisas sobre as Américas* 13 (1): 83–106.

Cruz, Taís Vella. 2020. "Longe de casa: Aspectos do devido processo legal de refúgio no Brasil e o sistema de garantia dos direitos da criança e do adolescente no contexto das solicitantes desacompanhadas ou separadas." Master's thesis, Universidade Federal do Paraná. https://www.acervodigital.ufpr.br/bitstream/handle /1884/67239/R%20-%20D%20-%20TAIS%20VELLA%20CRUZ.pdf.

Cruz, Taís Vella, and Tatyana Scheila Friedrich. 2018. "A criança refugiada desacompanhada ou separada: Uma análise do panorama contemporâneo e dos aspectos da prática brasileira." *Publicatio UEPG: Ciências sociais aplicadas* 26, no. 1: 22–32.

Defensoria Pública da União. n.d. "Migrações, apatridia e refúgio." Accessed December 1, 2021. https://www.dpu.def.br/migracoes-e-refugio.

Dench, Janet. 2006. "Ending the Nightmare: Speeding Up Refugee Family Reunification." *Canadian Issues* (Spring 2006): 53–56. http://search.proquest.com/open view/2871253de5d613829cc1c4f0dc359706/1?pq-origsite=gscholar&cbl=43874.

Dorussen, Han, Hartmut Lenz, and Spyros Blavoukos. 2005. "Assessing the Reliability and Validity of Expert Interviews." *European Union Politics* 6 (3): 315–37.

EMN (European Migration Network). 2017. *EMN Synthesis Report for the EMN Focussed Study 2016 Family Reunification of Third-Country Nationals in the EU Plus Norway: National Practices.* Brussels: Migrapol EMN. https://emn.ie/publi cations/family-reunification-of-third-country-nationals-in-the-eu-plus-norway -emn-synthesis-report/.

Grajzer, Deborah Esther. 2018. "Crianças refugiadas: Um olhar para infância e seus direitos." Master's thesis, Universidade Federal de Santa Catarina. https://repositorio .ufsc.br/bitstream/handle/123456789/188092/PEED1323-D.pdf?sequence=-1.

Haile, Andrew. 2015. "The Scandal of Refugee Family Reunification." *Boston College Law School Review* 56, no. 1. http://lawdigitalcommons.bc.edu/bclr/vol56/iss1/7.

Hsieh, Hsiu-Fang, and Sarah E. Shannon. 2005. "Three Approaches to Qualitative Content Analysis." *Qualitative Health Research* 15 (9): 1277–88.

Husserl, Edmund. 1962. *Ideas: General Introduction to Pure Phenomenology.* Translated by W. R. Boyce Gibson. New York: Collier, Macmillan.

IACHR (Inter-American Court of Human Rights). 2014. Advisory Opinion OC-21/14. August 19, 2014. https://www.corteidh.or.cr/docs/opiniones/seriea_21_eng.pdf.

IJJO (International Juvenile Justice Observatory). 2014. *Children on the Move, Family Tracing and Needs Assessment: Guidelines for Better Cooperation Between Professionals Dealing with Unaccompanied Foreign Children in Europe.* Brussels: European Commission. https://www.fundaciondiagrama.es/sites/default/files/netforu -report-childrenonthemove.pdf.

Jacobsen, Karen, and Loren B. Landau. 2003. "The Dual Imperative in Refugee Research: Some Methodological and Ethical Considerations in Social Science Research on Forced Migration." *Disasters* 27 (3): 185–206.

Jatobá, Daniel, and Patrícia Nabuco Martuscelli. 2018. "Brazil as a Leader in the Latin American Refugees' Regime." *The Journal of International Relations, Peace Studies, and Development* 4, no. 1. https://scholarworks.arcadia.edu/cgi/viewcontent .cgi?article=1041&context=agsjournal.

Kenny, Catherine. 2011. "Positive, Humane and Expeditious—an Analysis of Ireland's Implementation of Its Obligations in Relation to Family Reunification Under the CRC." *Northern Ireland Legal Quarterly* 62 (2): 183–98.

King, Shani M. 2009. "US Immigration Law and the Traditional Nuclear Conception of Family: Toward a Functional Definition of Family That Protects Children's Fundamental Human Rights." *Columbia Human Rights Law Review* 41 (2): 509–68.

Lazarin, Monique Roecker. 2019. "Quando a infância pede refúgio: os processos de cri-
    anças no Comitê Nacional para os Refugiados." Master's thesis, Universidade Federal
    de São Carlos. https://repositorio.ufscar.br/bitstream/handle/ufscar/11627/Disserta
    %c3%a7%c3%a3o-%20Vers%c3%a3o%20final%20-%20Monique%20Roecker%20
    Lazarin%20-%20Quando%20a%20inf%c3%a2ncia%20pede%20ref%c3%bagio.pdf.
Martuscelli, Patrícia Nabuco. 2014. "A proteção brasileira para crianças refugiadas
    e suas consequências." *REMHU: Revista interdisciplinar da mobilidade humana*
    22 (42): 281–85.
Martuscelli, Patrícia Nabuco. 2020. "Family Reunification as a Right or a Strategy
    to Limit Migration?" *IMISCOE PhD Blog*. IMISCOE PhD Network, March 25,
    2020. https://imiscoephdblog.wordpress.com/2020/03/25/family-reunification
    -as-a-right-or-a-strategy-to-limit-migration/.
Ministério da Justiça and Gabinete do Ministro. 2018. *"Portaria Interministerial n°
    12, de 13 de junho de 2018"* Digitized legislation, June 13, 2018. https://www.in.gov
    .br/materia/-/asset_publisher/Kujrw0TZC2Mb/content/id/25601924/do1-2018
    -06-14-portaria-interministerial-n-12-de-13-de-junho-de-2018-25601731.
Ministério da Justiça e Segurança Pública. n.d.-a. "Comitê Nacional para os Refugia-
    dos (Conare)." Accessed December 1, 2021. https://www.gov.br/mj/pt-br/assuntos
    /seus-direitos/refugio/institucional.
Ministério da Justiça e Segurança Pública. n.d.-b. "Conselho Nacional de Imigração."
    Accessed December 1, 2021. https://portaldeimigracao.mj.gov.br/pt/resolucoes
    /1711-conselho-nacional-de-imigracao.
Ministério da Justiça e Segurança Pública, Secretaria Nacional de Justiça e Cidadania,
    and Departamento de Migrações Coordenação-Geral de Assuntos de Refugiados
    Comitê Nacional para os Refugiados. 2017. "Resolução conjunta CONANDA,
    CONARE, CNIg, DPU n. 1, de 09 de agosto de 2017." Digitized legislation, August 9,
    2017. https://www.in.gov.br/materia/-/asset_publisher/Kujrw0TZC2Mb/content
    /id/19245715/do1-2017-08-18-resolucao-conjunta-n-1-de-9-de-agosto-de-2017
    -19245542.
Oliveira Silva, Gabriel. 2019. "Solicitação de refúgio em favor de crianças e adoles-
    centes desacompanhados(as): A atuação da Defensoria Pública da União." *Revista
    da Defensoria Pública da União* 12:110–18.
Presidência da República. n.d. "CONANDA—Conselho Nacional dos Direitos da
    Criança e do Adolescente (CONANDA/MMFDH)." Accessed December 1, 2021.
    https://www.gov.br/participamaisbrasil/conanda.
Santos, Isabelle Dias Carneiro. 2015. "As políticas públicas de proteção e inclusão
    das crianças refugiadas no Brasil." *Revista de direito sociais e políticas públicas* 1
    (1): 88–107.
Tansey, Oisín. 2007. "Process Tracing and Elite Interviewing: A Case for Non-
    probability Sampling." *PS: Political Science and Politics* 40 (4): 765–72.
Tapaninen, Anna-Maria, Miia Halme-Tuomisaari, and Viljami Kankaanpää. 2019.
    "Mobile Lives, Immutable Facts: Family Reunification of Children in Finland."
    Journal of Ethnic and Migration Studies 45 (5): 825–41.

UNCRC (United Nations Committee on the Rights of the Child). 2006. "General Comment No. 7 (2006): Implementing Child Rights in Early Childhood." CRC/C/GC/7/Rev.1. September 20, 2006. https://www.refworld.org/docid/460bc5a62 .html.

UNCRC (United Nations Committee on the Rights of the Child). 2013. "General Comment No. 14 (2013) on the Right of the Child to Have His or Her Best Interests Taken as a Primary Consideration (Art. 3, Para. 1)." CRC/C/GC/14. May 29, 2013. https://www.refworld.org/docid/51a84b5e4.html.

UNHCR (United Nations High Commissioner for Refugees). 2020. *Global Trends: Forced Displacement in 2019*. Geneva: UNHCR. https://www.unhcr.org/5ee200 e37.pdf.

UNICEF (United Nations Children's Fund). 2019. *Nota sobre crianças e adolescentes venezuelanos desacompanhados ou separados de suas famílias*. Press release, December 6, 2019. https://www.unicef.org/brazil/comunicados-de-imprensa/nota -sobre-criancas-e-adolescentes-venezuelanos-desacompanhados-ou-separados.

UNTC (United Nations Treaty Collection). n.d. "Chapter IV: Human Rights." Certified true copy of the Convention on the Rights of the Child, November 20, 1989. Accessed December 1, 2021. https://treaties.un.org/Pages/ViewDetails.aspx?src= TREATY&mtdsg_no=IV-11&chapter=4&clang=_en.

Viana, Rafaela Gomes. 2016. "A proteção das crianças refugiadas no Brasil por meio do controle de convencionalidade." *Revista de direitos e garantias fundamentais* 17 (2): 81–106.

CHAPTER 8

Unaccompanied Undocumented Immigrant Children and the Structural and Legal Violence of the U.S. Immigration System

A View from the Child Advocate

LINA M. CASWELL AND EMILY RUEHS-NAVARRO

As volunteer child advocates, we have a front-row view into the lives of unaccompanied immigrant children who are detained in the United States. We have worked inside, but not with, shelters run by the Office of Refugee Resettlement (ORR), where immigrant children are held. This position provides us a unique perspective on the experiences of detained children. Although ORR is meant to provide care and protection to unaccompanied children, we have witnessed the ways in which children remain vulnerable to the violences of the immigration system.

Over the years we have collectively worked on thirteen cases in the Midwest and the Northeast, the shortest lasting just weeks and the longest spanning over a year. We have worked with both boys and girls, children as young as eight and as old as seventeen, from countries across Latin America. In addition to our personal experience, in our scholarship we have interviewed ninety-one people, including eight unaccompanied children who were detained with ORR, thirteen child advocates, twenty professionals working with ORR, and fifty other professionals who work with unaccompanied children, including attorneys, educators, and social workers. We use both our personal experience and these interviews in this work.[1]

In this chapter we draw on the experiences of child advocates to show that despite their intentions and goals, the work of helping immigrant children is often limited in scope and exposes those involved to the structural and legal violences that pervade all border institutions and particularly the system of child detention. It is through the advocates' experiences with violence that we explore their role as it exists in the ambiguity of children's agency and the tension between the construction of the child through their life story and the protection of the states' sovereignty (Oswell 2013). The role reveals the paradox that arises in the context of child detention between the need to protect children's rights and to enforce sovereignty laws. We first provide a short overview of unaccompanied immigrant children in the United States and the emergence of the role of child advocate. We then frame this with a brief overview of research on structural and legal violence. Drawing upon our data, we follow by showing the ways in which advocates witness, participate in, and experience the violence of the immigration system. We end with a brief discussion of the implications of this work.

Unaccompanied Immigrant Children

Unaccompanied immigrant children are defined as unaccompanied alien children under Title 6 U.S.C. § 279(g)(2) as those who are under the age of eighteen, have no legal immigration status in the United States, and have no parent or legal guardian to care for them in the United States or have no parent or legal guardian (United States Government Publishing Office 2010). Since the inception of the American immigration system at the turn of the twentieth century, the government has documented the arrival of thousands of immigrant children at Ellis Island in New York and Angel Island in California (Menjívar, Abrego, and Schmalzbauer 2016, 126). Over the next century, young people arrived alone, seeking family, pursuing labor and higher wages, and escaping persecution, abuse, war, poverty, and other forms of exploitation. Children's migration, like adult migration, followed geopolitical changes around the world and American foreign policy interventions (Moreno 2005; Werner 2009). However, it was not until the 1980s and '90s, prompted in part by an increase in the number of children migrating from Central America, that significant attention was paid to the processing and treatment of these immigrants (Terrio 2015).

In 1984 the system of apprehension and detention moved from a "catch and release" model, which allowed minors to reunite with family members in the United States promptly after apprehension, to a system of detention and delayed release. The government saw the arrival of Central American and Mexican children as a threat to national security, justifying its policies as a state of exception framed as a "self-authorizing and a moral imperative" (Terrio 2015, 10). The new system of detention was fraught with violations, housing minors with adults, subjecting them to long detention, and denying them prompt family reunification. The policies faced various legal challenges, which culminated in 1997 with the Flores settlement, which set the new standards of apprehension, detention, and release of minors (Kandel 2019).

The migration of children and young people from Central America continued its steady influx at the turn of the twenty-first century, averaging 8,000 to 10,000 apprehensions per year until 2008. The first drastic increase in apprehensions came in fiscal year 2009, when the numbers more than doubled to 20,000 but plateaued for the next two years. Then, in fiscal year 2013, apprehensions peaked at 40,000; by 2014 the number soared over 65,000; and in fiscal year 2019, Customs and Border Protection reported 73,235 apprehensions (Kandel 2019, 25–29; U.S. Customs and Border Protection 2020). The increase in numbers was in part due to a variety of factors, including violence by criminal organizations, deprivation, abuse at home, and the need for family reunification (United Nations Refugee Agency 2013; Arana 2005). The increase in numbers of unaccompanied minors from 2017 to 2018 was exacerbated by the "zero tolerance" policy of the Trump administration. The policy artificially turned approximately 3,000 children seeking asylum with their families into unaccompanied minors, forcibly separating them at the border and placing them under ORR custody. Up until 2020 several hundred parents were seeking reunification with their children (Briggs 2020, 159–66).

Detention and Apprehension of Children and Young People

When children are apprehended by border enforcement, they are processed by U.S. Customs and Border Protection (CBP), where they are kept for up to seventy-two hours in substandard, prisonlike conditions. The infamous images of "kids in cages" come from CBP holding cells, known colloquially as *la perrera* (the dog kennel) and *la hielera* (the icebox) due to the inhumane and freezing conditions. Within seventy-two hours, the government must legally transfer the young person to a government shelter, run by ORR. These shelters are located across the country, in twenty-three states, and they are run by an array of organizations that have received government contracts.

While the standard is for children to be placed in the least restrictive setting possible, the determination of setting is made based on several dimensions, including a child's perceived danger to self, danger to others, risk of flight, and psychological needs. The vast majority of these facilities are on lockdown, with strict rules about who can go in and out. Shelters are often blinded on maps, so the public is often not aware of their existence. And parents and community members are never given information about where their children are located. The explicit purpose of the facility is to detain the children until a suitable arrangement has been made for release and while their deportation proceedings begin. On average the length of stay was sixty-six days in 2019, with an average high of ninety-three days in November 2018, but this varies dramatically, with some children being detained for over a year (U.S. Department of Health and Human Services 2019). Facilities across the country have been the sites of widespread scrutiny for sexual abuse, subpar living conditions, punitive environments, and lack of transparency (Elliott 2016; Grabell, Sanders, and Pensel 2018; Sanchez 2020).

Once a placement is secured, the young person will be transported to their new home, often on the other side of the country from the shelter in which they were detained. Historically, most children received no further services at this point, with the exception of children who raised red flags and thus qualified for limited postrelease services, including building action plans with families and sponsors and making community referrals for services such as legal assistance and mental health support. At this point children are in the midst of deportation proceedings but do not have the right to legal counsel at the expense of the government. The consequences of this policy are devastating for young people's legal outcomes. In fiscal year 2018, 90 percent of children without representation were ordered removed, compared to only 39 percent of children with representation (Kandel 2019). Children who do not qualify for legal relief begin the process of repatriation or return to their country of origin. The process requires the collaboration of consular offices to issue travel documents for children, as well as perform risk assessment interviews, consult Department of Justice travel advisories, and observe other safety considerations prior to the children's return (Baker 2019). Although safety is a key element of repatriation, the U.S. government has not developed clear policies and procedures to define safety beyond removal and does not deal with the aftermath of return and re-integration (Baker 2019). Thus, there is a clear lack of coordination between international and national institutions, as well as a lack of financial support to develop policies and procedures in the Northern Triangle countries and Mexico for the safe reintegration of children (Bak, Celesia, and Tissera 2015). Furthermore, the U.S. government lacks transparency in the repatriation of unaccompanied children and has provided only three reports over the expanse of ten years detailing its repatriation methods (Baker 2019).

The Emergence of the Child Advocate

In response to the particular vulnerabilities of unaccompanied children, the Department of Health and Human Services provided seed funds to develop a model project to provide guardians ad litem for unaccompanied children. The project, formerly known as the Immigrant Child Advocate Project, evolved into what is known today as the Young Center for Immigrant Children's Rights (Young Center 2011). The goal was to provide child advocates who represent what they view as the child's best interests and provide information to the Young Center staff to develop best-interests recommendations. Stakeholders choose whether or not to use those recommendations in the children's cases. The 2004 pilot served children in Chicago. In 2012, coinciding with the increase of young migrants, the project expanded to Harlingen, Texas; New York; Washington, D.C.; Houston; and Los Angeles (Young Center 2021). In 2013 the Violence Against Women Act reauthorized the appointment of child advocates, increased the program's budget, delineated new funding requirements on matching dollars and in-kind donations, and increased government accountability by requesting annual reports to Senate and House committees. The reauthorization marked the first time Congress appointed child advocates or guardians ad litem for vulnerable immigrant children (United States Government Accountability Office 2015, 1–9). It provided a framework for child advocates as well as legal protections by granting them access to all materials relevant to the child's case and protecting them from civil and criminal liabilities (Young Center 2011, 11).

The Young Center recruits, trains, and supervises volunteer child advocates who serve as independent parties to the immigration process. The task of the advocate is to build a relationship of mutual trust and respect with the immigrant child, becoming the one constant and reliable adult throughout the contentious and complex immigration process, which many children face alone. At the core of the relationship between the child advocate and the child is the advocate's main task: to uncover and contextualize the child's migration story and to consider the child's present circumstances so as to provide recommendations on the best interests of the child. Advocates are also tasked with supporting the child during the child's release to a sponsor within the United States, with ensuring the safety of children's voluntary return to their home country, and with advocating for children aging out of the system (Young Center 2011, 10).

In 2016 the Government Accountability Office released its first study of the child advocate program by ORR. The study focused on the program's efficacy after it received increased government funding to expand its services by opening new locations across the United States. The report concluded that to evaluate the efficacy of the program, it was necessary to address considerable bureaucratic challenges between the contracting agency carrying out the program and ORR. Some of the impediments described by the report include the inability for all vulnerable children to have an advocate, the need to streamline the referral process, and the need to cut unnecessary bureaucratic processes to access children's complete records by the contracting agency, including home studies and incident reports, and to increase ORR accountability in data collection and program oversight (United States Government Accountability Office 2015).

While these concerns are valid, we draw upon our qualitative research and personal experiences to argue that there are more fundamental problems with the system of immigration for unaccompanied children and the use of advocates to respond to these needs. In particular, we argue that structural violences pervade the system of immigration, such that advocates witness, perpetuate, and experience the violence of immigration.

Structural Violence and Children Migrants

In this chapter we use the work of interdisciplinary scholars who have broadened conceptualizations of violence to include not just willful, interpersonal, and culturally deviant harm but harm that is sanctioned by governments and carried out through social structures and that causes both direct and indirect suffering (Jackman 2002). The first conceptualization of violence by structural forces came from peace researcher Johan Galtung (1969, 168), who argued that "violence is present when human beings are being influenced so that their actual somatic and mental realizations are below their potential realizations." This broadened definition encompassed the ways in which social structures could enact violence by preventing the realized potential in a given situation. Galtung explained that if someone dies of a disease for which there is no cure, this is not violence, since the death was unavoidable; yet when someone dies of a disease for which a cure is available—but not available to that person—this is a violent death, as the potential and actual outcomes were determined by structural forces.

Violent structures do not perpetrate violence in equal ways for all people. As medical anthropologist Paul Farmer (2009) notes, the embodiment of structural violence into the personal experience is mediated by factors including class, gender, and race. Indeed, social forces mediate risk. In the case of unaccompanied child migrants, their identities as young people (along with the myriad other identities of race, nationality, migration status, etc.) create significant vulnerabilities within violent structures. Further, violence is not always a latent function of a structure. Structural violence can be utilized by powerful actors to create change or maintain the status quo. On the United States–Mexico border, both direct violence and structural violence are used as enforcement tactics (Slack et al. 2016). Trauma and death are increasingly legitimized as strategies to deter migrants.

More recently, sociologists Cecilia Menjívar and Leisy J. Abrego continued this theorization on violence with their concept of legal violence. Legal violence is meant to encompass the "instances in which laws and their implementation rise to practices that harm individuals physically, economically, psychologically, or emotionally" (Abrego and Menjívar 2011, 11). The authors suggest that this violence should also include less visible injuries, including psychological stresses such as fear, humiliation, and imprisonment (Jackman 2002; Menjívar and Abrego 2012). In immigration law specifically, legal violence is enacted as the laws that purport to emphasize the public good in fact target marginalized groups of people.

These conceptualizations of violence are useful for analyzing the observations that advocates share about their experiences working with unaccompanied children in the immigration system. Advocates frequently communicated to us a sense of unease as they described their work with children, but they often had a difficult time locating the exact source of their concern.

However, the patterns in their responses, which were reflected in our own experiences, pointed to underlying harms that were present in the structure and laws guiding the United States' response to unaccompanied immigrant children. Indeed, as advocates work to help children, they find that they witness, perpetuate, and experience the very same violence they wish to eliminate.

Advocates Speak

When speaking candidly about their experience working with detained children, advocates communicate profound concerns about the system of detention and care and their ability to provide meaningful help. Most of the advocates we interviewed communicated a feeling of alienation from their work and concerns about their inability to create change in the lives of children. We argue that these feelings stem from the expansive and ubiquitous violence underlying the system of detention. Advocates observe this violence in a way that very few others see, and they provide important testimony in understanding the indignities that unaccompanied children experience. First, they witness the ways in which violence is prolonged, rather than stopped, in detention. Second, advocates find that they are also complicit in perpetuating this violence, and at times their feelings of alienation stem from their own involvement in harmful structures. Finally, we develop the idea of structural shrapnel to show how the work advocates do is also shaped by violence, such that advocates experience their own pain when shards of the violent structure impact their relationships with children.

Witness

Because of their unique position in the immigration system, child advocates provide a view of violence not as it exists in an individual moment but as it exists on a trajectory—what geographers Kate Swanson and Rebecca Maria Torres (2016) call "spatially expansive" violence. Swanson and Torres explain that unaccompanied children face violence in their homes and communities, during their journey to the United States, while crossing the border, and while in the hands of CBP agents. Using the experiences of advocates, we extend Swanson and Torres's framework to add more depth to the understanding of violence as a trajectory that continues through the ORR shelters.

Advocates demonstrate that these experiences of violence exist as the continuation of migratory violences and not as isolated incidents. Advocate Sofia told a story about Diego, a teenager who had been detained and sent to an ORR shelter.[2] Early on in his time at the shelter, Diego was interviewed by a social worker, to whom he communicated that he had been beaten by an older brother. Because of this experience, there were questions about the safety of his release to his family, and so his release was delayed for months. Although Diego saw these experiences as abuse, he deeply regretted having mentioned them to the social worker. He felt like he had been tricked into talking about this painful history, and he was devastated that it had significantly delayed his release. Diego's mental health deteriorated, and when Sofia asked him whether he wanted to stay in the United States with his mom or return to his home country, he indicated that he preferred to return rather than continue his indefinite detention. Sofia reports that Diego exclaimed: "I am sick of being told to be patient." A week later, he had a violent outburst in response to a change in the shelter: he threw chairs and screamed. "Nobody yelled at me when I calmed down," he later reported to Sofia. "But they did warn me that I was destroying government property and that my behavior would slow my case." When Sofia talked over the incident with the supervising attorney on his case, the attorney commented, "It's like they ignore that he is angry because he is in detention."

Sofia and Diego's story points to the trajectory of violence and its perpetuation through immigrant detention. In this story violence in Diego's life started in the home, long before his decision to migrate. In fact, this experience with sibling violence was merely one form of violence in a community where shootings, confrontations between gangs and police, and structural barriers to adequate food, health care, and security were rampant. It was the particular experience of sibling violence that followed Diego into U.S. custody, when his reports of this violence triggered the system to flag his case, thus lengthening his stay in detention. Rather than providing relief for this trauma, his reporting to social workers created further psychological distress, both prolonging his indefinite stay and also contributing to feelings of guilt regarding the betrayal of his family. Finally, this psychological distress culminated in Diego's own violent outburst, during which, for a moment, he felt he could control his environment through his anger—what Slack and Whiteford (2011) call poststructural violence, in which individuals respond to violent structures in attempts to mitigate their effects. Sofia witnessed the trajectory of violence but could do little to stop it. She explained that Diego would beg her for information about his release, but in her role she had no additional insight into the bureaucratic process that often trapped young people in ORR facilities.

In another similar case, advocate Martha witnessed the deteriorating mental health of a young man named Abdi.[3] Abdi was a seventeen-year-old from Somalia who had no family in the United States. In order to be released, he needed to be placed in foster care, a task that was nearly impossible due to his age. As a seventeen-year-old, Abdi was a man in Somalia, yet in the United States, he was still a minor, which meant that other adults made important decisions for him. Since Abdi felt capable of making his own decisions, he believed that the shelter deprived him of his freedom and operated as a form of punishment. He expressed significant stress and depressive symptoms due to this detention. Martha worked to advocate for the young man, and eventually the shelter acknowledged that he might be experiencing signs of posttraumatic stress. Yet instead of contextualizing and responding to the immediate concerns, shelter staff sent Abdi to the doctor, where he was prescribed pills. Martha explained that this only caused further distress: "He did not understand. In Somalia you don't take pills if you are worrying. He would tell me, 'In Somalia everybody worries; this is normal.'" Once more the violence that was already present in the young man's life was prolonged through his detention. Martha had a front-row seat to observe ways shelters respond to children's psychological stress. Divorced from his particular cultural context and wrapped in the psychological stress of detainment, Abdi's experience of violence grew, and the safety claimed by ORR's shelter system shrank.

The trajectory of violence witnessed by advocates and experienced by adolescents under detention is both insidious and overt. Violence is often shrouded in misguided institutional policies of safety that deny self-determination to immigrant children and their families. As advocates witness the many forms of violence in the context of detention, they rarely feel as though their work has made a dent in the children's suffering.

Participate

Advocates expressed concern about their inability to disrupt the trajectory of violence, but they communicated even greater distress as they reflected on the ways in which they saw themselves as complicit in this same violence. As advocates carry out their work with the best intentions of providing support, voice, and care to children, they find that they must work so closely within the legal and detention systems that they become actors in these very structures. In particular, advocates expressed concern about their own participation in the system of detention and the use of children's suffering as a pathway to legal and social resources.

Advocates often expressed deep concern about the system of detention, and many wondered whether their very presence made them complicit in practices that they disagreed with. Advocate Salma told a story about a young woman who was so desperate to leave the shelter that she began conceiving a plan for escape.[4] Salma says:

> She is really having a hard time. She has been in the center for, I don't know, eight months now, and she is at the breaking point. She was talking about how she wanted to escape from the building. . . . This is something that kind of breaks the confidentiality agreement that I have to do. And that sucked! It was hard. I stumbled through it. . . . I asked her if anybody knows what she wanted to do, and she said, "No, because if they did, they would be watching me every five minutes, checking in on me." So, great. Now I know what is going to happen to you if I tell.

Another advocate shared a similar story of a young man who wanted to run away from the shelter and actually succeeded in doing so. In this case the young man was waiting to be released to his mother, who was having difficulty in complying with the strenuous requirements for parents attempting to be reunited with their children (Heidbrink 2017). Advocate Patricia felt deeply conflicted about the situation because she wondered whether running away might actually be in the best interests of the young man:

> Sometimes what we decide is their best interest is not aligned with what they want but is aligned with policy. And sometimes it is like a weird gray area. Like, the boy who ran away [from the detention facility]. Like for him . . . he did the right thing. It is not like I was going to say, "You should probably get out of here. . . ." [Not] like I propped the door open. (And I can't [prop the door open]. They have to key me out anyway.) But yeah. He did the right thing for himself. Maybe if he had stayed, I would have probably said,

"We should step in and try to make the requirements for his mother less strenuous."[5]

In both of these cases—those of the girl who suggested she wanted to run away and of the boy who actually did run away—the advocates wrestled with their own role. Salma knew that reporting ideations of escape would result in penalties that would further hurt the child, and Patricia felt that the act of running was actually better for the mental health of the child than staying in the limbo in which he found himself. Yet both felt stymied by their own professional obligations, and these very obligations contributed to their complicity in the young people's detainment. Patricia knew that she could not hold the door open for the young man, but did her inability and unwillingness to open the door and let the child return to his mother make her complicit in the violence of detention and family separation? Indeed, advocates uphold the system of detention when their presence normalizes the idea that detention is a necessary step in protecting the safety of children.

Advocates communicated the most concern about their complicity in the violence of detention in one particular element of their work: exploring the history of the child. A story told by Sofia demonstrates this tension.[6] Sofia had been matched with Yesenia, a teenager from Central America, whose detention spanned an entire year. ORR had requested a child advocate for her, as she was refusing release to her legal guardian, and she would not explain to anyone the reason. As her child advocate, Sofia's goal was to better understand her situation and provide guidance for her release. After some time Yesenia agreed to tell Sofia about her concerns for her placement, and in a long letter, Yesenia detailed abuse that she had suffered in her home. Sofia took the letter and handed it over to the supervising attorney on her case. A meeting was quickly scheduled to discuss the content of the letter and to review recommendations. Yesenia asked whether she could be at the meeting, and all the stakeholders agreed that she should be able to assert her opinion. During the meeting multiple stakeholders convened, several by phone, and the letter was disclosed. Sofia reflected on the moment, explaining that Yesenia's body language revealed immediately that she had not understood that this letter would be shared with others. When she was addressed and her opinion on the matter was requested, she refused to speak. Sofia felt heartbroken for having inadvertently broken the trust that she had built with

Yesenia. She was not surprised, during her visit to her in the following week, when Yesenia didn't want to see her.

In this particular story, Sofia was devastated by the ways in which her work in carrying out a policy caused further distress for Yesenia. This also reflects a reality of the legal violence and release from detention: children must tell stories about their lives that can be interpreted by social workers, attorneys, and others in order to leave detention and gain legal relief. However, these stories are deeply personal, and children are often hesitant to share them with strangers, who use the stories only for their productive purpose in the immigration system.

A child's story of migration is crucial to release and to obtaining legal relief, but the story in itself holds little value unless it meets stringent legal requirements that define its "worth" under American immigration law. The story must adjust to restrictive forms of legal relief in categories that narrowly recognize children as victims of crimes who suffered from substantial physical and psychological abuse (U visa), human trafficking (T visa), parental abuse and neglect (Special Juvenile Immigrant Status), and severe forms of persecution that could grant them asylum (Terrio 2015; Ruehs-Navarro 2022). The lived experiences of children who do not fall under those categories hold no legal value even when children have been deprived of basic needs and require protection (e.g., in cases of extreme poverty, illness, disabilities, and child labor).

Many other advocates expressed feeling deeply uncomfortable with the job of excavating appropriate stories for productive use. For some the issue was the ways in which the immigration system used these stories of violence to define the child. Advocate Lucia explained: "I think there is so much emphasis put on their stories that I worry that it is like . . . [long pause]. I feel like a lot of them have challenging histories, you know, that have happened to them, so just wanting to make sure that [there is] a recognition that this has happened but also not just making them their story. There is a lot more to them than the things that happened. So I feel like I struggle with that."[7]

For others the issue was the sharing of profoundly painful information among stakeholders, even though advocates seek explicit assent from the minors to share their stories. When explaining how the initial intake meetings go, Jessica commented:

> Those meetings are actually interesting because you just sat with a case manager, and they usually tell you all the gory details, and so you get this

image in your head of this, like, terrible details and all of these awful things have happened. And then, all of the sudden, there is this little girl just sitting in front of you, and it is this really strange experience. All of that stuff that I just heard about—this is you. And it always strikes me . . . it's almost upsetting because you hear the story in an abstract way, and all of the sudden you get a person, and that is their story. But then I also feel a little bit uncomfortable because they don't know that I know their story, and then I have to try to get it out of them. And so there is a little bit, almost guilt, that I already know all this stuff about you and maybe you would not want me to know all this.[8]

The need to push for information, especially when the case was time sensitive or when detention of the child was stretching out for months, was also uncomfortable. Cecilia explains:

One of the things that I struggled with was this idea that you would go, and you would visit a child once a week, and you kind of need information in order to advocate for them. So if the child had been abused in some way, that was information that you were often encouraged to seek out because you need it. There was almost like an ethical dilemma of, I don't know you, and you don't trust me. Do I push for this information, or do I just get to know you, and maybe at some point you get to trust me? But it is okay if you don't, too, right? But you have this urgency of time and not necessarily the tools to figure out how to get information from kids.[9]

Though each advocate's experience is slightly different, all these stories share the core concern that trauma and suffering become the defining characteristic of the children. To recover the story of trauma requires building a relationship, opening wounds, and acknowledging the story as fragmented and affected by both time and the child's detention. Advocates must work to contextualize this story despite being in a system that is otherwise decontextualized from children's lived experiences. This emphasis on biography reflects modern conceptualization of the child as an independent agent, endowed with voice, agency, and political rights (Oswell 2013, 239–40). However, the child's story is constructed and deconstructed by social service agents, including the child advocate, an action often shrouded in a discourse of protection. Thus, the child is presented as an individual, but this presentation is moderated by the institution in a paradoxical effort to both protect children's rights and enforce the state's sovereignty laws. Advocates' experiences revealed the subtle ways in which they participate in the normalization of detention and in the productive reconstruction of children's stories of trauma for the law. Instead of feeling as though they were a positive influence in children's lives, advocates worried that they became complicit in the violence exercised on children by institutions and the law.

EXPERIENCE

To say that advocates experience violence is not meant to suggest that the immigration system exerts the same effects on citizen volunteers that it does on undocumented children. In no way do advocates undergo the intense pain of family separation, the despair of detainment, or the guilt of surveillance that children experience. What we consider here is what cultural theorist Lindsay Balfour (2013, 70) discusses as the unfolding of violence: violence is "several movements *through* time rather than *one* moment of time." Balfour uses the metaphor of organic shrapnel—where in the aftermath of a bomb, the severed body of one becomes lodged in another—to suggest that violence forces our lives to become part of others'. Balfour invites us to consider the "shared precarity of bodies" and to wrestle with the "breaching of personal borders, the velocity of interpersonal relations and, most significantly, how we engage or disengage with the lives of others" (73). We argue that this theoretical intervention into understanding of violence is experienced by advocates as they engage in work through a violent system.

Advocates are prepared for and often experience emotional distress when they hear about traumatic events in children's pasts. Known as compassion fatigue, secondary traumatic stress disorder, or vicarious trauma, this is a well-known psychological phenomenon where people working with individuals who have been traumatized exhibit symptoms in line with post-traumatic stress disorder (Figley 1995; McCann and Pearlman 1990; Stamm 1995). When advocates begin their work, they are often trained on the basics of secondary trauma. Yet in our observations, advocates experience a distress that is not encompassed by the idea of secondary trauma. Rather, tiny shards of the structural and legal violences that shape the lives of children also impact the work and relationships of their volunteer advocates. This structural shrapnel is an indirect result of the violences of the immigration system, and it has consequences for practitioners working in the system.

There was one case in particular in which I (Emily) experienced these shards of legal and structural violence. For nearly a year, I had visited a young boy who had developmental delays and a variety of other physical and psychological needs. He had come to the United States with an uncle with the hope that an American doctor could provide assistance for some of his medical needs. When detained, he was separated from the uncle at the border and sent hundreds of miles away to a tender-age children's shelter. This separation and the disorientation of this move caused such trauma that he was unable to function; the facility responded through medical intervention, providing him medicine that calmed him so he could function in the institutional setting. There were questions about whether he should remain in the United States or return to his home country, and so I was tasked with building a relationship to help determine the best course of action. Because of his disabilities, the relationship I built with him had an intensity that others had not. He was happy to see me some days and begged me to come every day; other days he refused to meet with me. I poured energy, time, and, indeed, love into my work with him. Advocates work to uncover the desires of children, but due to this child's developmental delays, he was unable to communicate these. Instead, I used stories and art to help determine my recommendations. His case dragged on for months, and although my relationship with him grew, I often felt that I did little in the way of advocating for his needs and quickening his return to his family. My observations were written into case notes, and I hope, although I am not sure, that these made an impact. I was out of town when I received word that he would be returned to his home country. I could not see him before he left, and due to the nature of his release and his particular vulnerabilities, I was unable to initiate any further contact with him. The termination of our relationship was sudden and without closure.

Advocate Cecilia told a similar story of a severed relationship. In her 2016 interview with Lina M. Caswell, she explained that she had been working with a young man who was on the cusp of his eighteenth birthday. When a young person turns eighteen while in ORR custody, they are immediately removed from the shelter system and transferred to an adult detention facility. Despite the numerous concerns about the unaccompanied-minor system, adult detention has even fewer safeguards, and young people would dread their eighteenth birthday, on which they would be taken away in handcuffs. Cecilia explained that despite her attempts to speed the release of the young man, he was still in ORR custody on his eighteenth birthday. She felt impotent in her attempts to avert the moment in which he was escorted out of the shelter in handcuffs. "I actually don't know what happened to him after that," she explained. "Presumably he may have also been deported."

The severing of relationships, coupled with advocates' feelings of impotency in controlling the terms of their relationships with children, came up in other interviews as well. Uncertainty in the work of the advocate is framed by discretionary policies that determine advocates' interactions with children, such as visitation hours, time, space, privacy, and ability to provide objects to facilitate interaction with children. Advocate Sonia was frustrated when she would try to communicate to a young person about her visits and was never certain that the young person received messages that she left with facility staff.[10] She explained: "Sometimes my time with the child would change, and that would not be communicated to him, and so, like . . . I just really did not like it, because I just feel like it is like a consistency thing, and consistency is really important. . . . [I don't like] feeling that I don't have the agency in that situation to, like, make sure he finds that out. So I think it does influence the relationship with the child. I know for my first child, we did not get notified until after the child left the facility."

Sonia's reflection is telling in several ways. First, she clearly identifies feelings of impotency, which are located in the restrictions that prevent her from creating and maintaining the terms of her relationship with the child. She values consistency and believes it is essential to build trust with a child, but she feels that discretionary policies take the control away from her. Second, it is notable that in her final thought, she uses the possessive to refer to the child for whom she advocated. For Sonia this is not just any child; he was "my first child." The uses of this phrase reveal a level of intimacy, responsibility, and concern that is linguistically more reflective of a mother and child than of a professional and a client. In fact, the professional and deeply restrictive nature of the job belies the profound sense of care that advocates often experience.

This combination of the lack of control and the intensity of the relationships extends to the child's moment of release and after. Advocates reflected on the negative impact of terminating their relationship with a child in sudden ways, and sometimes without notice, after providing critical support during the trauma of detention. Jessica reflected on the release of "her" child:

But I have felt really emotionally burdened . . . emotionally connected or impacted by the cases, especially when I would say goodbye to them. That has always been very difficult, even for the girl I just could not connect with. The last time I saw her, I just had, like, the heaviest feeling because I could tell she was scared. Because she was being released to her dad, who she did not really know, and it was like . . . I felt like I was sending her off into this unknown, and I know . . . I thought she would be okay, but it is just hard to be like, I am never going to see you again. Good luck with your life. It always feels really heavy when I would leave those situations.[11]

Jessica has trouble searching for the word that describes her feelings about her work and the children. She is burdened, connected, and impacted, all at once. She says that she knows but then realizes that she only thinks that the young girl will be okay. Although all work between professionals and children must come to an end, there is a particular and devastating finality to this ending that was created not by the desires of those involved but by the limitations and violences of the immigration system. There are borders built between advocates and young people, such that, despite the depth of care they provide, advocates are compelled to carry out practices with which they disagree and to maintain distance. As we reflect today on our own painful experiences of child advocacy, which were echoed in interviews with advocates such as Cecilia, Sonia, and Jessica, we are struck by the particular violences that shape the work. Our own pain was a result not just of secondary trauma. It was about the fracturing of relationships that had been built in a secret facility; it was about the uncertainty that pervades the work; it was the guilt of powerlessness and complicity. When workers stand so close to the unfolding of violence, they themselves find that the violence becomes embedded in them.

Conclusion and Discussion

An analysis of structural and legal violence as experienced by advocates provides insight into the insidiousness of the system of apprehension and detention experienced by unaccompanied immigrant children. Advocates witnessed how the bureaucracy perpetuated trajectories of violence that were already present, and they often felt they had little agency to combat this violence. Rather, they found that their presence meant that they were sometimes folded into the violence, complicit in carrying out structural and legal harm. Indeed, the violence of the system is so interwoven into everyday practices that advocates themselves left the work carrying shards of the violent structures within them as well.

This chapter provides a framework for practitioners to understand the violent context within which the work is carried out. It is also essential to understand that the practitioner is a part of the immigration system, witnessing, perpetuating, and experiencing the violence in the system as well. Advocates are not separate from this system. We believe that to carry out the work, advocates must hold a deep understanding of the insidiousness of that violence, which can be prolonged, which can co-opt good intentions, and which can impact those who work with such proximity to the system.

Advocates are taught that their role is to provide companionship and a voice, but advocates in our research sometimes felt that their work was little more than a Band-Aid, at best, to a broken system. We argue that advocates must be aware of the trajectory of violence experienced by children throughout the process of migration. Advocates must know to expect and recognize that feelings of powerlessness and alienation exist because of the violence of this system. They will witness, participate in, and experience this violence, not because of their individual inadequacy as practitioners but because of the proximity to the violence.

The testimonies of advocates corroborate and expand on the conceptualization of structural and legal violence as experienced by practitioners who, though not the direct recipients, carry their shards. Yet despite the challenges and concerns shared by the advocates in our research, they understood their role as critical to protecting the most vulnerable children. We also believe that the work of the child advocate in the current system is necessary as civilian oversight of deeply flawed and violent immigration policies and the institutions that support them.

Notes

1. We use pseudonyms throughout this work to maintain confidentiality in the research.
2. Interview with Emily Ruehs-Navarro, 2016.
3. Interview with Lina M. Caswell, 2016.

4. Interview with Emily Ruehs-Navarro, 2019.
5. Interview with Lina M. Caswell, 2016.
6. Interview with Emily Ruehs-Navarro, 2016.
7. Interview with Lina M. Caswell, 2016.
8. Interview with Lina M. Caswell, 2016.
9. Interview with Lina M. Caswell, 2016.
10. Interview with Lina M. Caswell, 2016.
11. Interview with Lina M. Caswell, 2016.

References

Abrego, Leisy J., and Cecilia Menjívar. 2011. "Immigrant Latina Mothers as Targets of Legal Violence." *International Journal of Sociology of the Family* 37 (1): 9–26.

Arana, Ana. 2005. "How the Street Gangs Took Central America." *Foreign Affairs* 84 (3): 98–110. https://doi.org/10.2307/20034353.

Bak, Elizabeth, Alberto Celesia, and Mara Tissera. 2015. *Niños, niñas y adolecentes migrantes retornados: Un análisis de los contextos y las respuestas de servicios y las políticas de protección en El Salvador, Guatemala, Honduras y México.* Buenos Aires: RELAF, Save the Children, UNICEF, United Nation Children's Fund. https://resourcecentre.savethechildren.net/library/ninos-ninas-y-adolescentes -migrantes-retornados-un-analisis-de-los-contextos-y-las.

Baker, Karen S. 2019. "Is the United States Safely Repatriating Unaccompanied Children? Law, Policy, and Return to Guatemala." *University of Miami Law Review* 73 (3): 781–862.

Balfour, Lindsay. 2013. "Organic Shrapnel and the Possibility of Violence." *Affinities: A Journal of Radical Theory, Culture, and Action* 6 (1): 68–82.

Briggs, Laura. 2020. *Taking Children: A History of American Terror*. Oakland, Calif.: University of California Press.

Elliott, Joseph Carlton. 2016. "Sleeping with One Eye Open: The Result of Non-Transparent Oversight by the Office of Refugee Resettlement of Facilities Sheltering Unaccompanied Alien Children." *Administrative Law Review* 68 (1): 153–75.

Farmer, Paul. 2009. "On Suffering and Structural Violence: A View from Below." *Race/Ethnicity: Multidisciplinary Global Contexts* 3 (1): 11–28.

Figley, Charles R., ed. 1995. *Compassion Fatigue: Coping with Secondary Traumatic Stress Disorder in Those Who Treat the Traumatized*. New York: Brunner/Mazel.

Galtung, Johan. 1969. "Violence, Peace, and Peace Research." *Journal of Peace Research* 6 (3): 167–91.

Grabell, Michael, Topher Sanders, and Silvina Sterin Pensel. 2018. "In Immigrant Children's Shelters, Sexual Assault Cases Are Open and Shut." ProPublica, December 21, 2018. https://www.propublica.org/article/boystown-immigrant-childrens -shelter-sexual-assault.

Heidbrink, Lauren. 2017. "Assessing Parental Fitness and Care for Unaccompanied Children." *The Russell Sage Foundation Journal of the Social Sciences* 3 (4): 37–52.

Jackman, Mary R. 2002. "Violence in Social Life." *Annual Review of Sociology* 28: 387–415.

Kandel, William A. 2019. *Unaccompanied Alien Children: An Overview*. Washington, D.C.: Congressional Research Services. https://crsreports.congress.gov/product /pdf/R/R43599.

McCann, I. Lisa, and Laurie Ann Pearlman. 1990. "Vicarious Traumatization: A Framework for Understanding the Psychological Effects of Working with Victims." *Journal of Traumatic Stress* 3:131–49.

Menjívar, Cecilia, and Leisy Abrego. 2012. "Legal Violence: Immigration Law and the Lives of Central American Immigrants." *American Journal of Sociology* 117 (5): 1380–421.

Menjívar, Cecilia, Leisy J. Abrego, and Leah C. Schmalzbauer. 2016. *Immigrant Families*. Malden, Mass.: Polity.

Moreno, Barry. 2005. *Images of America: Children of Ellis Island*. Charleston, S.C.: Arcadia.

Oswell, David. 2013. *The Agency of Children*. Cambridge, UK: Cambridge University Press.

Ruehs-Navarro, Emily. 2022. *Unaccompanied: The Plight of Immigrant Youth at the Border*. New York: New York University Press.

Sanchez, Melissa. 2020. "At Least 19 Children at a Chicago Shelter for Immigrant Detainees Have Tested Positive for COVID-19." ProPublica Illinois, April 13, 2020. https://www.propublica.org/article/at-least-19-children-at-a-chicago-shelter-for -immigrant-detainees-have-tested-positive-for-covid-19.

Slack, Jeremy, Daniel E. Martínez, Alison Elizabeth Lee, and Scott Whiteford. 2016. "The Geography of Border Militarization: Violence, Death and Health in Mexico and the United States." *Journal of Latin American Geography* 15 (1): 7–32.

Slack, Jeremy, and Scott Whiteford. 2011. "Violence and Migration on the Arizona-Sonora Border." *Human Organization* 70 (1): 11–21.

Stamm, Beth H., ed. 1995. *Secondary Traumatic Stress: Self-Care Issues for Clinicians, Researchers, and Educators*. Baltimore: Sidran.

Swanson, Kate, and Rebecca Maria Torres. 2016. "Child Migration and Transnationalized Violence in Central and North America." *Journal of Latin American Geography* 15 (3): 23–48.

Terrio, Susan J. 2015. *Whose Child Am I?* Oakland: University of California Press.

United Nations Refugee Agency. 2013. *Children on the Run*. Washington, D.C.: UNHCR.

United States Government Accountability Office. 2015. *Unaccompanied Alien Children*. Washington, D.C.: United States Government Accountability Office.

United States Government Publishing Office. 2010. "Title 6—Domestic Security." United States Code, 2010 Edition. https://www.govinfo.gov/content/pkg/US CODE-2010-title6/html/USCODE-2010-title6.htm.

U.S. Customs and Border Protection. 2020. "U.S. Border Patrol Southwest Border Apprehensions by Sector." Accessed December 26, 2020. https://www.cbp.gov /newsroom/stats/sw-border-migration/usbp-sw-border-apprehension.

U.S. Department of Health and Human Services. 2019. "Unaccompanied Alien Child Shelter at Homestead Job Crops Site, Homestead, Florida." Press release, August 6, 2019. https://www.hhs.gov/sites/default/files/Unaccompanied-Alien -Children-Sheltered-at-Homestead.pdf.

Werner, Emmy E. 2009. *Passages to America*. Dulles, Va.: Potomac.

Young Center. 2011. *Child Advocate Training Manual*. Chicago: Young Center.

Young Center. 2021. "About the Young Center." https://www.theyoungcenter.org/about -the-young-center.

CHAPTER 9

U.S.-Citizen Children of Deportees in Mexico and in the United States

So Close and Yet So Far

IRASEMA CORONADO

> What is done to children, they will do to society.
>
> —*Karl Menninger, MD*

> . . . the infinitely complex red-tape existence of stateless persons
>
> —*Hannah Arendt*

As early as 1937, U.S. courts dealt with the welfare of U.S.-citizen children of immigrants in cases of deportation. In the Nunez case, the mother was in the country legally but, due to her husband's death, applied for social welfare benefits for her U.S.-born children; at the time, immigrants could not apply for these benefits, and therefore the mother was rendered deportable. District Judge Paul John McCormick wrote,

> If the mother is deported, the children should and probably must go with her to Mexico. The record shows that it is the children who are the major recipients of the public benefactions, and, if the deportation of this alien mother is sought to be justified upon the claim of public economy, this result will be attained only slightly. There is no one in the United States able to support the children. They must continue to be public charges in the United States or be forced to go to Mexico with their mother. The first eventuality is safer and more humane than the last. Sound public policy and the welfare

of the American-born children of the alien precludes as a matter of law her deportation at this time. (*In re* Nunez, 18 F. Supp. 1007 [S. D. Calif. 1937])

In 2002 Judge Jack B. Weinstein of the United States District Court in Brooklyn, New York, ruled that Immigration and Naturalization Service agents could not deport an immigrant felon unless they first considered the impact on his child, who would be left behind in the United States. Judge Weinstein's ruling that the "best interests of the child" principle be taken into consideration in deportation cases was well received by human rights advocates. Gerald L. Neuman, a professor of law at Columbia Law School and expert on immigration law, noted that "if immigration officials always had to account for the best interests of the child in weighing whether to deport someone, that would radically change immigration practice" (Glaberson 2002). Jennifer M. Green, a lawyer with the Center for Constitutional Rights, stated that consideration of the effects of a deportation was essential (Glaberson 2002). Critics included Mark S. Krikorian of the Center for Immigration Studies, and legal scholars noted that Judge Weinstein's ruling was an example of judicial activism and would circumvent U.S. immigration law (Glaberson 2002). The ruling especially carried implications for provisions included in the Illegal Immigration Reform and Immigrant Responsibility Act of 1996, which allows for the deportation of undocumented immigrants who commit a misdemeanor or a felony.

Judge Weinstein wrote, "The United States cannot expect to reap the benefits of internationally recognized human rights in the form of greater worldwide stability and respect for people without being willing to adhere to them itself" (Glaberson 2002). U.S. courts have long accepted the principle that American judges can rely on "customary international law" (Glaberson 2002). In this deportation case, citing the International Convention on the Rights of the Child expanded the principle of the best interests of the child. Article 3 of the United Nations Convention on the Rights of the Child (1989) details the principle as follows: "In all actions concerning children, whether undertaken by public or private social welfare institutions, courts of law, administrative authorities or legislative bodies, the best interests of the child shall be a primary consideration" (OHCHR 2021).

The United States is a party to this UN convention but has never ratified it. Mexico is a party and ratified the convention in 1990. However, both countries fall short of taking into account the principle of the best interests of the child as it relates to their respective immigration policy. I argue that the "best interests of the child" principle should be a primary consideration when governments develop and enforce immigration laws. Governments should mitigate the trauma and negative impacts that children suffer because of immigration policies and deportation processes. In addition, governments should consider the short- and long-term consequences that the implementation and enforcement of these policies entail. The impact on children who live in ambiguous situations because of the migratory status of their family members has been well documented. Additionally, there are children that are living in a semi-stateless status, albeit in some cases temporarily, because they lack official documents to prove their citizenship or are in the process of obtaining them.

This chapter argues for the need of the "best interests of the child" principle to be included in immigration law and embraced by both the United States and Mexico. Highlighted especially are families that live in fear of deportation and families that have been separated because of deportation, as well as those living under the threat of having a family member deported, leading to negative outcomes in the well-being of children's families. I present (1) the plight and hardship of living in mixed-status households in the United States, (2) children left behind in the United States that have ended up in the foster care system or under the care of relatives, and (3) the challenges of U.S.-citizen children residing in Mexico because of a family member's deportation. I provide examples of nongovernmental organizations that are working to unite families, albeit temporarily, who are separated by immigration laws and the political boundary, and I set forth recommendations to both governments for the development of humane immigration policies that take into account the "best interests of the child" principle. The challenges that deported parents face to advocate for family reunification are also discussed, as well as the quandary of U.S.-citizen children living with their deported parents in Mexico's border cities, specifically Tijuana, Baja California; Nogales, Sonora; and Ciudad Juárez, Chihuahua. Many of these U.S.-citizen children living in Mexico—if they are close to the border—can literally see their country of origin on a daily basis. While they can legally live in and return to the United States, it is difficult for them to do so because their deported parents or family members cannot accompany them through the port of entry. These children can and will probably eventually return to the United States; how they will fare socially and economically could be affected by the deportation process and impact life chances. U.S.-citizen children living in Mexico would be well served if both countries adhered to the best interests of the child as a human rights principle. Each country should develop binational public policy solutions to mitigate the negative impacts of the deportation process on families. This chapter concludes with policy recommendations for the United States and Mexico to negotiate a binational agreement that embodies the principle of the best interests of the child in regard to migration and deportations.

Methodology

Data gathering for this project has been a long-term process. Telephone and face-to-face interviews were conducted with deportees in Ciudad Juárez, Chihuahua; Tijuana, Baja California; and Nogales, Sonora. Additionally, volunteers and staff members who work in migrant shelters provided very useful information and insight regarding the challenges that deportees face upon their return to Mexico. These volunteers and staff members are affiliated with various Catholic church organizations, including the Kino Border Initiative in Nogales, Sonora; Casa del Migrante in Ciudad Juárez, Chihuahua; and Desayunador Padre Chava in Tijuana, Baja California. Participants shared their experiences but most requested that they not be individually identified by their names.

As part of the data gathering, in September 2017 a conference titled Familias Divididas was held in collaboration with the Universidad Autónoma de Ciudad Juárez. The focus of the conference was to provide a forum for deportees to share their concerns and the challenges they faced negotiating a new life in Mexico. Staff members of human rights organizations, as well as local, state, and federal officials, shared the programs and services that their respective institutions provide to migrants and *repatriados*. A panel of academics provided an update on the current research on the topic of deportations.

This type of qualitative data gathering requires a great deal of emotional fortitude. Many interviewees break down and cry during the process because it is so painful for them to talk about their families, which are at risk of disintegrating because immigration policies preclude family members from being able to visit and see each other. Some deportees have been banned from reentering the United States for twenty years. Deportees that reenter the United States illegally, if detained again by immigration officials, can be sentenced to federal prison for up to twenty years, depending on the circumstances of the first deportation. For many interviewees limited hope for family reunification exists. This type of research is also time consuming and is not a onetime data gathering experience, because family members are working and have other responsibilities, and taking time to meet with researchers is not a high priority. Another challenge that arises when conducting this research is that the expectations of families are raised because they feel that the researcher has the wherewithal to help them address their immigration issue, which is not the case.

Living in Mixed-Status Households—Fear of Deportations

A growing body of research is documenting the impact of current immigration policy on children in the United States. The negative impacts of a broken immigration system in the United States affects children in many ways. But it is not only actual deportation that can have an impact on children and the family. Children report that even the threat of deportability affects them profoundly. Roughly half a million U.S.-citizen children experienced the apprehension, detention, and deportation of at least one parent between 2011 and 2013. In 2013 U.S. Immigration and Customs Enforcement (ICE) reported that 72,410 people were deported who said that they had one or more U.S.-citizen children. The impact of deportation on children is unarguable. A study conducted by Harvard researchers concluded that more than five million children in the United States are "at risk of lower educational performance, economic stagnation, blocked mobility and ambiguous belonging" because they are growing up in immigrant families affected by illegal status (Suárez-Orozco et al. 2011).

Living in a mixed-status family has negative impacts on overall well-being. Family members that I have interviewed share the impact of living with *miedo* (fear) and the physical, emotional, and mental stress that they experience because of their undocumented status. Interviewees share their concerns about being stopped by a police officer for a traffic violation and getting deported. Others express the *miedo* they feel that their children will come home to an empty home if they are deported. *Miedo* was a common theme that emerged during my interactions with people: *miedo* of being deported, *miedo* of losing their children, *miedo* of someone finding out that they are undocumented. Fear of having a family member, parent, or sibling deported; witnessing the arrest of a family member (by immigration officials); the impacts of the deportation process; and the ultimate separation of families can have devastating consequences on children, emotionally and financially (Capps et al. 2015).

This *miedo* also leads families to make decisions that can have long-term negative consequences on their well-being. Scholars have found that the risk of deportation leads Mexican immigrant mothers to avoid using social services and benefits even if their children are eligible to receive them (Vargas and Pirog 2016; Xu, Pirog, and Vargas 2016; Vargas 2015). By not taking advantage of social services, families might be missing out on Supplemental Nutrition Assistance Program (SNAP) or Medicaid benefits. Additionally, research indicates that knowing a deported individual is linked to child mental health problems and that children who know deported individuals are more likely to be referred for learning-disorder tests (Vargas and Benitez 2019). If it is true that what is done to children, they will do to society, the fear generated by ambiguous immigration status and deportations should be of concern and frighten us.

A Pew Research Center report indicates that around five million U.S.-born children younger than eighteen were living with at least one unauthorized immigrant parent in 2016 (Passel, Cohn, and Gramlich 2018). Further research indicates that children who are living in mixed-status households are at risk for a wide variety of negative outcomes related to health, economic status, and educational attainment. For example, a study conducted in Postville, Iowa, the site of one the largest workplace raids conducted by ICE, shows that infants born to Latina mothers in Iowa had a 24 percent higher risk of low birth weight in the period following that raid.

Families report that after the deportation of a parent, they usually experience housing insecurity due to loss of income. It is clear that when enforcing U.S. immigration policy, the UN's "best interests of the child" principle is not taken into account. Undocumented immigrants report that their only crime is to work without the benefits of proper documentation in order to provide a better life for their children. Once family members are deported, some opt to leave their children in the care of friends or relatives, while other children end up in foster care.

Children of Deportees Left Behind in the United States

Seth Freed Wessler's 2011 *Shattered Families* report found that there were at least 5,100 children living in foster care in the United States because their parents had been detained or deported. This next section will focus on families separated through the deportation process. The following situations highlight the absolute disregard for the "best interests of the child" principle when a parent is deported.

Children Placed with Good Foster Parents

"Alberto" lives in Nogales, Sonora, Mexico. He moved to the United States with his parents when he was an infant. He grew up in the greater Phoenix area, attended school, married, and had two children. As an adult he was deported, with negative impacts on his family. His wife "lost it," as he put it, and became involved with a bad crowd and started using drugs. Their children were placed in foster care.

In Alberto's situation the hearing officer handling his children's case allowed him to participate in the hearings through videoconferencing. In order to have his children removed from foster care in the United States and join him in Mexico, the hearing officer required Alberto to fulfill a series of conditions. Among these conditions were having employment and a place to live with adequate space for the children. In this case a separate bedroom for each child, plus a bedroom for Alberto, is required because one child is nine years old and the other one is two years old. Alberto earns five dollars a day working in a maquiladora. Based on his current salary, he cannot afford to rent a house with three bedrooms. He is hopeful that he will be reunited with his children because of the friendly disposition of the hearing officer and the kindness of the foster parents, who allow him to communicate with the children. He mentioned how lucky his children are to be in the hands of good foster parents who allow them to communicate with him. Kino Border Initiative volunteers take cards and letters across the border and mail them from the Nogales, Arizona, post office so that Alberto can keep in touch with his children.

Lost in the System in the United States

A deported mother now residing in Tijuana cannot find her son. She believes her son is currently in the custody of the child welfare agency in the state of California. She was detained by the local police for a minor traffic offense and then turned over to Border Patrol. During that transition her child ended up in the California child welfare system. After she was deported to Tijuana, she enlisted the support of a pro bono lawyer to help her find her son. She is hoping that the U.S. consulate in Tijuana and the Mexican consulate in the community where her child was originally detained can assist her in this effort.

In these cases families are separated for long periods of time, causing undue stress and hardship to all concerned. In the case of children in foster care, caseworkers may petition the appropriate dependency court to terminate parental rights. Judges often move to terminate parental rights of deported Mexican nationals whose children are U.S. citizens. In some cases these children are put up for adoption in the United States.

The foster care system is an example of how bureaucracy and lack of formal policies and procedures leads to negative outcomes for many immigrant families—notwithstanding the example of Alberto and his children. The absence of such procedures prohibits deported parents from participating in the hearing process. This is an example of how bureaucracy and lack of formal policies and procedures in place to seek out and allow deported parents to participate in the hearing process can lead to negative outcomes for the family. The Adoption and Safe Families Act was passed in 1999 in response to cases of children languishing in foster care for years because hearing officers took too much time terminating parental rights. In the case of the deportees, the unintended consequence of the act was expedited removal of parental rights without regard to the best interests of the child.

In the Care of Relatives in the United States

Another possible scenario occurs when relatives of the deported family member claim the child. Not all these situations have positive outcomes. Children miss their parents and act out, or economic issues may unfold in the family when the child becomes a financial burden. Some deportees attempt to parent through videoconferencing, social media, or email, but this can become a problem, especially if the family is separated for a long time. Some children feel abandoned by their parents, and there can be a great deal of resentment and feelings of isolation. The possible long-term consequences of this forced family separation and its future impact on individuals and society are alarming.

These forced family separations due to deportations pose complications and challenges and are difficult to address. In some instances teenage children in the United States do not want to go live with the parent or parents in Mexico. Some families arrange for children to stay with a relative, godparents, or friends. In these cases deported parents worry that they will not ever see their children again, especially if the child or children who are left behind in the United States are undocumented. Children who are U.S. citizens may not have a passport, and some who do report that they are afraid to go to Mexico to visit their parents or do not have the economic resources to make the trip. On occasion, in desperation, a deported parent may reenter the United States illegally, and if caught by U.S. Border Patrol, they can be charged with reentry after deportation. Reentry after deportation is a federal crime and punishable with between two and twenty years of prison, depending on the circumstances surrounding their original deportation (U.S. Department of Justice 2008). Hence, many deportees insist on taking their U.S.-born children to Mexico to ensure family unity.

U.S.-Citizen Children of Deportees Living in Mexico

In an attempt to keep families together, some parents decide to take their U.S.-citizen children with them when deported (Freed Wessler 2011). On the United States–Mexico border, there is a human rights crisis and a group of stateless people; children who are U.S. citizens and are living in Mexico because of a family member's deportation find themselves on the margins of both countries. Some of these children are U.S. citizens, and several obtained legal Mexican citizenship because their parents registered their birth in a Mexican consulate in the United States. Families trying to obtain Mexican citizenship for their U.S.-citizen children after being deported find the process costly, time-consuming, and difficult—especially if they do not have birth certificates with them. It is important to note that not all deportees are undocumented; there are numerous legal permanent residents who have committed crimes, and the U.S. legal system renders them deportable. Some legal permanent residents were long-term residents of the United States and never imagined that they would be deported and, subsequently, their families separated.

U.S.-Citizen Children Living in Mexico with Deported Parent(s)

Over half a million children born in the United States are enrolled in public schools throughout Mexico. The border states of Baja California and Chihuahua receive the greatest number of students. U.S.-born children who possess double nationality when they arrive in Mexico have more legal protections than those children who have only U.S. citizenship. Double nationality allows children to attend Mexican schools and receive social benefits. However, they may be stigmatized socially because some of them do not speak Spanish, do not know the Mexican national anthem, and are unfamiliar with Mexican history. In some instances school officials in Mexico have denied admission to immigrant children if they cannot prove Mexican citizenship. Reports describe discrimination and bullying when children do not speak Spanish or speak accented Spanish.

According to a report that evaluates Mexico's social development policies, published by the Consejo Nacional de Evaluación de la Política de Desarrollo Social, public education in Mexico, while a constitutional right, has limitations. The report indicates that there is great variability across the country, as some schools do not have adequate building space, desks, bathroom facilities, or drinking fountains. Only four out of ten primary schools have access to computers and Internet. On average, class size is thirty-four students, while the average for OECD (Organisation for Economic Co-operation and Development) countries is thirteen. Teachers' salaries are 33 percent below the average salary in OECD countries. Additionally, limited programs exist for children with special needs or for children who speak an Indigenous language. Newly arrived children who do not speak Spanish find themselves in an environment that has limited capacity to meet their educational needs (Garcia 2018).

Another pertinent scenario is when U.S.-citizen children live in a Mexican city and cross the border every day into the United States to attend school. This has been documented in schools in border states such as California, Texas, Arizona, and New Mexico. Most school districts require that students live in the district they attend, and families may have to provide proof of residency, such as a utility bill, a rental payment, or a mortgage payment receipt. Students whose families reside in Mexico may have to lie or tell school officials that they are homeless. Some school officials embrace the notion that they educate those who show up at the schoolroom door; others exercise far more scrutiny in determining whether the child does indeed live within the boundaries of the school district. This can be dependent upon district, city, or state laws and regulations (Bailey 2013).

Living Under the Threat of Deportation: How to Prepare

The fifty Mexican consulates in the United States provide a guide for families so they can prepare in case parents are deported. This guide, titled "Elabora un plan para un posible retorno a México," encourages Mexican-citizen parents to register their children's births at the consulate to obtain Mexican citizenship for their U.S.-born children prior to any deportation event. Mexican nationals residing in the United States, in order to register their children's births at a Mexican consulate in the United States, must have their own valid ID and an original copy of the child's birth certificate and must pay a thirteen-dollar fee. Once a child is registered, the child then becomes a Mexican national by virtue of the fact that their parent or parents are Mexican citizens. Consulates tout the benefits of having dual nationality by highlighting that the children will then enjoy all the rights and privileges of Mexican citizenship, such as being able to attend school and receive health care if they reside in Mexico.

Once in Mexico it is difficult and costly to obtain Mexican citizenship for U.S.-born children following a deportation event. The cost is almost $400, and the child's birth certificate must be translated into Spanish and have an apostille. This apostille must be attached to the original birth certificate, certifying that it is legitimate and authentic, so that it will be accepted by the Mexican government. Acquisition of this apostille is dependent upon state guidelines and has its own associated costs. These transactions are time consuming and costly for poor families who are struggling to reintegrate into Mexican society.

Interviews with consular officials in El Paso, Texas, and Nogales, Arizona, indicate that few parents or legal guardians take advantage of these consular services. Many deportees avoid interaction with any government institution, including Mexican consulates in the United States. Undocumented people tend not to have official identification cards, or some of their documents are expired. It is difficult for them to start the process of registering their children if they do not have valid identification.

Families who are unable to prepare or that do not prepare for possible deportation are provided some assistance, once they are in custody, through U.S. Immigration and Customs Enforcement Policy 11064.2: Detention and Removal of Alien Parents and Legal Guardians. This directive provides guidance regarding the detention and removal of parents and legal guardians of minor children. ICE will allow a detainee responsible for minor children to make arrangements for guardianship, including providing the detainee access to consular officials and lawyers. ICE may also help facilitate obtaining travel documents for the children and the person accompanying them and may help make travel arrangements so that the deportee can be reunited with their children in the deportee's country of origin.

In cases where a parent or legal guardian is in long-term detention, reasonable efforts may be made to allow for children to visit their family member. ICE officials are acutely aware of the challenges that deported parents have in arranging for the well-being and welfare of their U.S.-born children, who will either remain in the country or travel to the country to which the parent will be deported.

Should a U.S.-born child enter Mexico and not have dual nationality, then he or she would enter as a tourist and be able to stay no more than six months on a tourist visa. This is another manifestation of statelessness. Tourists are not able to attend public schools or receive social benefits. Before the six months are up, the child must leave Mexico and reenter the country with another tourist visa. This poses a major problem for a parent or parents who cannot leave Mexico for financial reasons or are not able to visit another country. The child could conceivably be considered a visa overstayer in Mexico or even an undocumented person in Mexico and find themselves in a stateless condition.

Another situation in which children are rendered stateless is when U.S.-citizen children living in Mexico do not have a birth certificate or any document that proves their U.S. citizenship. This can cause additional problems. In one case parents registered their U.S.-citizen child as a Mexican national because they wanted her to start school. Later, when the parents tried to obtain her passport through the U.S. embassy, they were presented with evidence of her registration in Mexico. However, the parents had a birth certificate from Georgia indicating that the child had been born there. It is customary in Mexico for people to use both their father's and mother's last name. In the United States, that is not the case, and this led to complications when trying to obtain copies of the child's birth certificate in Georgia while living in Mexico.

Hope for the Future

There are examples of civil society organizations that are raising awareness and mobilizing in order to improve situations for families and children who have been separated by deportation. Four nongovernmental organizations emerged in the border region that provide support for deportees and their children.

One organization is DREAMers Moms International USA/Tijuana. This group was founded by Yolanda Varona, a deportee who left her children in the United States. Ms. Varona shared that she felt very alone and sad when she was deported. At a shelter she was inspired to start helping other mothers who had also been deported and had children in the United States. She started DREAMers Moms International USA/Tijuana with the purpose of helping other mothers who find themselves in very vulnerable situations, especially when they have been deported. In an interview Varona said that the point of entering Mexico is when women are the most vulnerable and can fall prey to drug dealers, smugglers, and pimps. The organization works with families to help them deal with this tragic situation and offers support and guidance. The group is also working to help people find their children who are lost in the child welfare system. On the group's California radio show, Ms. Varona shares the challenges and successes of these mothers and finds ways to get passports and/or documents for their U.S.-born children in order to visit their mothers in Tijuana.

Two other organizations working hard to address migrant families' needs are Border Angels / Angeles de la Frontera and Friends of Friendship Park. Friendship Park has historically been a meeting place for families on both sides of the border where they could meet on the United States–Mexico border and visit with family. This was a traditional meeting place for families who could not cross the border because they did not have documents. Friendship Park was the place where grandchildren could meet their grandparents and children could visit their parents. With time the U.S. government gated this area. Border Angels / Angeles de la Frontera and Friends of Friendship Park are working to extend the visiting hours, which now are only on Saturdays and Sundays from ten o'clock in the morning to two o'clock in the afternoon, and allow families to have a more private place to meet.

In May 2016 these two organizations arranged for five people residing in the United States to visit with their families in Mexico for three minutes. The gate on the border fence was open for the first time in order to arrange these visits. Though this is a small effort, it is an indication of baby steps leading to even bigger steps that will initiate meaningful interactions between the United States and Mexico, resulting in a positive effect on families.

Another nongovernmental organization in El Paso, Texas, the Border Network for Human Rights, has held very special and heartwarming events called Hugs Not Walls (BNHR, n.d.). Families from both sides of the border can come together in an area where the Rio Grande / Río Bravo has been channeled. Hugs Not Walls events require an inordinate amount of planning and collaboration with U.S. government officials and volunteers in Ciudad Juárez, who help facilitate these three- to five-minute family reunions. Families need to apply to be a part of this event; if selected, they attend a mandatory briefing. During the briefing the process and the rules are explained to participants: no exchange of money, pictures, or any other items is allowed.

On the day of the Hugs Not Walls Events, families are given color-coded T-shirts to wear so that U.S. officials can clearly distinguish participants' respective countries. Families are given numbers, lined up, and escorted to the meeting area. The same process takes place in Ciudad Juárez. Magically, family members are able to hug and kiss for three to five minutes. During Hugs Not Walls events, grandparents meet their grandchildren for the first time, parents are reunited with their children, and siblings who have not seen each other in twenty years hug each other. After three to five minutes, everyone is escorted back to their respective country. These opportunities are invaluable to families who have been apart for years (Sanchez 2019).

It is important to recognize the efforts of DREAMers Moms International USA/Tijuana, Border Angels, Friends of Friendship Park, and the Border Network for Human Rights in reuniting families for a few minutes. However, Mexico and the United States need to work on better policies to allow families to have more frequent visits and, better yet, to be reunited.

The hardships, heartaches, and pain that children suffer because of their immigration status and forced family separations due to deportations is difficult to measure. Coupled with being stateless, this, in some instances, certainly can affect children's well-being. The long-term consequences are difficult to predict, but these hardships certainly cannot have positive outcomes. Families in this situation can definitely relate to the "infinitely complex red-tape existence of stateless persons" that Hannah Arendt experienced (Koh 2001).

Binational Public Policy Recommendations Taking into Account the Best Interests of the Child

Mexico and the United States should appoint a binational task force to address the issue of mixed-status families. After all, this is a binational problem that requires a binational solution. Family unification should be the paramount goal of this task force; at minimum this task force could create mechanisms for family visits at the border on a regular basis.

Both countries should embrace the "best interests of the child" principle and make decisions and formulate policies that take it into account. Research overwhelmingly indicates that living in a mixed-status household has a negative impact on children not only at the moment of separation but also in the future. Keeping in mind the best interests of the child, Mexico and the United States should evaluate their policies and make changes when warranted in order to cause the least amount of harm to children. Both countries should help children and their families obtain birth certificates, passports, and dual citizenship documents in an affordable and timely manner.

Mexico and the United States should create a mechanism for instant communication with officials who will serve as advocates when children are put in foster care or in the care of the state so that parents can know the children's whereabouts. This task force should establish visiting centers close to the border so that families can visit. Families have suggested that it would be a good idea to have a binational meeting space where they can visit their loved ones. A visiting center could be established close to Chamizal National Memorial in El Paso / Ciudad Juárez, the Mariposa Port of Entry in Nogales, and in Friendship Park in Tijuana/California.

This task force should find ways for U.S.-citizen children to attend public schools in the United States if their parents wish them to do so. This task force would serve as a liaison between parents and school districts. School districts should provide transportation and monitors to ensure the safe movement of children across the border. Currently, school districts require that the child live in the district catchment area; an exception should be made for U.S.-citizen children of deportees.

References

Bailey, Ebony. 2013. "Crossing the Border for a U.S. Education." Neon Tommy: Annenberg Digital News. Annenberg Media Center, February 18, 2013. http://www.neontommy.com/news/2013/02/crossing-border-us-education.

BNHR (Border Network for Human Rights). n.d. "Hugs Not Walls." Accessed March 17, 2021. https://bnhr.org/hugs-not-walls-stories-of-family-reunification/.

Capps, Randy, Heather Koball, Andrea Campetella, Krista Perreira, Sarah Hooker, and Juan Manuel Pedroza. 2015. *Implications of Immigration Enforcement Activities for the Well-Being of Children in Immigrant Families: A Review of the Literature.* Migration Policy Institute. Research report, September 2015. https://www.migrationpolicy.org/sites/default/files/publications/ASPE-ChildrenofDeported-Lit%20Review-FINAL.pdf.

Freed Wessler, Seth. 2011. *Shattered Families: The Perilous Intersection of Immigration Enforcement and the Child Welfare System.* Applied Research Center, November 2011. http://www.asph.sc.edu/cli/word_pdf/ARC_Report_Nov2011.pdf.

Garcia, Ana Karen. 2018. "Educación en México: Insuficiente, desigual y la calidad es difícil de medir." *El economista*, December 25, 2018. https://www.eleconomista.com.mx/politica/Educacion-en-Mexico-insuficiente-desigual-y-la-calidad-es-dificil-de-medir-20181225-0028.html.

Glaberson, William. 2002. "Judge Gives Children Voice in Deportation: Ruling on 'Best Interest' Provokes Intense Debate; Child's Well-Being Is Called Factor in a Deportation Case." *New York Times*, February 12, 2002. https://www.nytimes.com/2002/02/12/nyregion/judge-gives-children-voice-in-deportation.html.

Koh, Jerome. 2001. "The World of Hannah Arendt." *Library of Congress Information Bulletin* 60, no. 3 (March). https://www.loc.gov/loc/lcib/0103/arendt.html.

OHCHR (Office of the High Commissioner for Human Rights). 2021. "Convention on the Rights of the Child." Digitized legislation. https://www.ohchr.org/EN/ProfessionalInterest/Pages/CRC.aspx.

Passel, Jeffery S., D'Vera Cohn, and John Gramlich. 2018. "Number of U.S.-Born Babies with Unauthorized Immigrant Parents Has Fallen Since 2007." Pew Research Center, November 18, 2018. https://www.pewresearch.org/fact-tank/2018/11/01/the-number-of-u-s-born-babies-with-unauthorized-immigrant-parents-has-fallen-since-2007/.

Suárez-Orozco, Carola, Hirokazu Yoshikawa, Robert T. Teranishi, and Marcelo Suárez-Orozco. 2011. "Growing Up in the Shadows: The Developmental Implications of Unauthorized Status." *Harvard Educational Review* 81, no. 3 (September): 438–73. https://doi.org/10.17763/haer.81.3.g23x203763783m75.

U.S. Department of Justice. 2008. "1912. 8 U.S.C. 1326—Reentry After Deportation (Removal)." The United States Department of Justice Archives. Archived content, last updated January 17, 2020. https://www.justice.gov/archives/jm/criminal-resource-manual-1912-8-usc-1326-reentry-after-deportation-removal.

Vargas, Edward D. 2015. "Immigration Enforcement and Mixed-Status Families: The Effect of Risk of Deportation on Medicaid Use." *Children and Youth Services Review* 57 (October): 83–89. https://doi.org/10.1016/j.childyouth.2015.07.009.

Vargas, Edward D., and Viridiana L. Benitez. 2019. "Latino Parents' Links to Deportees are Associated with Developmental Disorders in their Children." *Journal of Community Psychology* 47, no. 5 (July): 1151–68. https://doi.org/10.1002/jcop.22178.

Vargas, Edward D., and Maureen A. Pirog. 2016. "Mexican Mixed-Status Families and WIC Uptake." *Social Science Quarterly* 97, no. 3 (September): 555–72. https://doi.org/10.1111/ssqu.12286.

Xu, Lanlan, Maureen A. Pirog, and Edward D. Vargas. 2016. "Child Support and Mixed-Status Families: An Analysis Using the Fragile Families and Child Well-being Study." *Social Science Research* 60 (November): 249–65. https://doi.org/10.1016/j.ssresearch.2016.06.005.

CHAPTER 10

Working in Argentina

Bolivian Children in Garment Workshops, Vegetable Farms, Stores, and Domestic Work

MARÍA INÉS PACECCA

Child Work and Migration

Between 2008 and 2012, more than a hundred boys and girls born in Bolivia, aged between twelve and seventeen, received assistance from Argentina's federal child protection agency after undergoing labor exploitation in garment workshops, vegetable farms, and small retail stores or as domestic workers. Although these children's stories were not identical, where criminal charges were pressed, exploiters were prosecuted for trafficking in minors under Law 26,364/2008.

Based on a more extensive report,[1] this chapter focuses on the children's families of origin (their parents and siblings), their schooling and previous work in Bolivia, the people who offered them the jobs, their trips to Argentina (including the border crossing), the tasks they were employed in, and how they reached the child protection agency. The information comes from my systematization of 106 individual case files drafted by the professional staff of a children's rights protection service at the Secretaría Nacional de Niñez, Adolescencia y Familia (National Secretariat for Children, Adolescents, and Families, or SENAF, part of the Ministry of Social Development). Analyzed with due ethical and confidentiality standards, this corpus (a small part of a largely hidden universe) provides substantial insights on a long-term concern that is not disappearing: independent child migration linked to a job offer in a productive or commercial enterprise carried out by other migrants (in this case, also Bolivians) at the destination. Different reasons pushed many of these children and teenagers into the labor market at an early age, while the social networks and the migration dynamics between Argentina and Bolivia prompted them to cross an international border and placed them in jobs similar to those of adult migrants.

Almost all the children and teenagers whose trajectories I analyze (based only on the case files) had discontinued their schooling long before migrating to Argentina, and about half mentioned having worked in their hometowns in Bolivia. Coming from families they define as poor, at a young age they started working for their own and their families' maintenance, to help support their siblings, or to alleviate debt or domestic straits. In this context, mainly through relatives or acquaintances, and in many cases with their parents' acquiescence, they received offers to work in Argentina in entrepreneurial ventures that other Bolivian migrants were carrying out in different parts of the country. These job offers usually included transportation or bus tickets to the destination, housing, meals (provided by the employer), and wages that amounted to half the legal minimum wage in Argentina but doubled the income of those already working in Bolivia.

Once in Argentina they all worked where originally offered (there was no deception concerning what they would do), but few earned the wages promised. Most received either no payment at all or occasional (and scant) advances. All worked ten to twelve hours daily, and none returned to school. In short, all the offers led to child labor or exploitation, aggravated by noncompliance with the federal immigration law (Law 25,871), and qualified for prosecution for trafficking of minors, which entails a harsher sentence than for trafficking of adults.

Indeed, independent child migration is always closely linked to labor or sexual exploitation, a regrettable outcome that should not prevent us from looking into the motives and processes that led to it. Assuming that exploitation arises solely from coercion or deception, or that the job offer comes from an utter stranger and behind the parents' back, obscures a salient aspect of the process, namely, how these children and teenagers see themselves, their families, and their lives, and the steps they take toward what they hope will be a positive change. From this point of view, the cases analyzed also show the tensions between normative/legal categories and social perceptions. These children's agency overrides the fact that they are still legally minors and that, as such, their scope of action is limited.

Whereas for most legal systems (Argentina's included), the passage to adulthood and full legal autonomy occurs at age eighteen, the sequence of events and decisions leading to independent child migration shows the gap between regulations and agency. This complex and sensitive issue involves a wide range of actors (both of age and underage): parents, relatives, acquaintances, strangers, job givers, border authorities, judicial and assistance operators, and the children themselves. This variety of actors also points to the several social and legal frameworks that children and teenagers traverse in their crossing.

Several studies (Bhabha 2008; Levinson 2011; O'Connell Davidson and Farrow 2007; Van de Glind 2010; Yaqub 2009a) have pointed out the different ways children are part of migration:

- Children who migrate internationally with one or both parents.
- Children who stay in their place of origin when one or both parents migrate.
- Unaccompanied children, such as those who migrate through deception, threats, or coercion. They are the most vulnerable to various forms of violence and exploitation, including human trafficking, and some may be potential asylum seekers.
- Independent child migrants, encompassing those defined as "an individual below the age of 18, who has changed (permanently or temporarily) their place of residence without a parent or customary adult guardian also migrating to their current residence (usually in a different locality)" (Edmonds and Shrestha 2009, 1). These children voluntarily become internal or international migrants, usually motivated by job opportunities and quite frequently with acquiescence and support from parents. Unlike unaccompanied minors, their migration is not due to deception or coercion. Nonetheless, labor exploitation is a frequent outcome, since their employment rarely respects local regulations.

These four types consider children's internal or international migration either as part of larger family migration processes (decided and carried out by parents) or as indicative of immigration law violations, child labor, migrant smuggling, or trafficking in persons. In the first case scenario, child migration is barely visible, whereas in the second it is hypervisible. Around 2000, various research projects and investigations (often promoted by the United Nations International Children's Emergency Fund, or UNICEF, and the International Labour Organization) set out to analyze and understand the causes, motives, and mechanisms that link child work to independent internal or international child migration. Assuming that partial or biased descriptions pave the way for ineffective and even counterproductive policies, these studies combine statistical and qualitative information to understand the connections between poverty, child work, and labor migration of children and teenagers (see, among others, Edmonds and Shresta 2012; Yaqub 2009a, 2009b; Whitehead and Hashim 2005; Huijmans 2006, 2011; Thorsen 2007; Jacquemin 2004; Lescingland 2011; Flamm 2010).

These investigations have focused on finding out which children start working (boys or girls?), at what ages (older or younger siblings?), from which ethnic/class/racial groups, what information is available concerning potential migration destinations, and how their migration is decided. Is it an agreement between relatives, employers, and parents? Do children take part and have a say in the arrangements? Were advantages, costs, and drawbacks for parents, children, and other family members sorted out and balanced? Most of these studies have shown there are many noncoercive and nondeceptive reasons why children migrate to work (usually in agriculture, as domestic servants, or as street vendors), thus confronting a widespread and thinly documented narrative that points only to deceit and violence. It is usually argued that employers who resort to child work do so because it is cheaper and because children are easier to handle (and to exploit) than adults. However, there is comparatively less research analyzing whether the conditions originally agreed to were met and what children and teenagers (can) do when work effectively evolves toward exploitation (Jacquemin 2004).

While it is usually true that children migrate to the same destinations as adults, a review of the literature shows no specific focus on the connections between the migration patterns of adults and those of children. Thus, there seem to be two underlying assumptions: First, independent child migrants are employed (at destination) in the same jobs as their nonmigrant age peers. Second, employers seeking children and teenage workers are indifferent to whether they are migrants or not. The hypothesis that guided my research on the independent migration of Bolivian children and teenagers is different. I believe their migration must be analyzed within the context of a handful of job opportunities that are available in Argentina *because of* successful Bolivian ethnic enterprises in several parts of the country. These ethnic enterprises *prefer* migrant workers, whatever their age (adults or children). The next section summarizes certain aspects of Bolivian migration to Argentina in order to strengthen this point.

The Enterprises of Bolivian Migrants in Argentina

According to the last National Population Census, 1,470,000 migrants from South American countries lived in Argentina in 2010. A quarter of them came from Bolivia (INDEC 2022).

The census in Argentina has never collected information on residential status, but it is usually safe to assume that most of these migrants are legal residents. Migration Law 25,871, enacted in 2004, established a two-year work and residence permit for citizens of all Mercosur countries.[2] This temporary permit, granted on the basis of nationality, can be converted into permanent resident status if renewed before its expiration date. Between 2004 and 2010, this path provided 450,000 temporary and 340,000 permanent permits. Between 2011 and 2018, the National Immigration Department issued 1,000,000 more temporary permits and 900,000 permanent ones. Bolivian migrants accounted for 25 percent of the temporary permits and for 28 percent of the permanent permits (Pacecca, Liguori, and Vicario Caram 2019).

The 2010 population census shows a gender balance among Bolivian migrants (171,000 men and 173,000 women), of which 11 percent are children fourteen or younger. Although in 2000 more than 50 percent had settled in the Buenos Aires Metropolitan Area, during the following decade they spread toward new destinations in the provinces of Buenos Aires (such as Escobar, La Plata, and Mar del Plata), Mendoza, Córdoba, Chubut, Santa Cruz, Río Negro, and Neuquén (INDEC 2022).

For decades, Bolivian migration to Argentina has been mostly a family migration, drawn and assisted by ethnic networks that provide jobs and housing. These networks also played a key role in capital accumulation and access to labor, leading to productive ventures in vegetable farming (in the 1980s) and garment manufacturing (in the 1990s). Ethnic enterprises usually pivot around a husband and a wife, each assuming clearly defined productive and commercial responsibilities, and expand through kinship and ethnic ties that provide access to would-be migrants and future workers (Benencia 2006). Since vegetable farms and workshops include the commercialization of the product (small shops and street markets for clothes, wholesale markets and retail greengrocers for vegetables), a large portion of Bolivian migrants can find work with Bolivian employers, farming, manufacturing, or selling.

Vegetable farms and garment workshops share two features: First, un-skilled workers may start as day laborers or pieceworkers and then move up the ladder as they collect experience, capital, and business contacts. This is especially so in workshops, where start-up capital can be as low as USD 1,000—the market price for one or two essential sewing machines. Second, since both types of venture require intensive work, their expansion links di-rectly to access to cheap labor. Thus, producers organize their work in such a way that it stringently relies on migration and on the persistence of certain migration flows.

As in many other migratory processes, kinship and local ties are a social capital available to settled, recent, or potential migrants. Settled migrants rely on networks to contact workers interested in coming to Argentina. Re-cent or potential migrants find or receive through their networks an attrac-tive job offer that provides necessary footing since it also includes a bus ticket (or a travel loan) and some sort of housing at the destination. This way the ties that underpin local/transnational networks ensure the three fundamentals of any migration process: travel costs, immediate work, and housing at a reasonable cost. Of course, none of this implies decent work or quality housing.

Through this combination of ethnic enterprises and networks, the Boliv-ian community in Argentina creates jobs for its members, from the Bolivian contractors and building crews in construction (Vargas 2005) to the garment workshops (Dandler and Medeiros 1986) and the vegetable farms that supply fresh greens to the cities of Buenos Aires, La Plata, Córdoba, Río Cuarto, Neuquén, and so on (Benencia 2006; Ciarallo and Trpin 2010; Pizarro 2011). Bolivian migrants also own or manage many of the retail stores for vegetable farms and garment workshops (such as greengrocers and street stalls selling clothing) and have lately become involved in the distribution and whole-sale of vegetables and garments. Thus, many Bolivian migrants, especially the most recent arrivals, have high chances of working in vegetable farms, garment workshops, shops, or stalls, as employees of their countrymen and countrywomen.

In these cases kinship and local/transnational networks connect job giv-ers with those wanting to migrate to Argentina. Bolivian entrepreneurs seek and employ almost exclusively Bolivian workers. Their job offers combine low-paying work with extra "perks" or "benefits" (travel expenses, housing, and meals) in a way that can only be attractive for unskilled persons looking to migrate, for those who have recently migrated and have nowhere to live, and for families with young children that cannot afford childcare and rent.

For the workshop or vegetable-farm owners, and even for the shopkeepers, offering accommodation (in the workplace) is a way of profiting from an expense (rent) they cannot avoid. For the workers the (stark) living quarters offered provide a chance to save time and money, send remittances, and avoid exposure to the police or other controlling agencies. Living in the workplace also means working longer hours (owners demand piecework, but so do employees) and receiving a speed course on the skills of the trade. The faster workers learn, the faster they work; the faster they work, the more money they earn.

While attractive before migration, this combination of work and "benefits" is a frequent source of conflict that highlights the blurred (and abusive) small print of the arrangement. *Must* those who live in the workplace work twelve or more hours a day? What happens when the worker gets sick? Or when his or her child (also living there) needs a doctor? How are the bus ticket, housing, and meals factored into the hours worked and the wages earned?

As it is currently structured, the business model of vegetable farms and workshops is sustainable as long as employers can obtain underpaid labor, secured by offering "benefits" such as transportation, housing, and meals. Independent child migration takes place in this context. The following sections analyze the key role of the kinship ties through which Bolivian children arrive at the same destinations as adults, for the same jobs, and in many cases for the same wages.

Cases and Issues

The data analyzed in this chapter, relative to 106 Bolivian boys and girls, comes from 106 individual interview-based reports drafted by the intervening social workers at SENAF's child protective service.[3] Despite minor limitations, these reports offer extraordinary insights on several aspects of independent child migration. At what ages does it take place? Did the children abandon school because of their migration? Or had they already dropped out before? Did they get their first job in Argentina, or had they worked previously, in their home country? Besides poverty, are there any other factors pushing children toward international migration? Do children move in and through the same networks as adults? Or do they reach the same destinations (geographically and work-wise) through other channels and routes? What role do parents and relatives play? And since we are dealing with Bolivian boys and girls, how is their independent migration linked with the ethnic/entrepreneurial production summarized in the previous section?

Of the 106 cases analyzed, 35 refer to boys and 71 to girls. This considerable gender disparity points to two sets of issues: first, the different means by which boys and girls reached the child protective services; and second, certain risk factors that seem to affect girls more than boys. I will start with the first set since the second one requires looking into several other aspects.

Table 10.1 shows that 74 percent of the boys reached child protective services after a police raid mandated by a judge, and only a few of them actively tried to leave the place where they lived and worked / were exploited. As for the girls, 39 percent reached child protective services after police intervention and another 39 percent after escaping on their own when they felt they could take no more. In several cases the girls' escapes or requests for help were triggered by factual or imminent sexual abuse.

These children came to Argentina from rural areas or small towns throughout Bolivia. Around 70 percent of them had arrived between 2010 and 2012, when they were between ten and seventeen years old. The youngest were two girls aged ten and eleven: one of them had lost both parents, while the other one had lost her father and was part of a family with seven siblings. Apart from these two girls, 75 percent of the other boys and girls arrived and began to work at ages fifteen to seventeen.[4] All of them began working immediately or within two or three days after their arrival.

Almost all these children came from large families: approximately 60 percent had four or more siblings, a number that must be set against the presence or absence of one or both parents. Before moving to Argentina, 80 percent of the boys and girls had a mother with whom they lived or had regular contact. However, 44 percent of the girls had no father (due either to death or to long-standing absence), in contrast with 31 percent of the boys.

Regarding their education, boys and girls averaged seven years of schooling. However, this average blurs meaningful gender differences. On one hand 23 percent of the girls attended school for five years or less, compared to 17 percent of the boys. On the other hand, those with the longest school attendance (nine to twelve years) were also girls. Of the three children who

TABLE 10.1 Paths to child protective services: Percentage of children in cases analyzed

	Boys	Girls
Police raid	74	39
Escape or quest for help	17	39
Institutional intervention	9	6
Noninstitutional third-party intervention	0	13
Unknown	0	3
Total	*100*	*100*

had finished high school, two were girls, and the only child who had never attended school (and was illiterate) was also a girl. In the case of children who abandoned school early, there is a plausible connection with the death or absence of the father (a fact in the life of several children with five years of education or less) and with large groups of siblings. Most of these children had left school two or three years before migrating, often at the end of seventh or eighth grade.

Another relevant aspect relates to work before migration. On this issue 34 percent of the boys and 48 percent of the girls expressly mentioned working in Bolivia at a very young age and before their migration to Argentina. The girls had been domestic workers, nannies, waitresses, kitchen helpers, and street vendors. Some had even moved on their own between different Bolivian cities in search of work at such young ages as thirteen, fourteen, or fifteen. The boys reported having worked as bricklayers, in brick kilns, and as woodcutters. Those who came from rural areas had frequently moved around harvesting different crops (including coca leaves in the Yungas) or taking care of land and animals on small family farms.

None of the boys had children before migrating. Two of the girls had infant children (born in Bolivia), and three were pregnant when they reached child protective services.

Migration to Argentina

Why did these children migrate? Except for two who already lived in Argentina, where they had previously arrived with their parents, 90 percent of these boys and girls said they came to the country because they had been offered a job. Of the remaining 10 percent, some arrived for family reasons (such as moving in with adult siblings or other relatives after the death of a parent), some traveled to continue their education, and 3 percent said they had just come "for a visit." These 3 percent are some of the very few that did not start working immediately upon arrival.

The job offer as a migration driver is consistent with the rest of the data reviewed: rural origins or small communities, many siblings, discontinued schooling, and work at an early age. It should be noted that the job offer was made in Bolivia by a Bolivian person seeking either workers for his or her own business (garment workshop, vegetable farm, or retail store) or a domestic worker / nanny to help around the house so the wife could devote more time to the family enterprise. In addition, there was no deception whatsoever regarding the type of work: those who recruited for garment workshops, vegetable farms, or small shops effectively placed the boys and girls in such jobs.

In the case of the boys, 77 percent of the job offers were made directly to the children and 11 percent to their parents. In the case of the girls, 63 percent received the offer themselves, while their parents received it in 21 percent of cases, and 6 percent of the offers were made to another relative. It is worth analyzing who was involved in the job offer and whom it was made to: the child or a meaningful adult.

The values in table 10.2 point to two interesting issues. First, for both boys and girls, the subtotals included in "Relatives" add up to almost 45 percent of those who were involved in the job offer. Additionally, the category "Acquaintances" allows for slightly more than 30 percent of the cases. Second, both "Stranger" and "Employment Agency / Advertisement" are irrelevant for boys but account for almost 20 percent of the job offers received by girls. Who were these strangers offering jobs? In their stories the girls usually mentioned adult women (met on the street or in other public places) who, after making conversation, offered them a job. The case reports suggest that this process took just a few hours; at most, a day or two passed between the first encounter and the job offer in Argentina. Just like "Employment Agency / Advertisement," these offers reached the girls without the endorsement of relatives or acquaintances. The lack of mediation by a third party (such as family or acquaintances) results from the girls' own agency and autonomy as much as it derives from extremely weakened family ties, independent internal migration, and homelessness, all the more frequent in girls than in boys.

TABLE 10.2 Participants in the job offer: Percentage of children in cases analyzed

Participant	Boys	Girls	Total
Relative (uncle/aunt/godfather/godmother)	20	18	*43*
Relatives (cousins/siblings)	34	17	
Parents (mother/father)	0	3	
Acquaintance[a]	29	32	*31*
Stranger[b]	3	11	*9*
Employment Agency / Advertisement[c]	0	7	*5*
Not applicable	11	10	*10*
No information available	3	2	*2*
Total	*100*	*100*	*100*

[a] *Acquaintance* includes neighbors, friends, and employers (for those already working in Bolivia). Acquaintances were not defined in terms of kinship, but it was always someone the child or his/her family knew *before* the job offer was made.
[b] *Stranger* refers to people neither the children or their families knew *before* receiving the job offer.
[c] *Employment Agency / Advertisement* refers to the cases where the children themselves sought a job, either through an employment agency or by contacting someone requesting workers through radio or television ads.

Added together, "Relatives" and "Acquaintances" account for 74 percent of all job offers. This poses questions on the effectiveness of the widely publicized antitrafficking campaigns[5] warning against the perils of accepting job offers from strangers. Considering the context and the way in which so many of the jobs were offered, neither the children nor their parents had solid reasons to mistrust or to heed warnings that connected eventual exploitation with strangers.

The recruiters always made it clear that the job offered (garments, farmwork, vending, or domestic work) was in Argentina and that accepting it meant migrating. Unlike what happens in sexual exploitation, none of the children were deceived about the type of work they would do or where they would do it. In addition, 55 percent of them knew what their wages would be (I review later whether or not the agreed conditions were met). The information regarding their wages is expressed in U.S. dollars, Argentine pesos, and Bolivian bolivianos (the currencies the children mentioned to their caseworkers). The offers in U.S. dollars ranged from USD 100 to USD 200 per month. The offers in Argentine pesos went from ARS 100 to ARS

1,000 per month, with most between ARS 500 and ARS 700 per month. Finally, the offers in Bolivian bolivianos ranged from BOB 1,200 to BOB 2,000 per month, which roughly doubled the amount of the children's income in Bolivia.

Not all agreements involved payments made on a monthly basis. In some cases payday would be every three months, in others annually (due at the end of the year), and in still others the amount offered depended on working for the employer for at least four or six months. Children offered jobs in garment workshops were unclear on how their wages were set. In many cases the amount offered reflected the piecework earnings of fast and experienced workers, which was not the case of children who had never sat at the sewing machine before.

The job offer expressly included transportation, housing, and meals. As mentioned, this combination deal makes the proposal attractive, since it (apparently) reduces the costs of migration to zero. There is no need to raise money for the ticket, look for work upon arrival, or worry about accommodation, transportation, or food costs. For the person interested in migrating, this is solid ground for deciding and committing to the job giver, and it is certainly a reasonable trade-off for those who wish to migrate but lack the resources to do so. This offer is probably even more seductive for young people living in small towns where local job opportunities are scarce and purchasing and obtaining bus tickets may not be an easy task.

TRANSPORTATION AND BORDER CROSSING

In almost all cases where migration was driven by the job offer, the prospective employer provided transportation, usually by paying for the long-distance bus fare and occasionally by driving the child in his or her own vehicle, along with the employer's family. According to data available in SEN-AF's reports, 44 percent of the border crossings were through the Villazón (Potosí)–La Quiaca (Jujuy) pass, 13 percent through the Yacuiba (Tarija)–Salvador Mazza (Salta) pass, and 8 percent through the Bermejo (Tarija)–Aguas Blancas (Salta) pass. Unfortunately, there is no information on the crossing point for 35 percent of the cases.

Regarding the border crossing, regular crossings (with adequate personal identification and parental authorization, which was mandatory since all were underage) are significantly higher among boys than among girls. As many as 38 percent of the girls made irregular crossings, either because

MAP 10.1 Map of La Quiaca. Source: Google Maps.

they lacked parental permission or because they used fraudulent personal identification documents (usually an ID belonging to someone else of legal age or their own ID, tampered with to change the birth date and make them pass for adults).

SENAF's case reports also specify whether the border crossing was regular or not. For example, some children (both boys and girls) who had their own ID and parental authorization crossed *así nomás* ("just so," meaning avoiding immigration controls) despite having all the required papers. Of the irregular entries (due to fraudulent documentation or skipping controls), seventeen happened in the Villazón–La Quiaca pass, four in the Yacuiba– Salvador Mazza pass, and three in the Bermejo–Aguas Blancas pass. Another irregular crossing was also registered, but without specifying where. In short, almost 25 percent of the entries were irregular.

Destinations

After as many as three days of land travel, the children reached their destinations in Argentina. Slightly more than 70 percent arrived at the Buenos Aires Metropolitan Area (which includes the city of Buenos Aires and twenty-four other boroughs around it), 10 percent reached several destinations within the province of Buenos Aires, and the remaining 20 percent (all girls) were scattered throughout the country, in the provinces of Córdoba, Chubut, Santa Cruz, Río Negro, Santa Fe, La Pampa, San Juan, and Mendoza. These locations are consistent with long-standing destinations for Bolivian migrants in Argentina and are linked to the different types of jobs offered. Those arriving in the metropolitan area of Buenos Aires were employed in garment workshops and, to a lesser extent, retail greengrocers. For those arriving in the province of Buenos Aires, the work was in vegetable farms and small shops, while in the rest of the destinations (to which only girls arrived) the work was either in vegetable farms, in stores, or as domestic servants. It is worth noting that all the garment workshops were in the City of Buenos Aires or its suburbs.[6]

Boys were employed mostly in garment workshops and vegetable farms, while girls were employed in small shops (which employed thirteen of the girls and only three of the boys) or as domestic workers. There seem to be no gender preferences in garment workshops; boys and girls worked there alike. Sexual division of labor concerned only cleaning and cooking, which obviously fell on women.

Concerning store jobs, the few boys that worked there were employed by small retailers selling fresh fruits and vegetables, whereas the girls were also employed in clothing stores. It is difficult to trace any such age and gender patterns for vegetable farms since they represent only 10 percent of all cases and are greatly dispersed, both geographically and productively: some grew leafy vegetables, other olives, and others only onions, all of which involve very different tasks and time frames.

The cases of girls employed as domestic workers are probably the most complex. Since the tasks are carried out in private homes, neighbors often believe the girl is just another family member. They were also very young girls (eleven, twelve, or thirteen), less resourceful than sixteen- or seventeen-year-olds. Drawing from the colonial Hispanic practice of *criadazgo* (similar to indentured servitude but applying mostly to children) and carried out within the privacy of the employer's home, domestic work was the situation in which exploitation lasted the longest (an average of sixteen months) and the most severe forms of abuse were detected.[7]

In contrast, the absence of boys on construction sites (only 3 percent) is revealing since access to construction jobs and crews tends to be ethnically regulated and organized by Bolivian and Paraguayan contractors (Vargas 2005). Despite the relative informality of many hiring procedures, underage workers would not go unnoticed on construction sites, and they would certainly not be tolerated. Contractors, real estate developers, builders, and unions are frequently inspected by the labor department, are familiar with safety and legal issues, and are well aware of the consequences of employing children. Unlike workplaces that are less visible to the public eye (unidentified garment workshops or private homes) or mom-and-pop stores, where the boundary between family members and employees is blurred for clients, construction sites are conspicuous and regulated. Additionally, construction work is not organized exclusively or centrally according to the rules imposed by the Bolivian employer, as is the case in workshops, vegetable farms, and stores.[8]

How long did the children work in vegetable farms, garment workshops, small stores, or homes? Except for two children who never reached their intended destination because police or child protective services found them while still on their way, for the rest, the length of time varied from ten days to thirty-six months: 35 percent worked for up to three months and 50 percent between six and eighteen months, with no significant differences between boys and girls. There is, however, a gender difference for those who worked eighteen months or more: six of them were girls (three in garment workshops, three in domestic work) and only one a teenage boy, who worked briefly at a construction site and then sewed in several garment workshops.

A handful of the children working at garment workshops seemed to have worked for different employers, apparently moving at will from one to another. In addition, a girl who began working on a vegetable farm then found her way to a small store, where the tasks expected of her were less exhausting.

What happened with the wages originally promised? Outcomes have varied greatly. Even though continued and regular payment happened in very few cases, nonpayment was much more frequent among girls.[9] Regarding payment, the total cases include the 10 percent of children who did not migrate to work but who ended up working anyway. Almost half the boys (43 percent) received the wages originally agreed on, while girls were frequently not paid under one of two guises. Either the employer "kept"[10] their money for them (twice as often for girls than for boys) or the money was handed to another person (the mother, an aunt, an older sister, the father) with whom the initial agreement had been struck.

In the few cases where wages were paid regularly, payment was monthly. The amounts the children mentioned varied from ARS 100 (USD 20) per month to 400, 500, 700, 1,000, 1,200, or 1,500 Argentine pesos. One girl mentioned receiving a lump sum of ARS 2,200 for four months' work, while a boy on a vegetable farm (raided by the police a week after his arrival) claims to have received ARS 50 per day. On the other hand, many children mentioned employer "loans" of 50 or 100 Argentine pesos to spend during the weekend.

Working and Living Conditions

Both SENAF's reports and the indictments analyzed for the research refer to working and housing conditions. Whether in garment workshops, vegetable farms, or small shops, working conditions do not differ significantly between children and adults. The workplace is also the house where everyone lives, employees and employers alike, and extremely long working hours are the rule for almost everyone.

The workshops mentioned in the reports or indictments analyzed for this research vary in size. Some are small family workshops with five or six sewing machines operated by a husband and wife, some of their teenage children, and two or three other workers, possibly relatives. Others are somewhat larger, with twenty to thirty sewing machines of different types and a similar number of people to operate them. Finally, there are some considerably larger workshops, such as one operating on a huge corner lot in the southern part of the city of Buenos Aires, which had eighty machines and worked in association with an industrial laundry and an ironing shop. Some of the workers lived in the workshop, while others slept in one of two other houses that the workshop owner had rented for that purpose a few blocks away.

The garment workshops usually operate in large and dilapidated houses; rooms are organized into working areas, sleeping areas, and a kitchen. The bedrooms are small, with makeshift partitions holding several bunk beds each, and divided according to sex (for single persons) or for families, since it is not uncommon for workers to migrate with their children and live with them in the workplace. In some cases the teenage children of the workshop owners share bedrooms with the workers. The bathrooms (when more than one exists) also seem to be organized according to sex, although they are not always fully equipped and may lack safe means for providing hot water.

In addition to the garment workers and their assistants, many of them teenagers who sort the bobbins and fabrics, cut loose threads, fold, assemble bundles for the laundry, sweep, and tidy up, all workshops have at least one cook in charge of preparing and serving four daily meals for all workers. This is a specific job, undertaken by an adult woman, occasionally helped by a teenage girl. Many girls mentioned working as sewing assistants, sometimes as kitchen assistants, and cleaning the workshop, common spaces, and the owner's bedroom. Cleaning tasks not directly related to sewing activities were not reported by the boys, showing the traditional gender divide within the workshops.

In the workshops sixteen-hour-long workdays (from seven o'clock in the morning to eleven o'clock at night), with short breaks for breakfast, lunch, afternoon snack, and dinner, were frequent. Regular working hours are from Monday to Friday, with part-time work on Saturdays. Sunday is the day off and the day when the workers must buy and cook their own food. These very long hours are fueled by piecework (or per-piece pay rates), authorized only under very specific conditions specified in Labor Contract Law 20,774.

Vegetable farms show a similar picture concerning housing conditions and long working hours organized according to sunlight and temperature throughout the year. However, unlike garment workshops, vegetable farms have received little attention, resulting in fewer police investigations and raids.

In small retail shops, work differs depending on whether the shop is a greengrocer or a clothing store. At a greengrocer's the daily wholesale purchase in the very early hours (three or four o'clock in the morning) involves the loading and unloading of dozens of heavy boxes and sacks, followed by the preparation of the vegetables (these are peeled, sliced, and arranged in disposable trays of different sizes and weights) and the daily display inside the store and on the adjacent sidewalk. These are tasks additional to serving customers, cleaning the premises, and disassembling at the end of the day (discarding rotten vegetables, bringing in what is on display on the sidewalk, etc.). Almost all grocery stores have opening hours from eight o'clock in the morning to nine o'clock at night. Although sometimes those who work there take turns, this does not always mean that whoever is not in the store is resting. Some of the children who worked for greengrocers said their employers managed two stores and that they went from one to the other. Since greengrocers are generally small, rented stores (or are within self-service supermarkets owned by Korean, Taiwanese, or Chinese immigrants), they are rarely living quarters. This meant children and teenagers had an additional task: cleaning the owners' home, where they all usually lived.

In clothing stores the situation has been similar in terms of extended hours and the combination of serving customers, cleaning and tidying up the premises, taking care of cleaning and cooking, and sometimes looking after the employer's children.

Aftermath

The cases reviewed here show the nuances and complexities of independent child migration when looking beyond immigration regulations and simplifying dichotomies.

None of these children worked in compliance with the terms and conditions established by law. Regardless of the age limits (fourteen years until the enactment of Law 26,390 in June 2008, and sixteen years from then on), working hours always exceeded even those set for adults. There is also the matter of noncompliance with other provisions relating to decent work in general, such as ridiculously low wages, irregular payment, and nonpayment.

The analysis of SENAF's case files and the legal proceedings (included in the full research report) shows that, except for domestic work, job givers did not search specifically for child workers. In their respective workplaces, child migrant workers were a fraction of all employees: a comparatively small one in garment workshops and a slightly larger one in vegetable farms and stores, which require less labor. Likewise, the tasks they were assigned did not relate to their age but rather to their inexperience. Since they took on the same jobs as adults, there is no distinct evidence of a specific niche demanding child work—which is, in turn, consistent with the blurred separation between fifteen- or sixteen-year-olds and adults.

Indeed, in workshops, farms, stores, and private homes, there is no obvious distinction between teenagers and adults, only between children and adults. Whatever the age, those with the strength and physical ability to do the job are seen as adult workers for all practical purposes. There is, however, a difference in treatment: exploitation, abuse, and nonpayment affect children more frequently than adults, who have stronger personal and social resources to confront the employer. However, when it comes to job performance, the same is expected of both.

The normative framework that rules institutional interventions in these situations does not help to understand the process that leads to work-driven child migration. It is oblivious of the need or decision to work and migrate, of the family or parental dynamics behind it, and of the children's agency. As mentioned earlier, 70 percent of the job proposals were received directly by the children, and more than half of them had precise information regarding the work children would do and the wages they would receive. Additionally, in half the cases, the children crossed the international border with the written permission of their parents, who knew with whom and why they were crossing it. Thus, it is reasonable to believe that most of these boys and girls made choices and decisions on migration and work (or agreed with them) with the consent, knowledge, or direct involvement of their families. Moreover, when the family was not aware (as in the case of some girls), it was not because the recruitment had relied on deception or kidnapping but simply because those girls had already slipped from family guardianship and control and neither asked for permission nor requested counsel.

The actions of parents and other responsible adults, as well as some of their statements in court proceedings (analyzed in the full report), show that, from their point of view, childhood was a past stage. Being "no longer children," they were expected to help their families or at least not to be economically dependent on their parents. In this sense the adults and teenagers of these families shared common characterizations and expectations vis-à-vis early economic independence, considered one of the key transitions to adulthood.

Did fathers and mothers, sons and daughters, have any idea how hard that work in Argentina could be? Did they suspect that in many cases the economic agreements would not be honored? Had they known, would they have made other choices, including deciding not to migrate? Since this article draws on case files, not on interviews or ethnographic fieldwork, I have no explicit answers. However, the professional staff of child protective services in charge of returning these children to their families and hometowns and resettling them pointed out in several interviews that migration to Argentina is still an expectation. Despite these children's flawed first try, the conditions that led to migration did not change significantly, and a new migratory process should not be ruled out. It will be a matter of waiting to come of legal age, figuring out how things could have been different, expanding the network of contacts, and trying again. Crossing the international border will be less risky for those who are legally adults next time, and the demand for ethnic (and overworked) labor will continue strong in garment workshops, vegetable farms, and retail stores.

Notes

1. This chapter is based on previous research published in 2014 as María Inés Pacecca in *El trabajo adolescente y la migración desde Bolivia a Argentina: Entre la adultez y la explotación* (Teenage work and migration from Bolivia to Argentina: Between adulthood and exploitation) (Buenos Aires: CLACSO). The complete ebook can be downloaded from https://www.clacso.org.ar.

2. This work permit (the requirements of which include neither a job offer nor a formal work contract) is available to citizens of Bolivia, Brazil, Chile, Colombia, Ecuador, Paraguay, Peru, Uruguay, Venezuela, and Suriname.

3. I did not personally interview or contact any of the children or their families. My analysis draws on the systematization of more than a hundred of SENAF's case files.

4. Law 26,390/2008, the Prohibition of Child Labor and Protection of Adolescent Work, raised the minimum working age from fourteen to sixteen and forbade persons under sixteen years of age to work.

5. The federal immigration departments in Bolivia and Argentina frequently exhibit a variety of posters and messages in border crossings warning against human trafficking and migrant smuggling. Several local nongovernmental organizations and international organizations (such as the International Organization for Migration, the United Nations High Commissioner for Refugees, UNICEF, and others) have produced and broadcast ads on social media, radio, and TV networks emphasizing the perils of accepting work offers from strangers.

6. This does not imply there are no garment workshops managed by Bolivian migrants in other provinces. The fact that children have reached SENAF from a few jurisdictions (and not from all) is due to local prosecution policies (many of which emphasize sex trafficking) and to the availability and expertise of local child protective services. The same is true of the small number of children identified on vegetable farms, located in scantily populated rural areas and not among the top policing interests of prosecutors.

7. Law 26,390/2008 expressly forbids hiring persons under sixteen years of age as sleep-in domestic workers. Law 26,844/2013 extended this restriction to sixteen- and seventeen-year-olds.

8. Several sources have pointed out that Bolivian families frequently work in brick kilns in rural areas. Since these are rarely inspected, children may be working there, along with the rest of their families or on their own, as independent child migrants.

9. The disparity between payment and nonpayment among boys and girls poses an issue that is not mentioned in the caseworkers' reports but is part of my own fieldwork experience with adult migrants (men and women) and how they subtly nuance their own work narratives according to the interviewer's gender. Since all of SENAF's caseworkers were women, some teenage boys may have understated nonpayment situations in order to avoid feeling embarrassed or appearing weak.

10. When the children say their employer "kept" their money for them, it usually means they had no access to it.

References

Benencia, Roberto. 2006. "Bolivianización de la horticultura en Argentina: Procesos de migración trasnacional y construcción de territorios productivos." In *Migraciones regionales hacia la Argentina: Diferencia, desigualdad y derechos*, edited by Elizabeth Jelin and Alejandro Grimson, 135–67. Buenos Aires: Prometeo.

Bhabha, Jacqueline. 2008. "Independent Children, Inconsistent Adults: International Child Migration and the Legal Framework." Innocenti Discussion Paper No. 2008–02, May 2008. Florence: UNICEF Innocenti Research Centre.

Ciarallo, Ana, and Verónica Trpin. 2010. "Chacareros, empresas, horticultores y trabajadores: Territorios y representaciones en disputa en el Alto Valle de Río Negro." Unpublished manuscript.

Dandler, Jorge, and Carmen Medeiros. 1986. "Migración temporaria de Cochabamba, Bolivia, a la Argentina: Patrones e impacto en las áreas de envío." In *Fronteras permeables: Migración laboral y movimientos de refugiados en América*, edited by Patricia Pessar, 19–53. Buenos Aires: Planeta.

Edmonds, Eric V., and Maheshwor Shrestha. 2009. *Children's Work and Independent Child Migration: A Critical Review*. Innocenti Working Paper IWP-2009-19, December. Florence: UNICEF Innocenti Research Centre.

Edmonds, Eric V., and Maheshwor Shrestha. 2013. "Independent Child Labor Migrants." In *The International Handbook of the Economics of Migration*, edited by Amelie Constant and Klaus Zimmerman, 98–119. Cheltenham, UK.: Edward Elgar.

Flamm, Sarah. 2010. "The Linkage Between Migration and Child Labor: An International Perspective." *Stanford Journal of International Relations* 12, no. 1 (Fall): 15–25.

Huijmans, Roy. 2006. "Children, Childhood and Migration." Working Paper Series No. 427, ORPAS, Institute of Social Studies, The Hague, Netherlands, June 2006. https://www.researchgate.net/publication/44836772_Children_childhood_and _migration.

Huijmans, Roy. 2011. "Child Migration and Questions of Agency." *Development and Change* 42 (5): 1307–21.

INDEC (Instituto Nacional de Estadísticas y Censos de la República Argentina). 2022. "Censos." https://www.indec.gob.ar/indec/web/Nivel3-Tema-2-41.

Jacquemin, Mélanie. 2004. "Children's Domestic Work in Abidjan, Côte d'Ivoire: The Petites Bonnes Have the Floor." *Childhood* 11 (3): 383–97.

Lescingland, Marie. 2011. "Migration des jeunes filles au Mali: Exploitation ou émancipation?" *Travail, genre et sociétés*, no. 25 (April): 23–40.

Levinson, Amanda. 2011. "Unaccompanied Immigrant Children: A Growing Phenomenon with Few Easy Solutions." Migration Policy Institute. Migration Information Source, January 24, 2011. https://www.migrationpolicy.org/article/unaccompanied-immigrant-children-growing-phenomenon-few-easy-solutions.

O'Connell Davidson, Julia, and Caitlin Farrow. 2007. *Child Migration and the Construction of Vulnerability*. Sweden: Save the Children.

Pacecca, María Inés, Gabriela Liguori, and María Fernanda Vicario Caram. 2019. *Personas, "papeles," políticas y derechos: Las migraciones contemporáneas en Argentina desde la perspectiva de CAREF (2004–2015)*. Buenos Aires: Comisión Argentina para Refugiados y Migrantes.

Pizarro, Cynthia. 2011. "Sufriendo y resistiendo la segregación laboral: Experiencias de inmigrantes bolivianos que trabajan en el sector hortícola de la región metropolitana de la ciudad de Córdoba." In *Migraciones internacionales contemporáneas: Estudios para el debate*, edited by Cynthia Pizarro, 335–58. Buenos Aires: Ciccus.

Thorsen, Dorte. 2007. "If Only I Get Enough Money for a Bicycle! A Study of Childhoods, Migration and Adolescent Aspirations Against a Backdrop of Exploitation and Trafficking in Burkina Faso." Working paper no. 21, Development Research Centre on Migration, Globalisation and Poverty, University of Sussex, UK.

Van de Glind, Hans. 2010. "Migration and Child Labour: Exploring Child Migrant Vulnerabilities and Those of Children Left Behind." Working paper, International Labour Office, International Programme on the Elimination of Child Labour, Geneva, September. https://www.ilo.org/ipecinfo/product/download.do?type=document&id=14313.

Vargas, Patricia. 2005. *Bolivianos, paraguayos y argentinos en la obra. Identidades étnico-nacionales entre los trabajadores de la construcción*. Buenos Aires: Editorial Antropofagia.

Whitehead, Ann, and Iman Hashim. 2005. "Children and Migration." Background paper for DFID Migration Team, University of Sussex, Sussex, UK.

Yaqub, Shahin. 2009a. "Independent Child Migrants in Developing Countries: Unexplored Links in Migration and Development." Innocenti Discussion Paper No. 2009–01, January. Florence: UNICEF Innocenti Research Centre.

Yaqub, Shahin. 2009b. "Child Migrants With and Without Parents: Census-Based Estimates of Scale and Characteristics in Argentina, Chile and South Africa." Innocenti Discussion Paper No. 2009–02, February. Florence: UNICEF Innocenti Research Centre.

Conclusion

These chapters contribute to our understanding of the plight of migrant children as they leave their homeland, alone or with their families, and embark on crossing many borders: geographic, political, structural, linguistic, cultural, class, racial, and educational. What have we learned from this book project? What are the conclusions that we can draw from our research, and what hope do we have for the future of the well-being of migrant children in the Americas?

Throughout the Americas, drivers of migration are poverty, cartel and gang violence, and political instability. Migrant children's experiences with *miedo* (fear), violence, injustices, hardships, vulnerabilities, and anguish are palpable throughout the chapters. The prejudices they face, the lack of visibility and empathy, the strangeness, and the need of belonging shape the life experiences of migrant children. Migrant children and young border crossers confront many risks to endure and resist the harshness of the journey. Even when they have arrived in a relatively safe environment, another ordeal begins when trying to build a life and make their way in frequently unfriendly environments in which tolerance and comprehension do not abound. Surrounded by prejudices that come from news media, television, and film, as well as from relatives, friends, and neighbors, migrant children in the Americas find many obstacles in their path.

Governments should come together to develop economic development strategies that will promote human dignity and elevate the quality of life for all in the Americas. Policies that avoid the need for children to leave their home country to work to provide for families should be pursued.

Additionally, there should be a hemispheric policy that punishes exploiters of children. Drug smugglers as well as human, labor, and sex traffickers and other exploiters take advantage of vulnerable migrant children, who are forced to smuggle drugs or work under inhumane conditions or are physically and sexually abused.

Children's lived experiences crossing national boundaries and the response of the state, human rights workers, and immigration officials are embodied knowledge that can have positive and negative effects on children's future and life chances. These long-term consequences should be considered by policy makers and government officials when developing policies.

Institutional interventions need to take place at border crossings and in courts, detention facilities, and schools so that migrant children receive special attention at borders and during legal proceedings, and dedicated staff should be appointed to serve as advocates so that children are treated with respect and dignity. Avoiding the oppression of migrant children in schools should be a goal of educators at all levels and branches of the school environment. On a daily basis in the Americas, children cross linguistic borders in schools. To minimize trauma, educators should undergo special training and develop capacities to integrate migrant children into schools in a culturally sensitive and appropriate way. Schools can be a refuge and a safe haven for children if there are policies in place to make them so.

Artwork created by children cannot, perhaps, change border regimes, but children's creativity can touch and even soften someone's heart and mind to advocate for policy changes that are more amenable to the best interests of the child.

How can we create, make visible, and disseminate cultural productions for children and young adults (not only literature but also films, series, podcasts, music, and social networks) that question the stereotypes associated with migrant children's experiences and can help all children understand the experiences of migrants and combat racism, nationalism, and xenophobia? How can we ensure that migrant children are better understood and heard? Creating cultural works for migrant children that help them process their experiences can have powerful psychological benefits and validate those same experiences. At the same time, disseminating knowledge and the experiences of migrant children among the public can help to debilitate and question stereotypes, give visibility to migrant children's pleas, and also stimulate feelings of empathy and tolerance that can help every one of us in a sometimes cruel, unforgiving world.

The different methodologies and approaches employed by contributors to this volume are truly noteworthy: academics serving as advocates, interpreters, and companions; university professors working with and in elementary schools and conducting workshops with migrant children. All allow for a multitude of learning and sharing opportunities to help elevate the study of borders and migrants, especially migrant children.

We hope that this book contributes to elevating the status of migrant children, promoting their well-being, and ensuring prosperous, peaceful futures. We also hope that understanding the pleas of migrant children can help us all be more forgiving, empathetic, and comprehensive and to find every way we can to give others the opportunity to thrive.

CONTRIBUTORS

Marissa Bejarano-Fernbaugh is an EL educator, activist, and advocate in South Louisiana. A Mexican American who grew up in the United States–Mexico border town of Nogales, Arizona, she received her BA in political science from the University of the Incarnate Word in San Antonio, Texas, and her MEd in curriculum and instruction with a concentration in English as a second language from Louisiana State University Shreveport. Marissa's passion for creating equity and inclusiveness for all students and her love of education compel her to continue her work on behalf of immigrant and English-language-learning populations.

Nancie Bouchard has a BA in elementary education from the Université du Québec à Montréal as well as a certificate in children's literature from the Université du Québec à Trois-Rivières and has completed a graduate microprogram in cooperative learning at the University of Sherbrooke. She has been a primary school teacher at the Centre de services scolaire de Montréal for twenty-five years, and her pedagogical approach mobilizes children's literature and art in order to acquire knowledge and skills. She has set up several integrative projects incorporating knowledge and experience in a multidisciplinary learning approach that she has presented on several occasions at AQEP and AQOPS conferences.

Lina M. Caswell has a BA in human services from Springfield College and an MA in sociology and social justice from Kean University. Lina completed high school in Colombia, from which she emigrated in 1997. In the past twenty years, she served in Connecticut as an advocate for minoritized immigrant children and families and low-income Latinx communities for the Hispanic Health Council, the City of Hartford Office of Youth Development, the Refugee Assistance Center, and the Center for Children's Advocacy in Hartford. Currently, Lina works in New Jersey as an adjunct sociology professor at several community colleges and as a consultant for the Sisters of Charity of Saint Elizabeth Values into Action college internship program serving immigrant communities. Since 2012 she has served as a child advocate for unaccompanied immigrant children through the Young Center for Immigrant Children's Rights and the Children's Emergency Medical Fund of New Jersey.

Irasema Coronado, PhD, is a professor and director of the School of Transborder Studies at Arizona State University. Her research focuses on the politics of the U.S.-Mexico border region, focusing on binational cooperation, activism, human rights, environmental issues, and the role of women in politics. She is co-author of *Fronteras No Mas: Toward Social Justice at the U.S.-Mexico Border* and numerous academic articles. She is a member of the Association of Borderland Studies and the International Political Science Association.

Valentina Glockner is a Mexican anthropologist affiliated with the Departamento de Investigaciones Educativas at Centro de Investigación y Estudios Avanzados (CINVESTAV) in Mexico City. Her work focuses on the anthropology of childhood, (im)migration, and the state. She has published research on India, Mexico, and the United States. She has directed and coordinated research projects funded by the National Geographic Society, the Arizona-Sonora Interuniversity Alliance, ConTex, the National Science Foundation, and Consejo Nacional de Ciencia y Tecnología.

Alejandra J. Josiowicz, PhD, is an assistant professor (*professora adjunta*), coordinator of internationalization, and Prociencia Fellow at the Universidade do Estado do Rio de Janeiro (Rio de Janeiro State University) in Brazil. Her research focuses on childhood studies and children's literature in Latin America, particularly on the intersections of racial, gender, and class inequalities. She has published *La cruzada de los niños: Intelectuales, infancia y modernidad literaria en América Latina* (Universidad Nacional de Quilmes 2018) and articles in the *Journal of Lusophone Studies, Revista Iberoamericana,* and *Hispamérica,* among others. She has also contributed a chapter on Latin American children's literature to the Cambridge Literature in Transition series.

Patrícia Nabuco Martuscelli is a lecturer in international relations at the University of Sheffield. Patrícia holds a PhD in political science from the Universidade de São Paulo. She has a BA and an MA in international relations from the Universidade de Brasília. She was a visiting scholar at the Zukunftskolleg, the Jacobs Center for Productive Youth Development, and the Carolina Population Center. Her research interests are family migration, child migration, and asylum and migration policies in Latin America.

María Inés Pacecca is an anthropologist. She is professor and researcher at the Universidad de Buenos Aires (Argentina), where she teaches undergraduate and master's courses on migration, asylum, and human rights at the faculties of philosophy and literature (Facultad de Filosofía y Letras) and law and social sciences (Facultad de Derecho y Ciencias Sociales). She also teaches similar courses at the Universidad Nacional de Lanús. She has conducted and coordinated research on migration, gender, and labor; asylum; human trafficking; political rights; migration policies; childhood and borders; and foreign persons in the penal system. She has published five books (one as author, four as author and co-editor), numerous research reports, and more than thirty articles in national and foreign books and magazines. Since 1997 she has collaborated with the Argentine Commission for Refugees and Migrants (CAREF), where since 2017 she has been coordinator of the Research Area.

Marta Rodríguez-Cruz, PhD, is a professor and researcher at the Department of Social Anthropology of the Universidad de Sevilla (PAIDI 2020 Doctors Program, FSE-JDA). Her lines of research are migration, return, childhood, adolescence, interculturality, interethnic relations, bilingual intercultural education, and Indigenous peoples. She is the author and editor of numerous publications and winner of several awards on education, interculturalism, and indigenous peoples. Dr. Rodríguez-Cruz coordinates the international seminar Childhood, Adolescence and Migrant Youth, participated in by different entities of Universidad Nacional Autónoma de México, in Mexico, the United States, and Spain.

Emily Ruehs-Navarro is an assistant professor of sociology at Elmhurst University. She received her PhD in sociology with a concentration in gender and women's studies from the University of Illinois Chicago. She has worked with immigrant youth in various capacities, including as a case manager for a refugee resettlement agency and a volunteer child advocate with the Young Center for Immigrant Children's Rights. She is the author of the forthcoming book *Unaccompanied: The Plight of Immigrant Youth at the Border* from New York University Press.

Kathleen Tacelosky, PhD, is a professor of Spanish at Lebanon Valley College, Pennsylvania. Her work regarding the linguistic and educational realities of the children of return migrants in Mexico is the topic of numerous publications and presentations as well as a TEDx Talk. Tacelosky's ongoing work has been supported by two Fulbright grants.

Élisabeth Vallet is an associate professor at the Royal Military College Saint-Jean, director of the Center for Geopolitical Studies of the Raoul-Dandurand Chair in Strategic and Diplomatic Studies, honorary professor at the Department of Geography at the Université du Québec à Montréal, and Quebec lead for the Borders in Globalization program at the University of Victoria. She is also a regular columnist for the Canadian National Network (Radio-Canada) and for the newspaper *Le Devoir*. She is the recipient of the 2017 Richard Morrill Outreach Award from the American Association of Geographers' Political Geography Specialty Group. Her current research focuses on borders and globalization, border walls, and governance.

INDEX